# Using Resources to Support Mathematical Thinking

D1076518

### Primary and Early Years

# Using Resources to Support Mathematical Thinking

## Primary and Early Years

**Edited by Doreen Drews and Alice Hansen**

LearningMatters

# Acknowledgements

Diagram in Chapter 2 page 20 reprinted by permission of Sage Publications Ltd from Derek Haylock and Anne Cockburn, *Understanding Mathematics in the Lower Primary Years*, © Sage Publications, 2003.

First published in 2007 by Learning Matters Ltd

ISBN 978 1 84445 057 2

Cover design by Code 5
Project Management by Deer Park Productions, Tavistock, Devon
Typeset by Pantek Arts Ltd, Maidstone, Kent
Printed and bound in Great Britain by Bell & Bain Ltd, Glasgow

Learning Matters Ltd
33 Southernhay East
Exeter EX1 1NX
Tel: 01392 215560
info@learningmatters.co.uk
www.learningmatters.co.uk

# Contents

# Editors and contributors

The editors and contributors are all lecturers at St Martin's College.

**Doreen Drews** has taught extensively within the Foundation Stage, Key Stage 1 and Key Stage 2. She was a mathematics advisory teacher for four years before joining St Martin's. She has a particular interest in Early Years mathematics.

**Alice Hansen** has taught extensively at primary level in England and abroad. She has a particular interest in using ICT to effectively enhance the teaching and learning of primary mathematics. Her current research focus is on how children develop their understanding of definitions of shapes.

**Kellie Cunningham** taught in large urban primary schools before joining St Martin's as a lecturer in primary mathematics and education studies. Her specialist areas are mathematics education, PE and outdoor education but she has particular interest in developing curriculum enrichment through cross-curricular links.

**John Dudgeon** has taught at a wide range of primary schools and held a post of subject leader in mathematics before joining St Martin's. John has a particular interest in the effective use of mathematical resources to support teaching and learning across the full primary age range.

**Anne Gager** began her teaching career in secondary schools, teaching the core subjects to low attainers. Her interest in pupils' barriers to learning mathematics began at this stage and continued as she moved to work with both primary and secondary pupils in a variety of teaching and advisory teaching posts. Anne's interests are in inclusive education and valuing all pupils for what they can do and who they are. Anne is currently a lecturer in inclusion at St Martin's.

**Mike Toyn** has experience of working in a variety of primary schools. He was both a lead mathematics teacher and lead IWB teacher. He has extensive experience of using ICT in primary teaching. He has worked in the Division of Mathematics Education at St Martin's and currently lectures primary ICT for the Division of ICT at St Martin's.

# Introduction

Developing children's confidence and enthusiasm in mathematics is central to their ability to progress successfully in learning and applying mathematical knowledge, skills and concepts. Such development is dependent on many factors (see Reynolds and Farrell, 1996). This book aims to support teachers, trainee teachers and practitioners working within primary settings by bringing together what we believe to be two of the key elements involved in successful mathematical learning and teaching.

1. The need for teachers and practitioners to support children in developing their mathematical thinking;
2. The effective use of a wide range of mathematical resources to support learning and teaching.

## Key themes

Connecting these two elements are key themes which underpin the discussion and case studies within each chapter. These are as follows.

- **The role played by resources in providing different forms of representation of mathematical ideas.**
- **The need for teachers, trainee teachers and practitioners to plan for the connection between these different ways in which mathematical ideas can be represented.**
- **All children within primary settings can benefit from access to, and use of, a wide range of resources to develop their mathematical thinking.**
- **Resources act as a bridge to link children's own experiences, developing mathematical ideas, mental imagery and recall.**
- **Children's mathematical thinking is supported by teaching approaches which encourage reflection of ideas, learning from peers, communication of ideas, and which challenge thinking and exploration of possible outcomes.**

## The chapters

The book begins with two chapters which take each of the two key elements identified to explore in more depth. The areas explored in these two chapters create a framework for the rest of the book. The remaining chapters are more practical in nature; they present a series of case studies from Foundation Stage to Year 6 that utilise a resource. Each case study is followed by a discussion on the effective use of the specific resource to support and develop the children's mathematical thinking. While each case study focuses on a particular age group, the issues that are raised are also pertinent to a wider age range.

Within each case study you will find a section that outlines the appropriate learning objectives from the following documents.

| | |
|---|---|
| NC | National Curriculum for Mathematics |
| CGfFS | Curriculum Guidance for the Foundation Stage |
| 2006 PNS Framework | Primary National Strategy Primary Framework for Literacy and Mathematics |
| 1999 NNS Framework | National Numeracy Strategy Framework for Teaching Mathematics |
| Other | Any other reference to Curriculum Documentation such as other NC Programmes of Study or QCA Schemes of work |

These objectives have been indexed at the end of the book to assist your mathematics planning. We have included objectives linked to both the Primary Framework for Mathematics 2006 and the 1999 National Numeracy Framework as we recognise that schools are currently in a period of transition and are using both documents.

# Meeting the Professional Standards for the award of QTS

Making effective use of resources to develop your teaching and the children's mathematical thinking can be considered an inherent aspect of achieving the QTS Standards, which are listed below. As an opportunity to reflect on your practice to date, you may read through these Standards and consider the extent to which your mathematics teaching meets these. Any aspects you feel less confident in will help you set targets for your teaching on placements. Those recommended for the award of QTS should demonstrate all of the following:

## Professional attributes

**Q1** Have high expectations of children and young people including a commitment to ensuring that they can achieve their full educational potential and to establishing fair, respectful, trusting, supportive and constructive relationships with them.

**Q2** Demonstrate the positive values, attitudes and behaviour they expect from children and young people.

**Q3** (a) Be aware of the professional duties of teachers and the statutory framework within which they work.

(b) Be aware of the policies and practices of the workplace and share in collective responsibility for their implementation.

**Q4** Communicate effectively with children, young people, colleagues, parents and carers.

**Q5** Recognise and respect the contribution that colleagues, parents and carers can make to the development and well-being of children and young people and to raising their levels of attainment.

**Q6** Have a commitment to collaboration and co-operative working.

**Q7** (a) Reflect on and improve their practice, and take responsibility for identifying and meeting their developing professional needs.

(b) Identify priorities for their early professional development in the context of induction.

**Q8** Have a creative and constructively critical approach towards innovation, being prepared to adapt their practice where benefits and improvements are identified.

**Q9** Act upon advice and feedback and be open to coaching and mentoring.

# Professional knowledge and understanding

**Q10** Have a knowledge and understanding of a range of teaching, learning and behaviour management strategies and know how to use and adapt them, including how to personalise learning and provide opportunities for all learners to achieve their potential.

**Q11** Know the assessment requirements and arrangements for the subjects/curriculum areas in the age ranges they are trained to teach, including those relating to public examinations and qualifications.

**Q12** Know a range of approaches to assessment, including the importance of formative assessment.

**Q13** Know how to use local and national statistical information to evaluate the effectiveness of their teaching, to monitor the progress of those they teach and to raise levels of attainment.

**Q14** Have a secure knowledge and understanding of their subjects/curriculum areas and related pedagogy to enable them to teach effectively across the age and ability range for which they are trained.

**Q15** Know and understand the relevant statutory and non-statutory curricula, frameworks, including those provided through the National Strategies, for their subjects/curriculum areas, and other relevant initiatives applicable to the age and ability range for which they are trained.

**Q16** Have passed the professional skills tests in numeracy, literacy and information and communication technology (ICT).

**Q17** Know how to use skills in literacy, numeracy and ICT to support their teaching and wider professional activities.

**Q18** Understand how children and young people develop and that the progress and well-being of learners are affected by a range of developmental, social, religious, ethnic, cultural and linguistic influences.

**Q19** Know how to make effective personalised provision for those they teach, including those for whom English is an additional language or who have special educational needs or disabilities, and how to take practical account of diversity and promote equality and inclusion in their teaching.

**Q20** Know and understand the roles of colleagues with specific responsibilities, including those with responsibility for learners with special educational needs and disabilities and other individual learning needs.

**Q21** (a) Be aware of current legal requirements, national policies and guidance on the safeguarding and promotion of the well-being of children and young people.

(b) Know how to identify and support children and young people whose progress, development or well-being is affected by changes or difficulties in their personal circumstances, and when to refer them to colleagues for specialist support.

# Professional skills

**Q22** Plan for progression across the age and ability range for which they are trained, designing effective learning sequences within lessons and across series of lessons and demonstrating secure subject/curriculum knowledge.

**Q23** Design opportunities for learners to develop their literacy, numeracy and ICT skills.

**Q24** Plan homework or other out-of-class work to sustain learners' progress and to extend and consolidate their learning.

**Q25** Teach lessons and sequences of lessons across the age and ability range for which they are trained in which they:

(a) use a range of teaching strategies and resources, including e-learning, taking practical account of diversity and promoting equality and inclusion;

(b) build on prior knowledge, develop concepts and processes, enable learners to apply new knowledge, understanding and skills and meet learning objectives;

(c) adapt their language to suit the learners they teach, introducing new ideas and concepts clearly, and using explanations, questions, discussions and plenaries effectively;

(d) manage the learning of individuals, groups and whole classes, modifying their teaching to suit the stage of the lesson.

**Q26** (a) Make effective use of a range of assessment, monitoring and recording strategies.

(b) Assess the learning needs of those they teach in order to set challenging learning objectives.

**Q27** Provide timely, accurate and constructive feedback on learners' attainment, progress and areas for development.

**Q28** Support and guide learners to reflect on their learning, identify the progress they have made and identify their emerging learning needs.

**Q29** Evaluate the impact of their teaching on the progress of all learners, and modify their planning and classroom practice where necessary.

**Q30** Establish a purposeful and safe learning environment conducive to learning and identify opportunities for learners to learn in out of school contexts.

**Q31** Establish a clear framework for classroom discipline to manage learners' behaviour constructively and promote their self-control and independence.

**Q32** Work as a team member and identify opportunities for working with colleagues, sharing the development of effective practice with them.

**Q33** Ensure that colleagues working with them are appropriately involved in supporting learning and understand the roles they are expected to fulfil.

## REFERENCES REFERENCES REFERENCES REFERENCES REFERENCES REFERENCES

Reynolds, D. and Farrell, S. (1996) *Worlds apart? A review of international surveys of educational achievement involving England*. London: OFSTED.

# 1

# Children's mathematical thinking

Alice Hansen

## What is mathematical thinking?

In a recent seminar one of my students almost encapsulated what mathematical thinking is. Mark said, 'It isn't just about being able to get the answers in class. For me it is about being able to think more logically in life and being able to do everything more efficiently and effectively because of that.' I was impressed by Mark's comments for several reasons. First, Mark had seen how mathematical thinking has an impact beyond that of the classroom. Indeed, the aspects of mathematical thinking that will be discussed later in this chapter (such as problem-solving, communication and reasoning) should be integrated into how we encourage our children to use and apply mathematics in lessons, but they are also skills that pervade other aspects of the curriculum and our lives outside the classroom. Second, Mark saw a tangible outcome from being able to think mathematically. He saw that the process of mathematical thinking resulted in a product – that of being able to operate more effectively and efficiently in life. Being aware of this must provide motivation to hone the skills involved. Third, although Mark had focused on logical thinking, which is only one aspect of mathematical thinking, he had communicated his ideas to 24 other people in the seminar group. This sparked a number of comments from others, developing the group's shared understanding of what mathematical thinking is, and in doing so modelled another aspect of mathematical thinking: communication. Finally, Mark's comment alludes to one of the central tenets in this chapter: that mathematical thinking is a creative process and underpins mathematics as a creative subject.

## Chapter focus

By understanding how mathematical thinking enables us to be effective thinkers in the wider world, teachers can successfully consider how to ensure that children develop their mathematical thinking in their mathematics lessons. This chapter will discuss the nature of mathematical thinking and why it is so important. It will explore how mathematical thinking has been developed and presented in a range of curriculum documents from around the world. By comparing our own National Curriculum (NC) (DfEE, 1999a) with those of other countries it is possible to critically reflect on our own practice and look to how it might be improved from others'. The chapter will focus on:

- mathematical thinking in the National Curriculum for England and Wales;
- other countries' approaches to mathematical thinking;
- how children develop mathematical thinking;
- the teacher's role in developing children's mathematical thinking.

# Mathematical thinking in the curriculum

## The Mathematics Curriculum for England and Wales: Using and Applying Mathematics

The NC prioritises mathematical thinking into three areas: problem-solving, reasoning and communication. This section will consider each of those areas in turn. To introduce the NC, on the National Curriculum Online website the importance of mathematics is identified for us:

> *Mathematics equips pupils with a uniquely powerful set of tools to understand and change the world. These tools include logical reasoning, problem-solving skills, and the ability to think in abstract ways. Mathematics is important in everyday life, many forms of employment, science and technology, medicine, the economy, the environment and development, and in public decision-making. Different cultures have contributed to the development and application of mathematics. Today, the subject transcends cultural boundaries and its importance is universally recognised. Mathematics is a creative discipline. It can stimulate moments of pleasure and wonder when a child solves a problem for the first time, discovers a more elegant solution to that problem, or suddenly sees hidden connections.* (**www.nc.uk.net/nc/contents/Ma-home.htm**)

This powerful statement builds on Mark's comments in the opening lines of this chapter. It refers to mathematics as a 'powerful set of tools' with which to 'understand and change the world': Mark talked about being able to enhance his own life because he has become more elegant in his mathematical thinking, and this is likely to have a positive impact on the world in turn. In addition to building on Mark's words, the statement further challenges our understanding of the importance of mathematics. It highlights its cultural and social history and its current application. It also highlights the creative nature of mathematics and the potential pleasure that it can provide for children. What makes this statement so powerful and exciting is the understanding that mathematics allows us to make sense of our world, ourselves and each other as well as the impact that mathematics can have on our environment, our lives and more immediately in our classrooms. For example, it is vital that teachers take responsibility in their planning to allow children to experience the 'moments of pleasure and wonder' that mathematics (like any other subject) provides.

If we momentarily step back from the topic content of the NC, this statement holds true regardless of the area of mathematics that is being taught or learnt. Being able to use tools in everyday life, seeing links and connections within mathematics and between mathematics and other aspects of life, creativity, pleasure and wonder all transcend the topics of number, shape and space, measures and handling data. As a result they can together start to create a picture for us of mathematical thinking.

Focusing on the need for children to learn to apply mathematics, Hughes *et al.* (2000: 118) suggest that they:

> *attend school in order to acquire knowledge that will be useful to them in the rest of their lives ... we want children to be numerate, not so they can carry out feats of mental arithmetic in school, but so they can confidently apply their knowledge of mathematics to a range of situations in their subsequent working and domestic lives. There is no point in teaching children to be 'numerate' if they cannot apply what they know ...*

*Children learn mathematics in school with a view to going beyond classroom exercises and using mathematical knowledge in all aspects of their professional and domestic lives.*

This might be the case in some exceptions; however, in my experience the majority of primary school children undertake their mathematics work for many other reasons, most of which are very short term. For example, when I visit trainee teachers on school placements, I often ask the children why they are doing their maths work. The common responses I have received include: 'Because Miss told us to', 'It will help us learn the objective of the lesson', and 'I don't know'. I have never had anyone tell me that it will equip them for the world of work or their adult life.

While children tend not to state explicitly the link that Hughes *et al.* assert, over the last decade or so there has been a shift in emphasis from 'careful rehearsal of standard procedures to a focus on mathematical thinking and communication to prepare them for the world of tomorrow' (Anghileri, 1995: 2).

Both the NC and the Primary Framework for Mathematics (DfES, 2006a) support teachers to develop a learning trajectory for developing their children's mathematical thinking. In order to reflect the shift described by Anghileri, the most recent National Curriculum for Mathematics in England and Wales (DfEE, 1999a) made a significant adjustment to the way it presented Attainment Target 1: Using and Applying Mathematics. It altered the Using and Applying Attainment Target (Ma1) from a separate section that asked teachers to incorporate its aspects throughout the curriculum to a fully integrated part of all the programmes of study for mathematics. 'In addition to requiring teachers to pay attention to the range of mathematical contexts, using and applying mathematics also means making sure that children are developing their mathematical thinking' (Askew, 1998: 158). The level descriptions for Ma1 encapsulate this premise. The NC states that 'teachers should expect attainment at a given level in this attainment target to be demonstrated through activities in which the mathematics from the other attainment targets is at, or very close to, the same level' (DfEE, 1999a: Attainment Targets p9).

In addition to this intra-curriculum link there are references to cross-curricular and extracurricular work in Ma1. For example, at level 1, pupils are expected to 'use mathematics as an integral part of classroom activities' (DfEE, 1999a: Attainment Targets p9). This reflects comments made earlier in this chapter about mathematical thinking being one of the necessary aspects of operating successfully in the wider world rather than being encouraged only in mathematics lessons. By midway through their primary career, most children at level 3 will be expected to 'try different approaches and find ways of overcoming difficulties that arise when they are solving problems' (ibid.). Later in the same level a distinction is made about pupils discussing their mathematical work. Thus the first statement also refers to a wider context. This distinction continues. At level 4, 'pupils are developing their own strategies for solving problems and are using these strategies both in working within mathematics and in applying mathematics to practical contexts' (ibid.). More able pupils are also expected at level 5 to be able to 'show understanding of situations by describing them mathematically using symbols, words and diagrams' (ibid.).

## Problem-solving, reasoning and communication

The Using and Applying Attainment Target (Ma1) contains three sections: Problem-solving, Reasoning and Communicating. An overview of each of these is provided in Tables 1.1 and 1.2, with key themes emboldened.

**Table 1.1  An overview of using and applying mathematics in Key Stage 1 (DfEE, 1999a)**

| | Using and applying number | Using and applying shape, space and measures | Using and applying handling data |
|---|---|---|---|
| **Key Stage 1: 1) Pupils should be taught to:** | | | |
| **Problem-solving** | a) approach problems involving number, and data presented in a variety of forms, in order to **identify** what they need to do  b) develop **flexible approaches** to problem solving and look for ways to overcome difficulties  c) make **decisions** about which operations and problem solving strategies to use  d) **organise** and **check** their work | a) try **different approaches** and find ways of **overcoming difficulties** when solving shape and space problems  b) select and use appropriate **mathematical equipment** when solving problems involving measures or measurement  c) select and use **appropriate equipment** and materials when solving shape and space problems | Not applicable at Key Stage 1: Included in Using and applying number. |
| **Communicating** | e) use the **correct language, symbols and vocabulary** associated with number and data  f) **communicate in spoken, pictorial and written form**, at first using **informal** language and recording, then **mathematical** language and symbols | d) use the **correct language** and vocabulary for shape, space and measures | |
| **Reasoning** | g) **present** results in an **organised** way  h) understand a general statement and **investigate** whether particular cases match it  i) **explain** their methods and **reasoning** when solving problems involving number and data. | e) recognise simple spatial **patterns and relationships** and make **predictions** about them  f) use mathematical **communication** and explanation skills. | |

**Table 1.2  An overview of using and applying mathematics in Key Stage 2 (DfEE, 1999a)**

| Key Stage 2: 1) Pupils should be taught to: | | | |
| --- | --- | --- | --- |
| **Problem-solving** | a) make **connections** in mathematics and appreciate the need to use numerical skills and knowledge when solving problems in other parts of the mathematics curriculum<br>b) break down a more complex problem or calculation into simpler steps before attempting a solution; identify the information needed to carry out the tasks<br>c) select and use appropriate **mathematical equipment**, including ICT<br>d) find **different ways of approaching a problem** in order to overcome any difficulties<br>e) make mental estimates of the answers to calculations; **check results** | a) recognise the need for standard units of measurement<br>b) **select and use appropriate calculation skills** to solve geometrical problems<br>c) approach spatial problems **flexibly**, including trying **alternative approaches** to overcome difficulties<br>d) use **checking procedures** to confirm that their results of geometrical problems are reasonable | a) **select and use handling data skills** when solving problems in other areas of the curriculum, in particular science<br>b) **approach problems flexibly**, including trying alternative approaches to overcome any difficulties<br>c) **identify the data necessary** to solve a given problem<br>d) **select and use appropriate calculation skills** to solve problems involving data<br>e) **check results** and ensure that solutions are reasonable in the context of the problem |
| **Communicating** | f) **organise work** and refine ways of **recording**<br>g) use **notation diagrams and symbols** correctly within a given problem<br>h) **present and interpret** solutions in the context of the problem<br>i) **communicate mathematically**, including the use of precise mathematical language | e) **organise work** and **record or represent it in a variety of ways** when presenting solutions to geometrical problems<br>f) use **geometrical notation and symbols correctly**<br>g) **present and interpret solutions** to problems | f) decide how best to **organise and present findings**<br>g) use the **precise mathematical language** and vocabulary for handling data |
| **Reasoning** | j) understand and **investigate general** statements [for example, 'there are four prime numbers less than 10', 'wrist size is half neck size']<br>k) **search for pattern** in their results; develop logical thinking and explain their reasoning | h) use **mathematical reasoning to explain** features of shape and space. | h) **explain and justify their methods and reasoning.** |

From this overview it is possible to see how problem-solving, communication and reasoning are embedded within the mathematics content areas. The following section discusses the importance of these three aspects of mathematical thinking in more detail.

## Problem-solving

> *The ability to solve problems is at the heart of mathematics. The idea of investigation is fundamental both to the study of mathematics itself and also to an understanding of the ways in which mathematics can be used to extend knowledge and solve problems in very many fields.* (Cockcroft, 1982, Paragraph 250)

Although this quote from the seminal Cockcroft Report highlighting the need for children to solve problems was made over 25 years ago, the premise of solving problems being 'one of the core elements in the development of mathematical thinking' (Pound, 1999: 45) is still a key feature today. It is the purpose of the NC for children to be able to use the skills required to 'solve the problems they face in learning and in life'(DfEE, 1999a: 21).

Kelly and Lesh (2000: 28–29) remind us that 'mathematical thinking does not reside in [the] problems; it resides in the responses that students generate to problems'. As a result, it is 'crucial to develop in children the ability to tackle problems with initiative and confidence' (Anghileri, 2005: 2).

When the first National Numeracy Strategy Framework (NNS) was developed in 1999 (DfEE, 1999b), it placed a greater emphasis on solving problems. The Primary Framework for Mathematics (DfES, 2006a) responded to this by developing a 'Using and applying' strand. Problem-solving was embedded into this broader strand in order to 'bring an increased drive and momentum to mathematics, making adjustments to learning objectives, involving some scaling-up of expectations around ... using and applying mathematics' (DfEE, 2006b: 6).

## Communicating

There is no shortage of literature explaining the role of talk in developing mathematical thinking. Askew (1998: 3) refers to discussion as 'central' in 'helping children develop mathematical ideas'; Pound (1999: 63) explains how it is 'indispensable to both understanding and to the development of mathematical thinking'. In fact it has been widely accepted for many years that 'an essential part of developing mathematical thinking is communicating one's own thoughts both orally and in written records' (Floyd, 1981: 68). This is because it 'obliges children to make their thinking explicit to others, and to reflect upon their own reasoning and choice of strategies and approach' (Whitebread, 1995: 38).

Askew *et al.* (1997: 4) explain that highly effective teachers encourage 'purposeful discussion, in whole classes, small groups, and with individual pupils' because they believe that 'pupils develop strategies and networks of ideas by being challenged to think, through explaining, listening and problem solving'.

Hoyles (1985) identified how child language plays a role of conflict and co-construction in developing mathematical thinking. She explains two functions of talk during mathematical activity. The first, communicative language, involves a child explaining and justifying their own strategies and logically rejecting others'. The second function, cognitive talk, allows a child to 'step aside' and reflect on a piece of mathematics.

The Basic Skills Agency (cited in QCA, 2005) found that developing children's mathematical talk raises both their own achievement and the profile of mathematics. In addition to this, where schools adopted materials and approaches to learning that included thinking, questioning, collaboration, reflection and information processing, they created a climate of trust where making mistakes was seen as part of the process of learning. They also placed high value on mathematical talk and this effectively encouraged children to extend their mathematical thinking and explain their reasoning.

## Reasoning

Suggate *et al.* (2001) caution that children may well not be able to successfully use and apply number if they fall victim to rote learning and use certain mathematical rules 'without reason'. Reasoning allows children to make connections between areas within and out of mathematics. Daniel (in press) explains how reasoning provides the mechanism for them to organise different ideas into coherent systems. She states:

> To do mathematics is a way to imagine the world, to deal with reality, to reason about problems which are meaningful. When children, within a philosophical community of inquiry about mathematics, sit down and search together for the meanings of a mathematical problem, they develop their reasoning skills because, in order to succeed in their discursive activity, they have to extend the knowledge they already have (in regard with mathematics or with personal experience) through reasoning.

In this meaning-making process, children practise a number of skills and strategies such as classification, definition, questioning, comparing and contrasting (Lipman, 1991) that are all part of reasoning.

# Using and applying: to what extent has it been well integrated?

The rationale for integrating Ma1 thoughout the content areas of the NC was to demonstrate the relationship between and the balance required of the use and application of number, shape and space, measures and data handling. It has met with some success; however, the most recent evaluations of mathematics teaching and learning identify a number of aspects of using and applying that still need to be developed. For example, the Annual Report of Her Majesty's Chief Inspector of Schools 2004/05 reported:

> It still remains the case that too few pupils are able to connect the different skills they have acquired, remember the key things they have been taught, or use and apply their mathematics to solve problems in unfamiliar contexts. These features were reported in HMCI's most recent primary mathematics report and still remain pertinent. The challenge for the Primary National Strategy now is to ensure that the connectivity between different areas of the mathematics curriculum is emphasised and that pupils' learning progresses at an appropriate pace whilst they also develop the facility to understand, use and apply the skills to secure good progress through Key Stage 3. ... As has been reported on many occasions, pupils are not always able to connect the different skills they have acquired, or to use and apply their mathematics to solve problems in unfamiliar contexts. There remain many missed opportunities for both the application and development of mathematical skills in other subjects such as science, design and technology, geography and history.
> (www.ofsted.gov.uk/publications/annualreport0405/4.1.7.html)

In addition to this, OFSTED's mathematics subject report (cited in QCA, 2005) revealed that children's explanation is confined to the steps in methods and there is little expectation that they will need time to think and reason. The report suggests four main areas for development in primary mathematics, all of which have clear links with using and applying mathematics:

1 a clear focus on key mathematical concepts as well as computational techniques;
2 learning tasks that require children to think and reason about mathematics;
3 a classroom culture where children are given time to think and to work collaboratively with their peers;
4 a requirement for children to articulate their understanding and justify their strategies and solutions.

It appears that many of these weaknesses are due to teachers' lack of subject knowledge, which will be discussed later in the chapter.

# Other countries' approaches to mathematical thinking

Other countries have developed mathematical thinking in their curriculum documents in order to achieve similar outcomes. This section considers mathematical thinking from curriculum documents from a range of other countries. The relevant areas of five countries are outlined below. These countries were selected in order to consider a range of educational settings.

## An overview of mathematical thinking from other national curricula

### Australia (WA): Appreciating Mathematics and Working Mathematically
The Western Australian Curriculum Framework for mathematics is organised into seven 'clusters'. Two of these relate specifically to mathematical thinking. These are Appreciating mathematics and Working mathematically.

### Appreciating mathematics
Students appreciate the role mathematics has had, and continues to have, in their own and other communities. In particular, they:

• Show a disposition to use mathematics to assist with understanding new situations, solving problems and making decisions, showing initiative, flexibility and persistence when working mathematically and a positive attitude to their own continued involvement in learning and doing mathematics.
• Appreciate that mathematics has its origins in many cultures, and its forms reflect specific social and historical contexts, and understand its significance in explaining and influencing aspects of our lives.

### Working mathematically
Students use mathematical thinking processes and skills in interpreting and dealing with mathematical and non-mathematical situations. In particular, they:

• Call on a repertoire of general problem solving techniques, appropriate technology and personal and collaborative management strategies when working mathematically.

- Choose mathematical ideas and tools to fit the constraints in a practical situation, interpret and make sense of the results within the context and evaluate the appropriateness of the methods used.
- Investigate, generalise and reason about patterns in number, space and data, explaining and justifying conclusions reached.
  From **www.curriculum.wa.edu.au/pages/framework/framework08b.htm**

## Canada (Ontario): The Importance of Mathematics and the Process Skills

The Ontario Mathematics Curriculum for Grades 1–8 is organised into five 'strands' that focus on the knowledge and skills that pupils are required to know. At the beginning of every grade is a list of seven mathematical processes that children are expected to learn and apply as they work through the content of the strands. These are: problem-solving, reasoning and proving, reflecting, selecting tools and computational strategies, connecting, representing, and communicating. It is interesting to note that 'the mathematical processes can be seen as the processes through which students acquire and apply mathematical knowledge and skills. These processes are interconnected ... The mathematical processes cannot be separated from the knowledge and skills that students acquire throughout the year. Students must problem solve, communicate, reason, reflect, and so on, as they develop the knowledge, the understanding of concepts, and the skills required in all the strands in every grade.'
**(www.edu.gov.on.ca/eng/curriculum/elementary/math18curr.pdf)**

## Finland: Thinking Skills and Methods

In Finland, the curriculum considers the 'core contents'. 'Thinking Skills and Methods' is integral to this. In fact, the curriculum document places mathematical thinking at the heart of mathematics: 'The task of instruction in mathematics is to offer opportunities for the development of mathematical thinking, and for the learning of mathematical concepts and the most widely used problem-solving methods' (Finnish National Board of Education, 2004).

## New Zealand: Mathematical Processes

The New Zealand Mathematics National Curriculum is organised into 'strands'. There is one strand entitled 'Mathematical Processes' which is concerned with similar aspects to Ma1. These are listed below:

The mathematics curriculum intended by this statement will provide opportunities for students to:

- develop flexibility and creativity in applying mathematical ideas and techniques to unfamiliar problems arising in everyday life, and develop the ability to reflect critically on the methods they have chosen;
- become effective participants in problem-solving teams, learning to express ideas, and to listen and respond to the ideas of others;
- develop the skills of presentation and critical appraisal of a mathematical argument or calculation, use mathematics to explore and conjecture, and learn from mistakes as well as successes;
- develop the characteristics of logical and systematic thinking, and apply these in mathematical and other contexts, including other subjects of the curriculum;
- become confident and competent users of information technology in mathematical contexts;

- develop the skills and confidence to use their own language, and the language of mathematics, to express mathematical ideas;
- develop the knowledge and skills to interpret written presentations of mathematics.
(New Zealand Ministry of Education, 1995)

## USA

Within *Principles and Standards for School Mathematics* there are five 'Content Standards': number and operations, algebra, geometry, measurement, and data analysis and probability; and five 'Process Standards': problem solving, reasoning and proof, communication, connections, and representation:

**Problem solving:**
- build new mathematical knowledge through problem solving;
- solve problems that arise in mathematics and in other contexts;
- apply and adapt a variety of appropriate strategies to solve problems;
- monitor and reflect on the process of mathematical problem solving.

**Reasoning and proof:**
- recognize reasoning and proof as fundamental aspects of mathematics;
- make and investigate mathematical conjectures;
- develop and evaluate mathematical arguments and proofs;
- select and use various types of reasoning and methods of proof.

**Communication:**
- organize and consolidate their mathematical thinking though communication;
- communicate their mathematical thinking coherently and clearly to peers, teachers, and others;
- analyze and evaluate the mathematical thinking and strategies of others;
- use the language of mathematics to express mathematical ideas precisely.

**Connections:**
- recognize and use connections among mathematical ideas;
- understand how mathematical ideas interconnect and build on one another to produce a coherent whole;
- recognize and apply mathematics in contexts outside of mathematics

**Representation:**
- create and use representations to organize, record, and communicate mathematical ideas;
- select, apply, and translate among mathematical representations to solve problems;
- use representations to model and interpret physical, social, and mathematical phenomena.

**(http://standards.nctm.org/document/chapter3/index.htm)**

'The ... Curriculum should emphasise the development of children's mathematical thinking and reasoning abilities. An individual's future uses and needs for mathematics make the ability to think, reason and solve problems a primary goal for the study of mathematics ... The curriculum must take seriously the goal of instilling in students the confidence in their ability to think and communicate mathematically.' (National Council of Teachers of Mathematics, 2000)

# What can we learn from other national curricula?

The above section provides an overview of the particular mathematical knowledge and skills that pupils need to have in the curriculum documents of the five different countries. These are all similar in mathematical content, covering number, shape, handling data, measures, algebra. In addition to these, they all share a number of themes that reflect mathematical thinking. Some of these can be grouped together under the three sections of Ma1 of the National Curriculum for Mathematics in England and Wales, and this has been done, where appropriate, in Table 1.3. Others, however, do not sit so neatly with the existing Ma1 aspects.

These are disposition, making connections and evaluation. While these themes have been grouped in the table, it is necessary to remember that they all interrelate and are at work within mathematics contexts such as number, shape and space, measures, data handling, etc.

**Table 1.3  Mathematical thinking skills from the national curricula of the selected countries**

| | |
|---|---|
| **Problem-solving** | **Problem-solving techniques**<br><br>The majority of the curricula consider a need for having a repertoire of problem-solving skills, strategies or techniques available to pupils to use when solving problems. |
| | **Flexibility/creativity**<br><br>Having a flexible and creative approach to problem-solving and to mathematics in general is a strong theme of the antipodeans' national curricula. This is also a theme that schools in England are approaching through the Primary National Strategy's notion of Excellence and Enjoyment (EandE) (DfES, 2003). |
| | **Tools/technology**<br><br>Several of the curricula identified the need for pupils to be able access appropriate tools for the task. While this is not necessarily only in a problem-solving context, the use of tools (including technology) is part of a solving problems environment. |
| | **Investigating/generalising**<br><br>Key terms that are used in some curricula include 'investigation' and 'exploration'. Alongside these are 'generalising' and 'conjecturing'. While these have been placed within a problem-solving heading for the purposes of this table, they are also integral to reasoning. |
| **Reasoning** | **Reasoning**<br><br>The majority of the curricula placed an emphasis on reasoning. They focused on making sense of situations/problems through interpreting and through logical and systematic thinking. |
| **Communication** | **Expressing/explaining/justifying**<br><br>The majority of the curricula placed an emphasis on pupils explaining or justifying their ideas. In all the development was from their own everyday language to mathematical language. |
| | **Collaboration**<br><br>Several of the curricula explicitly considered the effect of collaboration on the development of mathematical thinking and mathematical understanding. This included being able to effectively manage working in a group as well as listening to and responding to others. |
| **Disposition** | **Disposition**<br><br>The majority of the documents highlighted the need for a positive attitude to mathematics, having persistence to solving problems (for example through trial-and-error) and confidence to do mathematics. In fact the TIMSS 2003 International study found that an important factor in mathematics achievement is pupils' self-confidence in the subject (Mullis *et al.*, 2005). |

| | |
|---|---|
| **Making connections** | **Making connections**<br><br>Many of the documents were concerned with teachers and pupils making links between mathematical thinking and all aspects of the mathematics NC as well as cross-curricular subjects and contexts out of the classroom. In addition to this, there were some links to the historical and cultural development of mathematics and how that impacts how we use mathematics in today's society. |
| **Evaluating** | **Evaluating**<br><br>Finally, there was a need from some of the countries for their pupils to evaluate their work. For example, the New Zealand Curriculum Framework for Mathematics referred to the pupils reflecting critically on their work and the work of others. In addition to this it explained how they should learn from their mistakes and successes. |

In this list, ten aspects of mathematical thinking have been identified. This book is concerned with the effective use of resources to develop children's mathematical thinking and the remaining chapters will consider in detail how these themes are supported where appropriate by resources.

# When do children begin to think mathematically?

*Young children continue to excite us with their enthusiasm and creative strategies for solving problems.*
(Clarke *et al.*, 2003)

Let me tell you a story. I witnessed my daughter's ability to solve a two-step problem when she was six months old! She had just learned to pull herself up to a standing position. One day she was in her cot and decided to stand up with Rosie, her favourite toy. But she had a problem: she wasn't strong enough to stand up while holding Rosie. Every time she got half-way up, she fell down again. After a number of failed attempts she tried a new method. She put Rosie in her mouth, stood up using both hands to pull her up and then, once upright, took Rosie out and stood holding Rosie while grinning from ear to ear!

Why did I want to share that story? Well, there are two important points I wish to make.

The first is that we are all born with the ability to think mathematically (see, for example, David *et al.*, 2003). My daughter did not receive any formal instruction from me or another adult/older child as to how to undertake this two-step problem but through trial and error (and sheer determination) she solved it. Skinner (2002: 24) explains how 'children have many wide-ranging mathematical experiences from the moment they are born. This can give a secure basis on which to build their further maths achievements.' DiSessa and Sherin (1998) call these early stages of learning mini-concepts, primitive concepts or p-prims. These are developed as our experiences increase and we mature. (To read more on this development of mathematical understanding, read Hansen, 2005.)

The second point is that children do not need to be articulate for teachers to gain an insight into the development of their mathematical thinking. Sometimes the trainees I work with struggle to assess and develop the mathematical thinking of younger children or children with special educational needs. They argue that they are unable to talk to them about their mathematical thinking and so cannot tell what the children are doing. Ironically, they often go on to share an episode where they observed a child doing something that provided a particularly insightful window into the child's mathematical thinking. When young children or children with special educational needs are given the opportunity to 'make their own representations of mathematical problems, processes and procedures before they are introduced to conventional symbols ... [this] holds enormous meaning for them [in gaining] an understanding and confidence in written symbols by first inventing and using their own' (Whitebread, 2005: 31–32).

An example of this comes from the influential research of Martin Hughes in the 1980s. Hughes (1986) demonstrated that young children have significant mathematical understanding before they start school and that they are even able to complete simple addition and subtraction if it is set in a context that makes sense to them. Anghileri (2005: 28) explains that 'in real situations, where the mathematics serves real purposes, young children quickly and easily develop their own informal and largely effective methods'. Carpenter *et al.*'s (1996: 3) research supports this, stating that children begin school with a 'great deal of informal or intuitive knowledge of mathematics', on which the more formal curriculum can be built.

Being able to build on this early mathematical thinking as part of the role of the teacher is discussed later in this chapter.

# What about children who demonstrate a low attainment level in number, shape and space, measures or handling data?

While the NC (DfEE, 1999a: Attainment Targets p9) expects 'attainment at a given level [in AT1] to be demonstrated through activities in which the mathematics from the other attainment targets is at, or very close to, the same level', there are a number of researchers (for example, Boaler, 1997; Ahmed, 1987; Watson, 2000; Harries, 2001) who provide evidence for 'lower attaining' pupils demonstrating mathematical thinking at a higher level than their level of content-specific mathematics work.

Indeed, Resnick and Collins (1996: 49) report research that claims that it may be possible to overcome the difficulties that lower-attaining pupils face (due to 'weak preparation' such as limited pre-school experience) by engaging them in 'intellectually challenging problem-solving while providing supporting "scaffolding"'. Recently a major Australian research project has developed this idea (Fleer *et al.*, 2006). Fleer *et al.* introduce the notion of 'optimal pathways'. In Figure 1.1 we see two children: A and B. Child A is at a lower attainment level than child B. The optimal pathway for both children is to reach attainment level C (Figure 1.1a). However, the less effective (but more commonly observed) pathway (Figure 1.1b) is where the optimal pathway is designed for Child B, and Child A is expected to catch up and follow it. Willis (2001) explains that this view 'does not treat the curriculum as neutral or "innocent" but suggests that every child is different and teachers need to understand and develop teaching that cater for their diverse pathways' (Willis, 2001: 4).

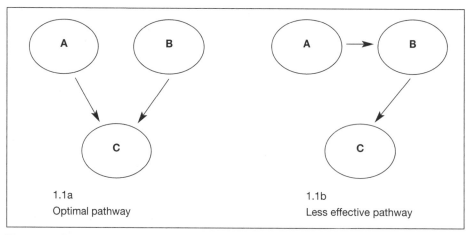

1.1a
Optimal pathway

1.1b
Less effective pathway

**Figure 1.1: Catering for diverse pathways (Willis, 2001)**

Within teachers' planning and assessment of work, it is necessary to ensure that consideration to 'using and applying' is given as an inherent part of all lessons. It is essential to be
aware that a pupil's NC level of attainment in Ma1 may not automatically correlate with the
level of attainment in other programmes of study.

It is concerning, therefore, to see that teachers are not taking heed of this. For example, in
their Mathematics Annual Report on Curriculum and Assessment, the Qualifications and
Curriculum Authority (QCA, 2005: 9) reported that 'using and applying mathematics does not
feature sufficiently in key stages 1 and 2'. They also report that 'many [Year 5] teachers use
optional test results rather than level descriptions to determine the level at which children are
working. The process of determining levels often does not draw on teachers' knowledge of
children's performance in class work over time or give appropriate emphasis to Ma1 (Using
and applying mathematics)' (QCA, 2005: 13).

# The role of the teacher in developing mathematical thinking

This section focuses on two aspects of how teachers can develop mathematical thinking in
their pupils: the importance of good teacher pedagogical and subject knowledge and the
need to build on children's existing knowledge.

## Good pedagogical and subject knowledge

Clarkson (1991: 147) proposes that 'if children are to develop as independent mathematical
thinkers, teachers need to know what are the processes of mathematical thinking, and how children
learn to use them'. Carpenter *et al.* (1996) suggest a solution for how teachers might begin to do
this. They purport that by understanding children's mathematical thinking, teachers can support
their own understanding of mathematics. By gaining insight into how children learn mathematics,
teachers will in turn learn how to support them to develop it. This section will introduce some
aspects of the teacher's role that you may wish to reflect on in light of your own experience.

Teachers have a statutory responsibility to deliver the requirements of the National
Curriculum. Unfortunately, the QCA report introduced earlier in this chapter (QCA, 2005) high-

lights a number of examples where teachers are not meeting these. The QCA explain that this might be because teachers may not have the necessary subject knowledge required in order to identify the connections within mathematics or between mathematics and other areas of the curriculum.

In their research into effective numeracy teachers, Askew *et al.* (1997) were interested in the pedagogy of effective teachers. They compared teachers with pupil attainment. In doing so, they identified three 'types' of teachers: those with connectionist, transmission or discovery orientation. This section will focus on the connectionist teachers, who were identified as achieving the highest gains with their pupils over the research period.

A connectionist-orientated teacher:

- has a conscious awareness of connections and relationships to develop pupils' mental agility and believes that this mental agility gives pupils the confidence in flexible mental methods so that they can tackle calculations positively;
- believes that all pupils regardless of their attainment level should be challenged in mathematics, has high expectations of all pupils and sees they all have the potential to succeed;
- values the place of discussion in the classroom, which includes teacher/class, teacher/pupil and pupil/pupil discussion, and keeps pupils focused through organising discussions around their work;
- recognises the importance of applying mathematical skills but does not see learning skills as a prerequisite to being able to apply it; the skill could be learnt through application.

## Building on young children's existing knowledge

Skemp (2002: 75) reminds us that 'children come to school having already acquired, without formal teaching, more mathematical knowledge than they are usually given credit for'. He explains, however, that the skills they come to school with are often practical skills and as a result their knowledge is 'not sufficient to take the weight of the lofty abstract structures we want them to build'.

The teacher needs to be aware of this and provide appropriate support for children to develop more school mathematics understanding. Engaging with school mathematics should not involve losing touch with understanding and meaning in what is being carried out. A range of research provides evidence that tells us this currently occurs in many situations. For example, Carpenter *et al.* (1993) identified that kindergarten children can successfully solve a variety of problems by modelling the problem. They draw on their personal experience of the world to evaluate the extent to which their solutions make sense. As children move through the school, however, children begin to see mathematics as not meaningful or relevant to them; they interpret it as an area of the curriculum involving meaningless symbols, rules and procedures (Greeno, 1988).

Vygotsky (1987) helps to explain why this development from home mathematics to school mathematics might be potentially difficult. He defines two concepts: the everyday concept and the scientific concept. Everyday concepts arise from children's daily experiences and are used without conscious realisation of the concepts. They are built out of everyday language and conversation. Scientific concepts, on the other hand, are removed from those meaningful, concrete situations and involve technical, domain-specific vocabulary. Vygotsky highlights the essential nature of the relationship between everyday concepts and scientific concepts, explaining that everyday concepts lay the foundations for building scientific concepts.

Vygotsky warns that it is impossible to teach a scientific concept without building on a child's own language from an everyday concept. He explains that doing so would achieve 'nothing but a mindless learning of words, an empty verbalism that simulates or imitates the presence of concepts in the child … It substitutes the learning of dead and empty verbal schemes for the mastery of living knowledge' (Vygotsky, 1987: 170).

## SUMMARY OF **KEY POINTS**

Mark Humble (2002: 25) identifies the need for children to be provided with 'well-structured learning contexts in which their existing mathematical knowledge and thinking can be applied, developed and enriched'. This chapter has begun to address some of the issues underlying how teachers might be able to do this. Initially it considered what mathematical thinking is in relation to the National Curriculum for Mathematics in England (DfEE, 1999a) and the national curricula of a range of other countries. It also highlighted how children's mathematical thinking exists, and why and how it should be developed (regardless of age, level of mathematical attainment or special educational need) in all children. It briefly considered the implications for teachers' pedagogical and content subject knowledge and the impact that connectionist teachers have on their pupils' mathematical thinking.

To summarise, mathematical thinking was identified as:

> using a range of problem-solving techniques;
> being flexible and creative in approaches to mathematics;
> understanding which tools are available and which are the best to use for the task at hand;
> being able to investigate patterns and to generalise findings;
> being able to work through problems using systematic, logical reasoning;
> the ability to explain and justify work to others verbally (in own language or mathematical language) or in written form (using pictures, diagrams, charts or symbols);
> working as a team to collaboratively undertake maths, not only being able to provide a point of view but to listen to those of others, questioning them and learning from their strengths;
> demonstrating an appropriate disposition towards mathematics through having the confidence and persistence to keep trying;
> being able to make connections within mathematics, between mathematics and other school curriculum subjects, between mathematics in school and out of school, between mathematics and cultural/historical contexts;
> constantly improving mathematical attainment through evaluating process.

## REFERENCES REFERENCES REFERENCES REFERENCES REFERENCES REFERENCES

Ahmed, A. (1987) *Better mathematics*. London: HMSO.

Anghileri, J. (1995) *Children's mathematical thinking in the primary years*. London: Cassell.

Anghileri, J. (2005) *Children's mathematical thinking in the primary years*. London: Continuum.

Askew, M. (1998) *Teaching primary mathematics: A guide for newly qualified teachers*. London: Hodder and Stoughton.

Askew, M., Brown, M., Johnson, D., Rhodes, V. and Wiliam, D. (1997) *Effective teachers of numeracy: Summary of findings*. London: King's College, pp2–3.

Boaler, J. (1997) *Experiencing school mathematics*. Buckingham: Open University Press.

Carpenter, T. P., Ansell, E., Franke, M.L., Fennema, E. and Weisbeck, L. (1993) Models of problem solving: a study of kindergarten children's problem-solving processes. *Journal of Research in Mathematics Education*, 24(5): 428–441.

Carpenter, T. P., Fennema, M.L. and Franke, M.L. (1996) Cognitively guided instruction: A knowledge base for reform in primary mathematics instruction. *The Elementary School Journal*, 97(1): 3–20.

Clarke, D.M., Cheeseman, J., McDonough, A. and Clarke, B.A. (2003) Assessing and developing measurement with young children, in Clements, D.H. and Bright, D.W. (eds) *Learning and teaching measurement*. Reston, VA: NCTM, pp68–80.

Clarkson, M. (1991) *Emerging issues in primary education*. London: Falmer Press.

Cockcroft, W.H. (1982) *Mathematics counts: Report of the Committee of Inquiry into the teaching of mathematics in schools under the chairmanship of Dr W.H. Cockcroft*. London: HMSO.

Daniel, M-F. (in press) A primary school curriculum to foster thinking about mathematics thinking. *Encyclopedia of Philosophy of Education 2006*. **www.vusst.hr/ENCYCLOPAEDIA/mathematics.htm** (accessed 01/08/06).

David, T., Gooch, K., Powell, S. and Abbott, L. (2003) *Birth to three matters: A review of the literature*. London: Department for Education and Skills.

Department for Education and Employment (1999a) Mathematics. *The National Curriculum for England: Key Stages 1–4*. London: DfEE Publications.

Department for Education and Employment (1999b) The National Numeracy Strategy. *Framework for Teaching Mathematics from Reception to Year 6*. London: DfEE Publications.

Department for Education and Skills (2003) *Excellence and enjoyment: A strategy for primary schools*. London: DfES Primary National Strategy. Ref. DfES0377/2003. Available at **www.gov.uk/primarydocument** (accessed 25/09/06).

Department for Education and Skills (2006a) Primary Framework for Mathematics. **www.standards.gov.uk/primaryframeworks**.

Department for Education and Skills (2006b) Draft framework for teaching mathematics: consultation document. DfES Ref. 0358-2006BKT-EN. London: DfES Publications.

diSessa, A and Sherin, B. (1998) What changes in conceptual change? *International Science Education*, 20(10): 1155–1191.

Finnish National Board of Education (2004) *National Core Curriculum for Basic Education*. Finland.

Fleer, M., Ridgway, A., Clarke, B., Kennedy, A., Robbins, J., May, W. and Surman, L. (2006) Catch the future: literacy and numeracy pathways for preschool children. Commonwealth of Australia. **www.dest.gov.au/NR/rdonlyres/8B6619B3-A2F9-4DCA-B76E-A9535D98F9DF/9461/catch_future2.pdf** (accessed 27/07/06).

Floyd, A. (ed.) (1981) *Developing mathematical thinking*. Wokingham: Addison-Wesley.

Government of Western Australia (1998) Curriculum framework: mathematics learning area statement. WA: Curriculum Council. Available at: **www.curriculum.wa.edu.au/files/pdf/maths.pdf** (accessed 04/08/06).

Greeno, J.G. (1988) The situated activities of learning and knowing mathematics, in Behr, M.J., Lacampagne, C.G. and Wheeler, M.M. (eds) *Proceedings of the Tenth Annual Meeting of PME-NA*. DeKalb, IL: Northern Illinois University, pp481–521.

Hansen, A. (ed.) (2005) *Children's errors in maths: understanding common misconceptions*. Exeter: Learning Matters.

Harries, T. (2001) Working through complexity: an experience of developing mathematical thinking through the use of Logo with low attaining pupils. *Support for Learning*, 16(1): 17–22.

Hoyles, C. (1985) What is the point of group discussion in mathematics? *Educational Studies in Mathematics*, 16: 205–214.

Hughes, H., Desforges, C. and Mitchell, C. (2000) *Numeracy and beyond*. Buckingham: Open University Press.

Hughes, M. (1986) *Children and number: children's difficulties in learning mathematics*. Oxford: Blackwell.

Humble, M. (2002) Investigating numeracy in key stage 2, in Koshy, V. and Murray, J. (eds) *Unlocking numeracy*. London: David Fulton, pp24–34.

Kelly, A. and Lesh, R. (2000) Purposes and assumptions of this book, in Kelly, A and Lesh, R. (eds) *Handbook of research design in mathematics and science education*. Mahwah, NJ: Lawrence Erlbaum, pp17–34.

Lipman, M. (1991) *Thinking in education*. Cambridge, MA: Cambridge University Press.

Mathematics Association (1992) *Maths talk* (2nd ed.). Cheltenham: Stanley Thornes.

Ministry of Education Ontario (1997) The Ontario Curriculum Grades 1-8: Mathematics. Ontario: Ministry of Education. Available at: **www.edu.gov.on.ca/eng/document/curricul/curr97ma/curr97m.html#import** (accessed 04/08/06).

Mullis, I.V.S., Martin, M.O. and Foy, P. (2005) IEA's TIMSS 2003 International Report on Achievement in the Mathematics Cognitive Domains Chestnut Hill, MA: TIMSS and PIRLS International Study Center, Boston College.

National Council of Teachers of Mathematics (2000) *Principles and standards for school mathematics* (3rd ed.). Reston, VA: NCTM.

New Zealand Ministry of Education (1995) *Mathematics in the New Zealand Curriculum*. Wellington: Ministry of Education. Available at: **www.tki.org.nz/r/maths/curriculum/statement/contents_e.php** (accessed 04/08/06).

QCA (2005) *Mathematics 2004/5 annual report on curriculum and assessment*. London: QCA. Ref. QCA/05/2171.

Pound, L. (1999) *Supporting mathematical development in the early years*. Buckingham: Open University Press.

Resnick, L.B. and Collins, A. (1996) Cognition and learning, in Plomp, T. and Ely, D.P. (eds) *International encyclopedia of educational technology* (2nd ed.), pp48 – 51.

Skemp, R. (2002) *Mathematics in the primary school*. London: Routledge Falmer.

Skinner, C. (2002) *More than numbers: Children developing mathematical thinking*. London: Early Education.

Suggate, J., Davis, A. and Goulding, M. (2001) *Mathematical knowledge for primary teachers* (2nd ed.). London: David Fulton.

Vygotsky, L.S. (1987) Thinking and speech, in Rieber, R.W. and Carton, A.S. (eds) *The collected works of L.S. Vygotsky, Vol. 1, Problems of general psychology*. New York: Plenum Press, pp39–285.

Watson, A. (2000) Going across the grain: mathematical generalisations in a group of low attainers. *Nordic Studies in Mathematics Education*, 8(1): 7–20.

Whitebread, D. (2005) Emergent mathematics or how to help young children become confident mathematicians, in J. Anghileri (ed.) *Children's Thinking in primary mathematics: perspectives on children's learning*. London: Cassell.

Willis, S. (2001) *Becoming numerate: Who's at risk and why?* Paper presented at the Early Years Numeracy Conference, May 2001. Melbourne: Monash University, Victoria.

# 2

# Do resources matter in primary mathematics teaching and learning?

Doreen Drews

It has been common practice for many years for primary school teachers and Foundation Stage practitioners to view the use of resources as an essential part of teaching and learning mathematics. Foundation Stage and lower primary teachers, in particular, have drawn upon aspects of constructivism to validate the argument that children operating in the Piagetian stages of 'pre-operational' and 'concrete operational' modes of thinking need to manipulate objects to make sense of, and develop, mathematical ideas. While acknowledging that the teaching and learning of mathematics does benefit from effective use of visual and practical aids, recent research has questioned whether such use is always needed, or helpful, to children's mathematical understanding. Crucial to the debate is the rationale which teachers use to support the planned use of mathematical resources within their lessons (Moyer, 2001), teacher beliefs about how best to teach mathematics to assist children's learning (Askew *et al.*, 1997), and assumptions which teachers may make regarding children's interpretations of the use of mathematical resources (Cobb *et al.*, 1992).

## Chapter focus

This chapter will explore the role that a wide range of resources could play in effective mathematics teaching and learning in the primary years. Current research will be reviewed to support, and challenge, the contention that the manipulation of practical aids is helpful, and often necessary, to the development of children's mental images of mathematical concepts. It will ask the question whether or not practical work and the use of iconic imagery directly link to symbolic understanding. It will focus on:

- **the value of resources to the teaching and learning of primary mathematics;**
- **the issues involved in the use of resources to support mathematics teaching and learning;**
- **the critical aspects involved in the choice and use of resources to support effective mathematics teaching and learning.**

# The value of resources to the teaching and learning of primary mathematics

## A rationale for using mathematical resources

In the area of mathematical learning, Jerome Bruner's three modes of representing our experiences (1964) are considered important to the development of children's understanding: the enactive mode involves representation of ideas through undertaking some form of action (such as manipulating physical objects); the iconic mode involves representing those ideas using pictures or images; and the symbolic mode involves ideas represented through utilising language or symbols. By the 'representation of ideas', Bruner was referring to the outcomes of the processing of past experiences. For Bruner (1966), these modes of representation are mutually supportive in assisting the storage of 'pictures in the mind'. This entails the development of a mental 'storage system' which allows learners to make predictions and to retrieve relevant information from past experiences to extrapolate to new situations. The use of physical resources, models and images in mathematics teaching and learning relate well to the enactive and iconic modes of representation, with mental imagery and language supporting the understanding and use of symbols.

The interconnections between manipulation of objects, iconic imagery, use of language and symbols can, perhaps, be more commonly seen in activities involving young children, although Edwards (1998: 18) argues that mathematical understanding is brought about for all children by connections being made between these modes of representation. Haylock and Cockburn (2003) suggest that the network of connections between concrete experiences, pictures, language and symbols could be significant to the understanding of a mathematical concept (Figure 2.1).

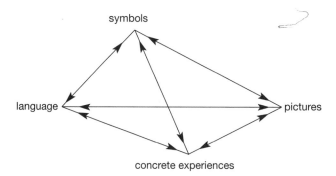

**Figure 2.1: Significant connections in understanding mathematics**

Central to this is the notion that 'when children are engaged in mathematical activity ... they are involved in *manipulating* some, or all, of the following: concrete materials, symbols, language and pictures' (Haylock and Cockburn, 2003: 3). It is this act of manipulation that allows for connections to be made through the different experiences. Moyer (2001: 176) supports this by stating that it is the active manipulation of materials that 'allows learners to develop a repertoire of images that can be used in the mental manipulation of abstract concepts'.

It would seem, therefore, that a key aspect to the value of children using practical resources within mathematics is a need for such activity to have a role to play in the development of mental imagery and mental strategies. Beyond this, a review of research undertaken by Askew and Wiliam (1995: 10) showed that 'practical work can provide images that help pupils contextualise mathematical ideas. It can also provide experiences out of which pupils can abstract mathematics.' In order for this to happen, Delaney (2001: 128) suggests that mental imagining of the given resource, and any action undertaken with the resource, need to be 'internalised and used to process mathematics when the resource is not physically present'. This would suggest that an important part of a teacher's role is to plan activities and conversations which refer to previous experiences of practical activity and encourage children to develop mental images.

Chapter 3 develops this idea further with specific case studies focusing on children building, and using, internal resources.

While concurring that practical activity has a clear role in aiding children's mathematical development, Anghileri (2000: 10) cautions against an overuse of concrete materials: 'It is important that children do not come to rely on using such materials for modelling numbers but that they develop mental imagery associated with these materials and can then work with "imagined" situations.' Hughes (1986) showed that young children were capable of imagining objects within a 'box game': this appears to be an important stage between manipulating objects and abstract work.

Askew (1998: 8) agrees that practical work on its own is not enough and suggests that practical activity should have an element of 'in the head' to avoid giving young children, in particular, the impression that mathematics is only about practical work.

The selection and effective use of appropriate mathematical resources requires careful consideration and planning on the part of the teacher. As Bottle (2005: 84) points out, the appropriateness of the resource should be 'judged by the extent to which the mental images that children form as a result are likely to be helpful or unhelpful in structuring their thinking'.

# Types of mathematical resources and how they may be used effectively

The term 'mathematical resource' is defined here as any form of specific mathematical apparatus (structured or unstructured), image, ICT, game, tool, paper, or everyday material which could be utilised to provide a mathematical teaching or learning aid.

## Manipulatives

Specific mathematical apparatus, or manipulatives, are 'objects designed to represent explicitly and concretely mathematical ideas that are abstract.' (Moyer, 2001: 176). They can be used as models by both teachers and learners, hold a visual and tactile appeal, and, as such, are designed primarily for hands-on manipulation.

Structured mathematical apparatus is specifically designed to embody one particular conceptual structure. Through manipulation of the apparatus the learners, or teachers, 'directly reflect the equivalent mathematical manipulations within that structure'. (Bottle, 2005: 87). Examples of this type of apparatus are Multibase 10 (Diene's) material and Cuisenaire Number Rods. Both types of material reflect the relationships within our base 10 number system: for example, Multibase 10 can be used to model the base 10 place value system and the relationships between, e.g. one hundred and ten tens. This structure is particularly helpful in helping children make sense of decomposition as a strategy for subtraction where it needs to be understood that i.e. four tens and three ones is worth the same as three tens and 13 ones.

Cuisenaire Rods enable children to explore the properties of numbers and relationships between numbers. Number pairs, inverse operations and number patterns can be explored and familiarity with/use of the apparatus can assist mathematical understanding (Delaney, 1992).

Unstructured mathematical apparatus is often more versatile and 'open' in its use as it has not been designed to focus on particular conceptual structures. Examples include Multilink, many counting materials or collections of shapes. In all these examples the materials can be used in specific ways, i.e. to aid counting, or in more exploratory ways such as investigating number/shape patterns, construction and design, or relationships between types of numbers or shapes. Variety of the same type of resource is important in the selection in order that children do not form misconceptions based on experiences with limited resources. As Hansen (2005: 85) indicates, where children are only exposed to prototypical examples/images of shapes, they are likely to form incorrect generalisations. The ability to use these materials in diverse ways can promote greater opportunities for investigational and collaborative work: such activities are more likely to encourage purposeful mathematical discussion and development of logic and reasoning. (Examples can be found in the case studies in Chapter 4.)

## Images

Young children will link an acoustic image (sounds, rhythms) to a concrete image of something meaningful such as fingers or objects (Harries and Spooner, 2000: 49). Visual and tactile images, such as an abacus or bead string, assist children in linking counting to movement. Such resources help children develop a sense of number order and number pattern, particularly where the beads are blocked in groups of fives or tens as evident on bead strings or a Slavonic abacus. Through the use of colour and/or groupings of beads, the concepts involved are embedded within the image. In order to connect this sense of order with symbolic representations of number a more abstract image is needed.

An abstract image gives an opportunity for particular aspects of mathematics to be presented as either visual or 'hands-on' teaching and/or learning aids. These could include pictorial images of shapes/objects or images more closely connected to our symbolic number system, e.g. number tracks, number lines, digit cards, 100 squares and place value arrow cards. As Delaney (2001: 132) points out, the latter abstract representations appear to be favoured by the National Numeracy Strategy (NNS) (DfEE, 1999) over more 'concrete' specific mathematical apparatus without a clear rationale evident for the choice. The value of connecting concrete images (as described above) with abstract images is that children learn to relate the number symbols, and order, to the acoustic and concrete images that they have experienced. (Examples of this can be found in case studies in Chapters 3, 5 and 6.)

As children develop their understanding of the number system, progression in the level of sophistication of an abstract number line is needed. More powerful images that illustrate how numbers are related in a logical structure act as a model for both teaching and learning. Consequently, number tracks need to be superseded by calibrated number lines as the latter allow for negative integers and intermediate values to be represented. A number line can therefore be a helpful teaching and learning aid beyond counting on and counting back. One aspect of fractions and decimals which children find difficult is the notion that they are numbers which fit within our number system (Frobisher *et al.*, 1999). As Lawton (2005: 40) points out, this lack of understanding is more evident when dealing with fractional/decimal values greater than one. Activities which demonstrate and which allow for rational numbers to be positioned on a number line can support a greater understanding of place value, relationships between 'numbers of a different kind' and our overall number system: this is true for all children including the more able in mathematics. An empty number line allows for the modelling of mental calculations where the order of numbers remains true but numbers and intervals are not marked. Children do not need to work to a correct scale in their size of 'jumps' between numbers. Harries and Spooner (2000: 50–51) view empty number lines, in particular, as providing children with flexible thinking tools: decisions need to be made at the point of construction regarding which numbers to use, how to place them and the intermediate numbers to be shown.

Abstract images, therefore, provide reference tools and thinking tools for children to work with as they develop understanding of the number system and perform calculations with numbers. Such images can act as visual cues/memory aids which, in turn, act as a basis for reflective thought. In addition, models, images and diagrams should assist understanding of how a particular strategy or method was used to solve a problem and why it worked. Research undertaken by Clausen-May (2005: 84) shows that visual and kinaesthetic thinkers are more likely to benefit from teaching and learning approaches which make effective use of models and images 'that make key mathematical concepts manifest'.

## ICT

A wide range of information and communication technology (ICT) is available in most primary schools as useful resources and tools to support the teaching and learning of mathematics. This can include programmable robots, calculators, television, radio, audio tape, video, digital cameras as well as computers, software, access to the internet and interactive whiteboards (IWBs). The NNS (DfEE, 1999: 32) advocates the use of such resources providing that 'it is the most efficient and effective way to meet your lesson objectives'. Bottle (2005: 95) lists some appropriate uses of ICT in mathematics lessons and suggests that there need to be connections between the tasks/activities undertaken using the ICT device and mathematical activities independent of the device. This is supported by Higgins and Muijs (1999: 112), who advocate that more explicit links need to be made between computer activities and other planned activities in order that pupils develop a greater awareness of mathematical connections. Anghileri (2001: 186) suggests that calculators are at their most effective as cognitive tools when they are used to provoke thinking rather than as simple machines to obtain answers to given calculations.

While there is little doubt that ICT offers powerful visual images and that children are motivated by ICT devices, on its own this will not necessarily lead to increased understanding of any mathematical aspect or concept. As with the use of all resources or tools, it is the choice of task, effective use of the resource/software, quality of teacher intervention and opportunities for discussion which are fundamental to successful learning. OFSTED (2005) continue to report that too few teachers use ICT effectively in their mathematics lessons. There does appear to be, however, a greater use of IWBs within whole-class lessons or sections of lessons, particularly for demonstration and review purposes. Chapter 8 provides more focus on creative and effective use of IWBs to develop mathematical thinking.

### Mathematical games

Mathematical games can be played in whole-class, small group or paired settings. They are a resource which is usually highly motivating to children and, consequently, encourages greater levels of concentration and engagement with mathematics. Games can be used in different ways to consolidate learning, practise skills, explore mathematical relationships and develop problem-solving strategies. Many board games, commercially produced games and some computer games are designed to practise particular aspects of mathematics; Parr (1994: 29) sees this as a major advantage of games as they 'can stimulate people to give repeated practice to skills of mental arithmetic and then do the whole thing again simply because they want to do better the second time around'. While such games do allow for the use and application of skills in a different context, when choosing these types of games, teachers and practitioners need to give consideration to the mathematical content and the level at which the children are working. The best games will allow for different levels of challenge.

One enjoyable aspect of games for children is that they are put into situations where they can control their own learning: there is often no 'one way' to solve the problem or achieve a winning solution. As Hatch (1998) and Anghileri (2000) note, this control encourages flexibility of thinking and mental fluency. The more effective games encourage mental work as calculations are tackled in children's heads. As much as possible, children should be encouraged to discuss the mathematics inherent in the game, and the strategies employed, in order to help the development of mathematical language and reasoning skills.

While many mathematical games are designed as competitive games, they can often turn into co-operative games where pupils support each other to obtain the greatest success. Carefully planned, these types of games can provide opportunities for developing skills related to mathematical thinking – predicting, generalising, justifying and explaining. (Chapter 4 has examples of such types of games in whole-class settings.) For Ainley (1988: 243), the main value of mathematical games lies in the linking together of mathematical problems which are 'real' to the children, the use of such process skills as listed above, and the need such activities present for children to think in a mathematical way.

While there are benefits in mathematical games being used as homework activities or 'stand-alone' free-choice activities in the classroom, the most effective use of games is when they are incorporated into the planned mathematics curriculum. Teachers and practitioners need to be clear on the intended learning outcomes of the game, how all children can benefit from appropriate games (not just the 'fast finishers'), and plan opportunities for adult support, discussion and pupil explanations.

## Worksheets and textbooks

These feature strongly as mathematical resources in many Key Stage 1 and Key Stage 2 classrooms. As Harries and Spooner (2000: 46) point out, worksheets and textbooks play an important role in influencing teachers' thinking with regard to the teaching and learning of primary mathematics. Many commercial schemes exist, usually comprising of a teacher's guide (usually the most useful, but, ironically, often the most underused part of the scheme), children's textbooks/workbooks, and additional resources such as photocopy masters for worksheets/CD-ROM materials. As Liebeck notes (1984: 16), such resources focus primarily on pictures and symbols rather than on 'concrete' experiences and language. This is problematic for Atkinson (1992: 13), who views meaningful mathematics as 'maths with reason [which] is rooted in action – learning through doing'. She suggests that schemes of work, therefore, need to start off with activity.

A teaching/learning approach that relies on a predominant use of textbooks and worksheets for mathematics can produce difficulties for all children, not just young children:

- children with visual and kinaesthetic learning styles often struggle with a 'print-based curriculum' (Clausen-May, 2005);
- there are syntactic and semantic levels of reading and interpretation of the illustrations involved in textbooks which can lead to confusion (Santos-Bernard, 1997, cited in Harries and Spooner, 2000);
- a predominant use of worksheets can 'persuade' children that mathematics has nothing to do with the real world but, perversely, encourage an attitude that 'real' mathematics is textbook/worksheet work;
- work from worksheets and textbooks does not always reflect an accurate view of what children can do.

In addition, problems can lie in the way in which textbooks and worksheets are used as activities/tasks. OFSTED (2005: para 63) notes that less effective teaching relies too heavily on worksheets, with children sometimes struggling to interpret the sheet/text or sustain interest in the work. An overuse of texts/worksheets also encourages teachers to view independent work as children working on their own, rather than simply independent of the teacher.

A more effective approach to the use of children's textbooks and worksheets is to view them as resources which may be useful to support, consolidate or extend children's mathematical learning through linking selected aspects to the unit of work planned by the teacher. Such an approach allows for teachers to make decisions on the appropriateness of the material, which groups of children may benefit from the set task, and to plan for independent work that is paired based/group based focusing on explanation of understanding. In these ways textbook activities, in particular, are used as a springboard into further problem-solving/investigational tasks with the benefit of children making stronger connections with 'textbook maths', other forms of mathematical activity, the use of mathematical thinking skills and doing 'real' mathematics.

## Everyday materials

These can be brought into the classroom and used successfully as resources to support and develop children's understanding of some of the purposes of mathematics in real-life contexts. The examples of materials which help relate 'school' mathematics to everyday applications are endless, but could include packaging materials, patterned fabric or paper, timetables, receipts, catalogues, scaled plans, photographs of shape/number in the environment and any form of container or measuring device. Such types of resources have use in whole-class teaching, small group activities, displays and cross-curricular role-play situations. The value of resources in role-play and other cross-curricular activities is explored further in Chapter 6.

In addition to these real-world artefacts, many resources not specifically designed for mathematical learning can be exploited to assist with early learning in particular. Toys, stories, environmental or malleable materials such as sand, water and play-dough can be used to support early concepts in aspects of number, shape and measurement. The advantages here are that they are tactile and more likely to connect with children's home/prior/real-world experiences. For Edwards (1998: 8), the value here lies in the fact that 'handling of familiar "everyday" objects enables children to learn about their properties and components'. Through manipulating familiar objects and materials, children are helped to rationalise their experiences. Aubrey (1997: 26) sounds a word of caution, however. Her research indicates that young children do not often relate their classroom interactions with the associated use of materials to their existing out-of-school problem-solving. In children's real-world experiences objects and materials are used in problem-solving situations, often play-based, and often self-initiated. This suggests that the use of everyday (and specific mathematical) resources is more successful in supporting children's learning through the type of teaching approach, and classroom environments, which put high priority on solving problems which are meaningful to the children.

Through reviewing a wide range of resources, it is possible to identify their potential to:

* motivate children;
* provide variety to teaching and learning experiences;
* connect 'classroom mathematics' with application to the real world;
* act as a visual aid to allow children to build up a store of mental images;

- enable teachers and children to model mathematical processes involved in specific number operations or calculations;
- encourage mathematical communication to take place;
- support teacher assessment of children's knowledge and understanding of aspects of mathematics;
- support the understanding of mathematical ideas through allowing children to make connections between, what for them may be, disconnected aspects of mathematical learning.

Anghileri (1995: 7) argues that it is 'active participation in problem solving through practical tasks, pattern seeking and sharing understanding' that enables children to make their own sense of the relationships that underlie all mathematical knowledge. Crucial to this argument is the belief that effective use of resources provides a forum for the acquisition and use of mathematical language and purposeful discussions. Anghileri (2000: 8) believes that 'mathematical understanding involves progression from practical experiences to talking about these experiences, first using informal language and then more formal language ... Talking about their experiences will help children establish the significances of the vocabulary used and how they relate it to the visual imagery being created.' This process takes time. It is important to remember that 'there is no mathematics actually in a resource' (Delaney, 2001: 124). Abstraction is needed from all these experiences. This signals a clear need for teachers and practitioners to:

- be clear as to why they provide specific resources;
- recognise the links between the practical task, the visual imagery created and the abstract mathematics involved;
- view the use of such resources in part as a social activity which can assist with reflective discourse between children and adults;
- give high priority to questioning and discussion linked to how the children used or worked with the resource to support their mathematical thinking.

# The issues involved in the use of resources

This section will focus on the necessity for children to abstract the mental mathematics from their practical experiences and the research undertaken in this area.

Hart *et al.* (1989) investigated children's ability to make the transition from practical work and pictorial images to more abstract mathematics. Many of the 11- to 12-year-old children in the project had difficulty in moving 'from the concrete or pictorial representations to the more formal (general) aspects of mathematics' (Hart *et al.*, 1989: 218). The research showed that many children were unable to link these stages in the learning process. Cobb *et al.* (1992) suggested that some of these difficulties derive from the use of particular materials which are used within a 'representational' approach. In this approach children would work with an external representation (e.g. Multibase10) in order to give meaning through 'internal' representations to a particular aspect of mathematics (in this example, aspects of place value). Cobb *et al.* suggest that there is an assumption here, on the part of the teacher, that specific mathematical meaning is actually embodied in the external representation: this may be true for the teacher, but not necessarily the child. Gravemeijer (1997: 316) concurs that 'concrete embodiments do not convey mathematical concepts' and that it is the 'experts' who already have those concepts who will make sense of the ideas being modelled.

How materials are used, therefore, and the ability of the teacher to negotiate their differing interpretations, would appear to be important factors in helping children translate their thinking processes from handling objects/using images to symbolic representations. Children need to see through the objects to the mathematics which underpin the representation (Harries and Spooner, 2000: 46). They need to be able to think with the representations.

For Ball (1992), too many teachers believe that children will reach 'correct' mathematical conclusions simply by manipulating resources. As she points out, 'although kinaesthetic experience can enhance perception and thinking, understanding does not travel through the fingertips and up the arm' (Ball, 1992: 47).

In itself, therefore, the physical exploration of concrete materials will not lead to children 'discovering' mathematical concepts. For MacLellan (1997), the crucial element is accompanying mental activity. Without some accompanying mental activity to reflect on the purpose and/or significance of the physical activity, concrete materials will not actually enable the child's mathematical understanding to develop (MacLellan, 1997: 33). In order for this to happen, there needs to be a discourse between the child and the teacher/practitioner which will allow the child to bridge the gap between the materials and the abstract ideas.

The need for teachers to be aware of the different meanings that children can ascribe to the same resource is highlighted by research undertaken by Ahmed *et al.* (2004). This study suggested that 'different children will engage with the same materials in different ways depending on the conceptions they bring with them and, hence, will establish different understanding'. The same research indicated a lack of clarity in many teachers' thinking regarding the 'subtle distinction between the way mathematical ideas are constructed from objects and the particular characteristic of the objects' (Ahmed *et al.*, 2004: 320). This would suggest a clear need for children to describe the different ways in which they perceive the material and its relationship to the mathematical idea under discussion.

Threlfall (1996) examined the reasons why the theoretical benefits of practical activity in mathematics did not always translate into practice. The use of specifically structured apparatus as an aid to finding the answers to calculations was highlighted as unhelpful to children's understanding. 'If children with little awareness of number patterns or the structure of our place value system, who do not have much idea about the meaning of the arithmetic operation, are being taught how to do "sums", the use of the apparatus to demonstrate the procedures will not make any difference to the success of the task' (Threlfall, 1996: 7). For Threlfall, using structured apparatus in such situations only obscured the real value of the resource; namely, to provide 'contexts in which meanings can be established and extended, in which relationships can be exemplified and explored and in which techniques can be demonstrated' (ibid.: 11). The contention here is that, having had sufficient exploration of possibilities in number through engaging with the apparatus in suitable contexts, children should be able to work on the calculations without the use of the apparatus. If they cannot, then the children should not yet have been expected to work on such calculations. More effective exploration and use of the apparatus would help them to succeed on similar calculations at a later date.

The need for children to develop and use calculation strategies eventually without the aid of concrete 'manipulatives' was identified in research undertaken by Carpenter and Moser (1982). They found some evidence that young children who could mentally apply sophisticated counting or calculation strategies reverted to more 'primitive' counting or calculation strategies when materials were available. In such situations it could be argued that the availability of concrete resources is inappropriate as they act to 'slow down' the children's thinking processes. This would suggest that teachers need to give careful consideration not only to the types of resources to have available, but also as to whether they should always be available to all children. A problematic issue arising out of this is the impact on children's self-esteem and the desire of most children, particularly in Key Stage 2, to be 'seen' to be undertaking the same tasks as their peers in the class. In such situations, children who would benefit from using appropriate resources may be unwilling to use them even if they are available.

Moyer (2001) found evidence that some teachers did not choose to provide resources to aid the children's mathematical learning (even when they acknowledged they might be helpful) as such materials were deemed babyish for older pupils. The research highlighted that teacher decisions on using, or not using, mathematical resources stemmed from their inherent views on why they teach mathematics, and how it can be learned effectively. These views influenced their teaching approaches. For many of the teachers in this study, resources were used to simply add 'fun' into lessons rather than using them to relate to the mathematical ideas being explored. Through observations, questionnaires and interviews, it was concluded that the underpinning issue here was a lack of understanding on the part of these teachers as to how to represent mathematical concepts. Without this understanding, the resources became used as little more than a diversion.

The importance of teacher beliefs into the 'why' and 'how' of teaching mathematics was clearly demonstrated by research into effective teachers of numeracy undertaken by Askew *et al*. in 1997. One of the characteristics of the most effective teachers in this study (deemed to be 'connectionist' teachers) was their ability to use and move between a wide range of different representations of mathematics – concrete objects, images, language and symbols – and to make connections being these different representations for their pupils.

# The critical aspects involved in the choice and use of resources

It is clear from the previous section that 'practical work is not at all useful if the children fail to abstract the mental mathematics from the experience' (Askew, 1998: 15), and that teachers need to be clear as to the purpose of using specific resources. This section will explore the critical aspects involved in teacher decision-making with regard to making the most effective use of mathematical resources to support teaching and learning.

Moyer's research alerts all practitioners that choosing to use resources in mathematics education on the basis that they provide more 'fun' for children is a simplistic approach at best and, at worst, can lead to situations in which both teacher and pupil are confused as to how such resources are beneficial to mathematical learning (Moyer, 2001).

For Delaney (2003), part of the decision process revolves around being clear as to whether resources are more effective when used in teacher demonstrations or used by children to engage with mathematical ideas. The latter is advocated as giving children a feeling of personal involvement and providing greater scope for the development of skills related to mathematical thinking. The disadvantage of an over-reliance on a 'demonstration' approach is that 'if a resource is only ever used to demonstrate how to do something you will only know from the child's actions whether they understood the *instructions* given' (Delaney, 2003: 41).

In addition, when selecting resources, teachers need to be secure in the purpose behind using a particular resource and being clear as to the support it can offer children. For example, place value arrow cards are useful to emphasise how number names are written and how the number value can be represented in hundreds, tens and ones, but they cannot offer a concrete sense of the size of the number. (An example of this can be found in one of the case studies in Chapter 3.)

Diversity is important in choosing resources to support children's learning. Children can form incorrect generalisations if they are only presented with limited examples. It is therefore important that children are given, and talk about, examples and non-examples so that they can investigate relevant and irrelevant features (Askew and Wiliam, 1995).

A greater use of mathematical resources in open-ended tasks may encourage teachers and children alike to view objects/images as tools or representations to help thinking. Flexible uses of resources can encourage flexible thinking. This approach can help develop a classroom 'culture' in which it is recognised that there are many paths to reach the same mathematical solution. In turn, some of those paths may involve the use of resources for some children. Turner and McCullouch (2004: 65) suggest that allowing choice in resources (either from a wide range or a selection chosen by their teacher) 'enhances the ability of children to apply their knowledge to new situations'. Choice may often depend on the child's preferred learning style.

Above all, actions as well as the intentions of the teacher are important when using resources as teaching or learning aids. Whatever the material provided or the context chosen, assumptions should not be made that children will draw the mathematical conclusions from the resource simply by interacting with it. The use of any form of mathematical resource (as defined in this chapter) needs to be accompanied by child–child and child–adult dialogue in order to:

- diagnose any misconceptions perhaps more evident through use of the resource;
- establish the level of mathematical understanding;
- use and apply relevant mathematical vocabulary;
- assess the effectiveness of the resource as an aid to learning and as a mechanism to support the development of mathematical thinking.

---

**SUMMARY OF KEY POINTS**

Resources have an important role to play in allowing teachers to model or demonstrate representations of mathematical ideas, and in supporting children's developing mathematical understanding and thinking. The effective use of any resource will depend on teacher understanding of how the particular representation helps develop mental imagery, and how to utilise the resource to assist with children's understanding of particular mathematical concepts. The process of abstracting mathematical ideas from practical aids or images is difficult for many children: all teachers and practitioners need to be mindful that 'just because the child is presented with some concrete materials it does not follow that the child will abstract the mathematical ideas from the materials' (MacLellan, 1997: 33). Significant to assisting this process of abstraction appears to be choices made by teachers regarding the type of resource to be used, the role which teachers see themselves as having while children are engaging with the resource(s), and the social culture of the class.

## REFERENCES REFERENCES REFERENCES **REFERENCES** REFERENCES REFERENCES

Ahmed, A., Clark-Jeavons, A. and Oldknow, A. (2004) How can teaching aids improve the quality of mathematics education? *Education Studies in Mathematics*, 56(2/3): 313–328.

Ainley, J. (1988) Playing games and real mathematics, in Pimm, D. (ed.) *Mathematics, teachers and children*. London: Hodder and Stoughton/Open University Press, pp239–248.

Anghileri, J. (ed.) (1995) *Children's mathematical thinking in the primary years: perspectives on children's learning*. London: Cassell.

Anghileri, J. (2000) *Teaching number sense*. London: Continuum.

Anghileri, J. (2001) *Principles and practices in arithmetic teaching. Innovative approaches for the primary classroom*. Buckingham: Open University Press.

Askew, M. (1998) *Teaching primary mathematics. A guide for newly qualified and student teachers*. London: Hodder and Stoughton Educational.

Askew, M. and Wiliam, D. (1995) *Recent research in mathematics education 5–16*. London: OFSTED.

Askew, M., Brown, M., Rhodes, V., Johnson, D. and Wiliam, D. (1997) *Effective teachers of numeracy*. Final report. King's College London.

Atkinson, S. (ed.) (1992) *Mathematics with reason. The emergent approach to primary maths*. London: Hodder and Stoughton.

Aubrey, C. (1997) Children's early learning of number in school and out, in Thompson, I. (ed.) *Teaching and learning early number*. Buckingham: Open University Press.

Ball, D. (1992) Magical hopes: Manipulatives and the reform of math education. *American Educator*, 16(2): 14–18, 46–47.

Bottle, G. (2005) *Teaching mathematics in the primary school*. London: Continuum.

Bruner, J. (1964) *Towards a theory of instruction*. London: Belknap Press.

Bruner, J. (1966) On cognitive growth, in Bruner, J., Oliver, R., and Greenfield, P. (eds) *Studies in cognitive growth*. New York: John Wiley.

Carpenter, T. and Moser J. (1982) The development of addition and subtraction problem solving skills, in Carpenter, T., Moser, J. and Romberg, T. (eds) *Addition and subtraction: a cognitive perspective*. Hillsdale, NJ: Lawrence Eribaum.

Clausen-May, T. (2005) *Teaching maths to pupils with different learning styles*. London: Paul Chapman.

Cobb, P., Yackel, E. and Wood, T. (1992) A constructivist alternative to the representational view of mind in mathematics education. *Journal for Research in Mathematics Education*, 23(1): 2–33.

Delaney, K. (1992) The missing piece. *Strategies*, 3(1): 28–29.

Delaney, K. (2001) Teaching mathematics resourcefully, in Gates, P. (ed.) *Issues in mathematics teaching*. London: Routledge Falmer, pp123–145.

Delaney, K. (2003) How should we really use resources within the NNS? *Education 3–13*, March, 31(1).

Department for Education and Employment (1999) *The National Numeracy Strategy. Framework for Teaching Mathematics from Reception to Year 6*. London: DfEE Publications.

Edwards, S. (1998) *Managing effective teaching of mathematics 3–8*. London: Paul Chapman.

Frobisher, L., Monaghan, J., Orton, A., Orton, J., Roper, T. and Threlfall, J. (1999) *Learning to teach number*. Cheltenham: Stanley Thornes.

Gravemeijer, K. (1997) Mediating between the concrete and the abstract, in Nunes, T. and Bryant, P. (eds) *Learning and teaching mathematics: an international perspective*. Hove: Psychology Press.

Hansen, A. (2005) Shape and space, in Hansen, A. (ed.) *Children's errors in mathematics. Understanding common misconceptions in primary schools*. Exeter: Learning Matters, pp76–102.

Harries, T. and Spooner, M. (2000) *Mental mathematics for the numeracy hour.* London: David Fulton.

Hart, K., Johnston, D., Brown, M., Dickson, L. and Clarkson, R. (1989) *Children's mathematical frameworks 8-13. A study of classroom teaching.* Nottingham: Shell Centre for Mathematical Education.

Hatch, G. (1998) Replace your mental arithmetic test with a game. *Mathematics in School*, 27(1): 32–35.

Haylock, D. and Cockburn, A. (2003) *Understanding mathematics in the lower primary years. A guide for teachers of children 3–8.* London: Paul Chapman.

Higgins, S. and Muijs, D. (1999) ICT and numeracy in primary schools, in Thompson, I. (ed.) *Issues in teaching numeracy in primary schools.* Buckingham: Open University Press.

Hughes, M. (1986) *Children and number.* Oxford: Basil Blackwell.

Lawton, F. (2005) Fractions, in Hansen (ed.) *Children's errors in mathematics. Understanding common misconceptions in primary schools.* Exeter: Learning Matters, pp37–42.

Liebeck, P. (1984) *How children learn mathematics.* London: Penguin Books.

MacLellan, E. (1997) The role of concrete materials in constructing mathematical meaning. *Education 3-13*, October: 31–35.

Moyer, P. (2001) Are we having fun yet? How teachers use manipulatives to teach mathematics. *Education Studies in Mathematics*, 47(2): 175–197.

OFSTED (2005) *The national literacy and numeracy strategies and the primary curriculum.* HMI 2395.

Parr, A. (1994) Games for playing. *Mathematics in School*, 23(3): 29–30.

Threlfall, J. (1996) The role of practical apparatus in the teaching and learning of arithmetic. *Educational Review*, 48(1): 3–12.

Turner, S. and McCullouch, J. (2004) *Making connections in primary mathematics.* London: David Fulton.

# 3

# Using models and images to support children's mathematical thinking

## Alice Hansen

*Close your eyes and visualise the number twenty-four. Do that now. What did you 'see'?*

When asking some trainee teachers this question I was genuinely taken aback by the variety of their responses. A small selection of these follows:

'Two dozen eggs.'
'A page in a large book with page 25 opposite it.'
'A number line from 0–100 with a mark about a quarter of the way along.'
'An array of squares six by four.'

This illustration perfectly introduces the focus of this chapter. By having images like those above, people are empowered to use number in a creative and powerful way (Gray *et al.*, 1999). For example, understanding the relationship between 24 and 12 is a useful relationship that can be applied numerous times in our everyday lives, such as calculating with a dozen. By thinking about 24 as a page in a book, there is an immediate focus on odd and even and the role that numbers play in systematically identifying place and order. We can undertake quick but effective estimations and calculations when we see numbers as part of a whole or near to milestones (such as 24 being about a quarter of 100, or near 25). Finally, identifying a relationship between numbers and shape provides a useful tool for exploring factors in a rectilinear arrangement.

English and Halford (1995: 57) explain that:

> the essence of understanding a concept is to have a mental representation or mental model that faithfully reflects the structure of that concept. Number is the core of mathematics, and to understand number is to have a mental model of it that includes all the essential relations of numbers, at least within the domain where the concept is used. A 5-year-old's concept of number is presumably much more restricted that that of a pure mathematician, but the 5-year-old may still have a representation of those number relations that are important within the particular domains in which she uses number (emphasis in original).

Anghileri (2003: 90) relates this to resources in the classroom:

> *Some children find it a lot easier to explain their thinking if they have equipment available to touch and move so that they can describe their actions rather than try to formulate abstract thoughts ... These objects also provide images that make it easier for children to follow the thinking of others and to recall situations they have experienced before'.*

It is the interaction of these objects that create mental models. Although models are formulated from these specific content-based experiences, 'this does not necessarily restrict their power to deal with abstract concepts ... *The important thing about mental models, especially in the context of mathematics, is the relations they represent*' (italics added) (English and Halford, 1995: 57).

## Chapter focus

This chapter will focus on:

- using models to develop mathematical talk in place value;
- pupils developing their own models and images to support mental calculation strategies;
- using models to support making connections in number patterns;
- using models to support children's reasoning in shape and space
- using models and images to solve problems.

# Using models to develop mathematical talk in place value

Lesh *et al.* (2000: 609) define a model as a 'system' that is used to describe, think about, make sense of, explain, or make predictions of another system. In this section, the use of a resource to support children's understanding of the value of digits in numbers is explored. This resource, place value arrow cards, represents a model in these terms as it helps children to make sense of number by making connections with the value of the digits in certain columns. In addition, the resource is used as a basis for a whole-class discussion that develops the children's understanding of place value, some related vocabulary and the teacher's expectations for communication in the classroom.

## Case Study 1: Reading three-digit numbers (Y2)

### Context

It is the last week of the school year for this Year 2 class and Marion (an NQT who will be their class teacher next year) has the opportunity to spend a day with them. She wants to find out what her new class understands of the place value of three-digit numbers. Below we see part of the introduction to the main part of her lesson.

## Curriculum links

| | |
|---|---|
| NC | **KS1 Ma2:** Pupils should be taught to:<br>**1e** use the correct language, symbols and vocabulary associated with number<br>**2c** read numbers to 100 or beyond; recognise that the position of a digit gives its value and know what each digit represents, including zero as a place-holder |
| 2006<br>PNS Framework | **Y2** Read and write two-digit and three-digit numbers in figures and words; describe and extend number sequences and recognise odd and even numbers |
| 1999<br>NNS Framework | **Y2** Read and write numbers to at least 100 in figures |

**Marion:** Who can tell me what this number is? *[She holds up a set of arrow cards to show 538]*

**Sara:** Five hundred and thirty eight

**Marion:** Well done, Sara. How did you know that so quickly?

**Sara:** I just knew it

**Marion:** OK, who in the class didn't know that this number was five hundred and thirty eight? *[A few hands go up, others nod]* Sara, can you explain to the rest of class how they might be able to read the number?

**Sara:** You know that it is the hundreds 'cos there are three numbers

**Marion:** Three digits

**Sara:** Yeah. And then the first one is the hundreds and then you can read the rest like normal off that *[She points to the hundred square on the wall in the class]*

**Marion:** Thank you, Sara. Let's see if we can use these cards to help your explanation. Can you please repeat your explanation for us?

**Sara:** Well, the 5 is five hundred because the digit that is in that space is always a hundred

**Marion:** *[Shows the 500 place value arrow card separately to the class]*

Well done, Sara. The digit 5 represents five hundred. Can you see that? Who can tell me what the digit 3 represents? Michel?

**Michel:** That is three, no, thirty

**Marion:** That's right, Michel. How did you know that?

**Michel:** I know that's how you write thirty eight. We've done loads of those numbers

**Marion:** I'm really pleased to hear that you are confident with your numbers, Michel. Who else thinks they are good at reading numbers? *[Most of the pupils' hands go up]* So we know that we read the 3 as thirty. We read the 5 as five hundred, or 5 hundreds. How else could we read the 3? 3 ...?

**George:** *[Calling out]* Tens!

**Marion:** Can you remember what we do when we want to say something to the class, George?

**George:** We put up our hand

**Marion:** Thank you, George. Now, how did you know the answer was three tens? [*Marion goes on to show the 30 place value card, the children read each of the numbers separately, '500, 30, 8', and then she puts them together again. This is repeated with other three-digit numbers*]

## How was the resource used effectively?

Sfard's (2001) 'thinking-as-communication' metaphor is helpful to discuss this case study. Her metaphor is first defined 'by its exceptional reliance on symbolic artefacts as its communication-mediating tools'. Marion's main focus of this part of the lesson was to assess the children's knowledge of place value for supporting her planning for next year. She was aware that the extent to which the children are able to explain their understanding is important to help her assessment. Additionally, she understands that it encourages a culture of shared understanding where the children can help each other to develop their mathematical knowledge and mathematical thinking (Yackel and Cobb, 1996). This is the second part of the definition of Sfard's 'thinking-as-communication' metaphor. It is concerned with 'the particular meta-rules that regulate this type of communication' (Sfard, 2001). There are several examples throughout the case study where the teacher has used this to great effect. For example, Marion initially used the resource to capture the children's attention. To do this, she ensured that the place value arrow cards were large enough for all the children to see. The separate colours of the ones/tens/hundreds cards further supported her discussion with them.

Another example is when, for whatever reason, Sara responded that she 'just knew' the answer. Marion wanted to understand what the children knew about place value and how well they were able to explain their thinking about place value. By refocusing her questioning, she persevered to gain a fuller response from Sara. This helped Marion in her assessment but it also served a wider purpose. Marion was developing the class ethos for the year about her expectations of talk and interaction in the classroom. During her period of questioning Sara, Marion continued to involve the other children by asking them supplementary questions. This was important to encourage them to listen to one anothers' ideas and to compare their thinking with others.

When necessary, Marion specifically addressed errors, such as Sara's incorrect use of the term 'number' to more effectively develop her reasoning through using 'digit'. Marion reinforced this through further questioning. Being able to use the correct mathematical terminology enables children to be accurate in their explanation so that it is more likely that others will understand their justification (Nelson-Herber, 1986).

The resource also supported Sara's explanation. By asking Sara to repeat her explanation to the class, Marion encouraged Sara to refine her response. This is important to help Sara and the other children to focus on Marion's learning intentions and to practise using the appropriate mathematical vocabulary herself. The resource also reiterated that the '5' represented 500 because it showed the two place-holding zeros after the 5 (Thompson, 1998). This was repeated with 30 and 8 and then later with different three-digit numbers.

The place value arrow cards were more effective than writing a number on the board and talking about the value of the digits because the children could see the three-digit number being partitioned by the cards and the digits being overlapped. This helped the children to see a model of the number being partitioned and put back together in a way that writing on the board would be more abstract. This helps to create a stronger mental image than something written on the board, regardless of how it might be presented.

# Children developing their own models and images to support mental calculation strategies

In the previous section the class were presented with a model from which to work. It was the teacher's intention that the resource might help the children to understand place value through providing them with an image on which to base their discussion. This section takes a different focus. Lesh *et al.*, (2000) believe it is important for children to create their own models to work from. They consider planning activities that create the need for children to 'develop, revise, refine, and extend a mathematically significant tool' (Lesh *et al.*, 2000: 609). They contend that this is because 'model-eliciting activities emphasize the fact that mathematics is about seeing at least as much as it is about doing' (ibid.: 611).

# Realistic mathematics education

The Realistic Mathematics Education (RME) philosophy shares a similar fundamental underpinning. RME sets out a curriculum based on several principles (van den Heuvel-Panhuizen, 2000). One of these is the guidance principle. This is concerned with giving students a 'guided' opportunity to 're-invent' mathematics through teacher-led tasks that meet the intended learning trajectories. By teachers providing tasks that allow for reinvention, children are able to 'construct mathematical insights and tools by themselves' (van den Heuvel-Panhuizen, 2000).

The RME approach applies Freudenthal's (1981) theory that mathematics should be drawn from the environment. Freudenthal (1979) recognised mathematics as 'a natural and social activity which develops according to the growth needs of an expanding world'. The use of 'realistic' within the name of the approach comes from the Dutch 'to imagine': *zich realiseren* (van den Heuvel-Panhuizen, 2000). The emphasis within the RME approach is to offer students a context problem: a 'problem situation that is experientially real' to them (Gravemeijer and Doorman, 1999). This may be as varied as a real-world scenario, a fantasy or from a pure mathematical problem: the crux of the matter is that it is 'real' to the children. Gravemeijer and Doorman explain that the purpose of context problems is more than just usefulness and motivation. They believe that they should be used from the very start of a unit of work as an anchoring point for reinventing mathematics in order to help children to lead to a formal understanding of mathematics as well as to preserve the connections between the concepts and contexts which the concepts describe (Treffers, 1987).

Some of the models from RME design research have been integrated into the National Numeracy Strategy Framework (NNS) (DfEE, 1999). One of these is the use of the empty number line. It is necessary to cast a word of caution at this stage. Lesh and Kelly (2000: 215) explain:

*mathematics entails seeing at least as much as doing. Or, to state the matter somewhat differently, one could say that doing mathematics involves (more than anything else) interpreting situations mathematically; that is, it involves mathematizing. When this mathematizing takes place, it is done using ... models ... explanatory systems for making sense of patterns and regularities in real or possible worlds ... These constructs must be developed by the students themselves; they cannot be delivered to them through their teachers' presentations.*

There is much difficulty in transferring a model from the Dutch curriculum, which is totally integrated in the ways it uses models of this kind, into England and Wales. It is largely problematic because teachers in England and Wales have a very different knowledge base to teachers in the Netherlands. As a result, they are likely to use the Dutch models as yet another set of 'unintelligible rules' (Skemp, 1971) in which the children are 'routinely drilled' (Freudenthal, 1981). In situations such as this, children who have been taught a skill or strategy in a specific context (and who have even performed it to specification) tend not to use or spontaneously apply it in other situations (Resnick and Collins, 1996).

It is important, therefore, to understand the philosophy underpinning the creation of models for mathematisation. Gravemeijer and Doorman (1999) explain the role of the teacher well: this role is one of guided reinvention, offering what they call a more reliable way to bridge the gap between informal and formal mathematics. In the following case study the teacher is using the children's own developing model to find the difference between two numbers.

## Case Study 2: Using an empty number line to find the difference (Y3)

The children have been looking at sums that have a missing addend, for example, 17 + ☐ = 26, with their teacher Robert. Up to this point, all the sums have totalled less than 30 because they have been using their ruler to help them 'count on' (Fusion, 1998). We join them in the plenary.

## Curriculum links

| | |
|---|---|
| NC | **KS2 Ma2:** Pupils should be taught to:<br>**1b** break down a more complex calculation into smaller steps; identify the information needed to carry out tasks<br>**3e** Pupils should be taught to work out what they need to do to add or subtract any pair of two-digit whole numbers |
| 2006 PNS Framework | **Y3** Develop and use written methods to record, support or explain addition and subtraction of two-digit and three-digit numbers<br>**Using and applying mathematics**<br>Describe and explain methods, choices and solutions to puzzles and problems, orally and in writing, using pictures and diagrams |
| 1999 NNS Framework | **Y3** Use informal pencil and paper methods to support, record or explain HTU+/– TU |

**Robert:** What have we been thinking about in today's lesson as you have solved the number sentences that I have given you?

| | |
|---|---|
| **Sajad:** | How many more we need to count on to find the answer |
| **Robert:** | Thank you, Sajad. We have been focusing on counting on to find the missing addend, the missing number in the sum. What have we used to help us to count on? |
| **Class:** | Our rulers! |
| **Robert:** | And how have they helped us? |
| **Mary-Jane:** | We put our finger on the first number in the sum and then we counted up how many more jumps we needed until we got to the answer |
| **Robert:** | And what information did that give us, Mary-Jane? |
| **Mary-Jane:** | It told us what the missing number was |
| **Robert:** | Thank you. Now, I have a problem that I want you to help me with. Can you help me, do you think? |
| **Class:** | Yes! |
| **Robert:** | I was thinking on my way to school today about a sum that used a number bigger than 30! [*Writes 17 +* ☐ *= 45 on the board*] |
| **Class:** | [*Gasps all round*] |
| **Robert:** | But the problem is, my ruler only goes to 30, so I wasn't so sure what I could do to solve the answer |
| **Jack:** | You could use the big ruler in there [*Points to the store cupboard where the metre rulers are kept*] |
| **Robert:** | That is a good idea, Jack. I could use the metre ruler to help me solve this because the answer is less than one hundred. What if I didn't have a metre ruler with me? What if I needed to know the answer when I was at home? |
| **Caitlin:** | You could use your fingers! |
| **Robert:** | Let's try that idea, Caitlin. What number do we all need to start from, to put in our heads? |
| **Caitlin:** | 17 |
| **Robert:** | So let's put 17 in our heads ... have we all done that? OK, let's count up to 45. Are you ready? |
| **Everyone:** | 18, 19, 20 [*On each count, one finger is raised*] ... 25, 26, 27 [*Now everyone's fingers go down and they continue to count*] 28, 29 ... 36, 37 [*Robert takes an intentionally loud sigh and everyone's fingers go down and they continue to count*] 38, 39 ... 44, 45 |
| **Robert:** | OK, how many have we counted on? [*There is a long pause. Some hands go up hesitantly*] Hmmm. That is a good strategy when we have two numbers that are close to each other, but it is hard to keep track of how many we have counted on when there is a big difference between them. Does anyone else have a suggestion? [*Pause*] Remember I don't have a metre ruler with me |
| **Erika:** | You could draw a ruler! [*Some children snigger*] |
| **Robert:** | That is an excellent idea, Erika. Let me draw a ruler on the board |

```
┌──────────────────────────────────────────────────────┐
│                                                        │
└──────────────────────────────────────────────────────┘
```

| | |
|---|---|
| | Now what do I need to do? |
| **Erika:** | You can show where the 17 is. Then where the 45 is. Then draw all the centimetres in between them |
| **Robert:** | [*Has been writing in the 17 and the 45 as Erika speaks. He stops at her final suggestion*] Do I need to do that? |
| **Erika:** | Oh, um ... |
| **James:** | I know! You don't have to put them all in. You can put in the 20 and the 30 and the 40 |

| Robert: | Show me what you mean |
|---|---|
| James: | [*Comes to the whiteboard and writes:*] |

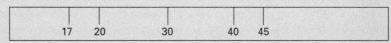

| Robert: | How does that help? [*James is keen to answer*] Can anyone else think about what James has done and why that might help us? |
|---|---|
| Tariq: | Ooh, I know! You know that there are three to 20, then ten to 30 and ten to 40. Then five more to 45 so the answer's 28 |
| Robert: | Who understood what Tariq was saying? [*Very few nods*] Can you come up to the board Tariq, and use the pen on our ruler to help us see? |
| Tariq: | *Goes up to the front and explains:* Well, you jump from 17 to 20 and that is three. [*Draws a curve from the 17 to the 20*] |
| Robert: | OK, can you write a 3 above that to remind us? |

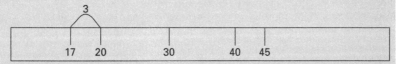

Then you go from 20 to 30 and you know that you count on 10 to get to that. And then the same to get to 40. Then it is five more to 45

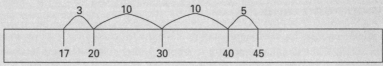

| Robert: | Thank you Tariq. What do we need to do now, then? |
|---|---|
| Tariq: | Well, you add them all up: 20 and 5 ... 8. 28 |
| Robert: | Why do we do that? |
| Tariq: | Because we are working out the difference between 17 and 45, so we need to count up all of them |
| Robert: | Thank you very much. Who can come and rewrite our number sentence? |

After a pupil has successfully written $17 + 28 = 45$, Robert goes through some more examples on the whiteboard. The next time he intentionally draws a blank number line instead of a 'ruler' and the children adopt this in their later work on the board. Robert begins to refer to the work on the board as a 'number line' rather than a 'ruler' and some of the children also do this.

## How was the resource used effectively?

Earlier in the lesson Robert had encouraged the children to use a resource that they were already familiar with using to 'count on' (Fusion, 1998) – the ruler. This provided an opportunity for the children to access a resource that bridged their understanding of number tracks to number lines.

By carefully constructed questioning, Robert took the children along a journey of his intended learning trajectory. This wasn't straightforward. When posed with a challenging problem to solve, the children initially referred to strategies that were familiar and previously successful to them (such as using their fingers or using a longer ruler). Robert's response to Jack's suggestion of using the metre ruler was thoughtful. He had considered ways in which the children could move into a position to use a generalised model that would work for any numbers (and indeed for any of the four operations).

The children were able to apply their previous knowledge of using the ruler to 'count on' in a context that was not dissimilar from the rulers they were all confident using. The children were also able to apply their knowledge of counting up in tens and identify significant numbers (such as the tens numbers) to effectively solve the problem of finding the missing number. A small number of higher-attaining children were able to use this informal model mentally in order to quickly and efficiently calculate the answers. This demonstrated that they were using their flexible understanding of number to manipulate the empty number line in their heads.

# Using models to support making connections in number patterns

Chapter 2 considers how it is generally accepted that resources can facilitate the development of mathematical thinking. English and Halford (1995: 98) explain how resources can help children to 'understand the meaning of mathematical ideas and their applications, can increase flexibility of thinking, can be used generatively to predict unknown information, and can reduce children's anxiety towards mathematics'. Earlier, this chapter highlighted the power of models to show connections within mathematical ideas. This section will discuss how shape models can create an environment for children to explore algebraic patterns.

## Shape and algebra

Many researchers have demonstrated the benefits for children in making an explicit connection between shape and algebra (for example, Arnold, 1996; Asp and McCrae, 2000; Bishop, 2000; Kieran and Sfard, 1999; Oldknow, 2003). Gray and Pitta (1997) used an approach encouraging more flexible thinking in arithmetic. They used a graphic calculator that could display several successive calculations. They worked with a pupil for six months and through this intervention it became obvious that she was beginning to 'build new images, symbolic ones that could stand on their own to provide options that gave her greater flexibility' (Gray *et al.*, 1999). The evidence suggested that 'if practical activities focus on the process of evaluation and the meaning of the symbolism they may offer a way into arithmetic that helps those children who are experiencing difficulty' (ibid.)

### Case Study 3: Triangular numbers (Y5)

#### Context

Liz's Year 5 class have been working on a unit on number patterns for nearly two weeks and she really wants to provide an open-ended task to them on the last day. She wants to introduce triangular numbers to them and she hopes that several of the children already working at level 4 of the National Curriculum will be challenged to formulate a general rule. Below is an excerpt of her planning sheet.

#### Curriculum links

| 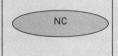 | **KS2 Ma2:** Pupils should be taught to:<br>1k search for pattern in their results; develop logical thinking and explain their reasoning |
| --- | --- |

| | **Y5 Using and applying mathematics** |
|---|---|
| 2006 PNS Framework | Represent a puzzle or problem by identifying and recording the information or calculations needed to solve it; find possible solutions and confirm them in the context of the problem<br>Plan and pursue an enquiry; present evidence by collecting, organising and interpreting information; suggest extensions to the enquiry<br>Explore patterns, properties and relationships and propose a general statement involving numbers or shapes; identify examples for which the statement is true or false |
| 1999 NNS Framework | **Y5** Recognise and explain patterns and relationships, generalise and predict |

## INTRODUCTION TO MAIN PART OF LESSON:

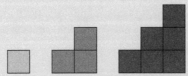

Ask pupils to look at the pattern I've made with the Multilink cubes. What can they tell me about it? Estimate how many cubes will be needed to make the next one? Make the next in the sequence, thinking about how they constructed it. (Focus on 'adding four' to the side, bottom or diagonal). Write the sequence 1, 3, 6, 10 on the board. Encourage pupils to make a link between the adding 2, 3, 4 onto their Multilink shapes to the +2, +3, +4 in the number pattern on the board. Predict further numbers in the sequence. Introduce name of sequence. Explain that the shapes look a bit like triangles. (A quick reminder of square numbers.)

## MAIN:
## Collaborative Group Work

| Lower-attainment group: *Independent work* | Middle-attainment group: *Working with TA* | Higher-attainment group: *My focus group* |
|---|---|---|
| 1. What is the biggest shape you can [physically] make? Why is that the biggest? Is there another way of recording your work? With your partner, make a list of all the possible ways of recording. Carry one through to show to the class in the plenary. | 1. Look what happens if I put the first and second shapes together. What shape does it make? What about the second and third shapes?<br><br> | 1. How many Multilink cubes are required for the fourth shape? The fifth shape? The tenth shape? What about the tenth and then hundredth shape?! What patterns can you see? *Possible solutions for the tenth shape:*<br>*– Making the shape from Multilink* |
| Extension: What ways can you put two of the shapes together? What shapes can you make? Can your friend make those shapes? How can this help you find out how many cubes are in other shapes in the sequence? | 2. What happens if I put two the same together? What if I put shapes together in different ways?<br>3. If I had made a square that had 25 Multilink in it (5x5), which two shapes would have made it up? Can you make it up to show us all? | *– Drawing the shape (on plain or squared paper)*<br>*– Using the pattern to count the number of cubes in it (10+9+8+7+6+5+4+3+2+1)*<br>*– Knowing that putting two of the tenth shapes together can make a rectangle 10x11. Halving this gives the number of cubes in one shape.* |

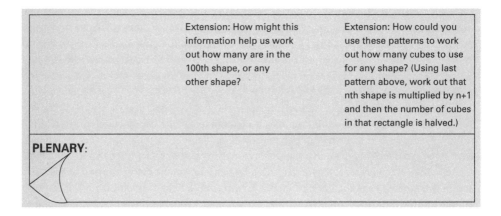

Extension: How might this information help us work out how many are in the 100th shape, or any other shape?

Extension: How could you use these patterns to work out how many cubes to use for any shape? (Using last pattern above, work out that nth shape is multiplied by n+1 and then the number of cubes in that rectangle is halved.)

PLENARY:

## How was the resource used effectively?

The Multilink was being used by all of the children in the class. Often teachers avoid using some resources in older classrooms or with more able children because of the myth that the children might think it is 'babyish' or that they might not need them. This example, however, demonstrates how the resource was the prompt for the whole lesson; the number sequence was introduced through its shape element.

In the introduction of the main part of the lesson, Liz asked the children to construct the fourth shape in the sequence and explicitly asked them to explain what they did. This opened up opportunities to consider that there was more than one strategy of making the next shape and it also allowed some children to make links between the construction of the shapes and the incremental increase in the number sequence.

In addition to this, a resource that could be manipulated was necessitated due to the children being asked to 'fit shapes in the sequence together'. Being able to physically manipulate the resource enabled some of the children in the class to see how when adding two consecutive triangular numbers a square number was created. (If this manipulation had not been made possible, many of the children would have found visualising the shapes together too difficult to do.) They created the following rule in words: 'If you have the fifth shape and put it together with the fourth shape you get 25 (because 5 × 5 = 25). If you halve 25, you get $12\frac{1}{2}$, then add on another half of 5 (which is $2\frac{1}{2}$) and you get 15, which is the number of cubes in the fifth shape.' This may appear a rather long-winded and complicated way to describe what was happening, but the children were rather confident in their explanation and could apply it to any other shape in the sequence. With the teaching assistant guiding them, they were able to begin to understand that 'the $n$th term had ($n^2$ divided by 2) + ($n$ divided by 2) cubes'.

Some other children identified that if you put two of the same triangular number together, you created an oblong. Using the Multilink provided them the opportunity to explain that the number of cubes in the $n$th shape was: $n \times (n + 1)$ divided by 2.

Whichever way the general rule was created, the children were supported by their Multilink models. While some children at this age (and younger) can see the patterns within the numbers themselves alone, the resource supported many of them to discover the general rule, which they wouldn't have done if they had been presented with the data in a tabulated format. Other resources were also available for the children to use, such as squared paper and coloured pencils as another method on recording their work. Some children chose this as a more efficient method of recording their thinking.

The lower-attaining children were not ready to be able to construct rules or formulae in this way. Instead, the resource allowed them to explore the number pattern through shape in a way that engaged them all. In this case, a sense of competition prevailed, with children striving to create the largest triangular number through using the physical resources (which raised discussion about patterns going on and on) and through paper-based work and mental work. The children moved away from Multilink when they realised that there was a physical limitation to how big it could be made. Several children realised that recording on squared paper was also time-consuming and that it resulted in a finite representation of an infinite pattern. One pair of those children began to write an addition number sequence to represent what they had been doing when adding a row to their Multilink each time (1 + 2 + 3 + 4 + 5 + ...) and most of the group followed suit. This first pair reached +234 by the end of the lesson and in the plenary they explained to the whole class the links between their work with the Multilink, drawing on squared paper and the number sentence. They were rather stunned when Liz asked them to calculate how many Multilink were indeed in the 234th shape! Over lunchtime, several children in the whole class chose to become involved in Liz's challenge to find the answer. Again, they used a variety of methods that included finding patterns and making generalisations. Others chose to use a calculator and checked their findings by repeating the calculation. Liz worked with three gifted and talented children to set up a spreadsheet to calculate any triangular number.

# Using models to support children's reasoning in shape and space

## The complex nature of naming shapes

One aspect of naming shapes that compounds the complex nature of this aspect of mathematics is the inclusivity and exclusivity of definitions (Whiteley, 2006). Children find it difficult to understand, for example, that a square is a rectangle (demonstrating the inclusive nature of the definition of rectangles), particularly when they are faced with images in and out of school where what they call a rectangle is, again, a prototypical oblong (illustrating the exclusive nature of the definition of 'oblong': a rectangle that is not a square). In addition to this, some quadrilaterals belong in more than one subset. For example, a square is a rectangle but it is also a type of right-angled trapezium. A square is a rhombus and is a rectangle, but not all rhombuses are rectangles. No wonder it is so confusing.

## The van Hiele levels of geometric understanding

Van Hiele (1986) offers a widely accepted framework to explain how pupils develop in their geometric understanding. At primary school level, the framework identifies three levels of understanding.

### Level 1 (visualisation)
Pupils are able to name and recognise shapes by their appearance, often comparing them to a prototypical shape. For example, when a pupil says, 'That is a rhombus' what they actually mean is, 'that is a shape I have learned to call a rhombus' (van Hiele, 1986: 109). They cannot explicitly identify the properties of shapes and although they may be able to recognise characteristics, they do not use them for recognition and sorting. Rather, decisions are made on perception: 'There is no why, one just sees it' (van Hiele, 1986: 83).

## Level 2 (analysis/description)

Pupils begin to identify properties of shapes and learn to characterise shapes by their properties. Irrelevant features (for example size, orientation, colour, texture, etc., or 'incidental properties', as Handscomb (2005) refers to them) become less important, as pupils are able to focus on all the shapes within a class. For example, they are able to think about what properties make a rectangle. However, they do not make connections between different shapes and their properties and so they may dispute that a square is a rectangle. Another example comes from van Hiele (1986: 109): a pupil may use the word 'rhombus' when referring to the collection of 'properties that he has learned to call "rhombus"'.

## Level 3 (informal deduction/abstraction/relational)

Pupils are able to recognise relationships between and among properties of shapes or classes of shapes. They are able to follow logical arguments using such properties. They can also distinguish between necessary and sufficient conditions. They can also classify figures hierarchically according to their properties. At level 3, pupils use properties of classes of figures with which to reason. The 'properties are ordered, and the person will know that the figure is a rhombus if it satisfies the definition of quadrangle with four sides' (van Hiele, 1986: 109).

# The impact of instruction on geometrical understanding

Fischbein (1993) blurs the edges of van Hiele's levels and reiterates the complex nature of geometry by observing that a geometrical figure 'possesses a property which usual concepts do not possess, namely it includes the mental representation of space property'. Fischbein argues that all geometrical figures are characterised by the interaction between their figural and conceptual aspects, leading to the notion of figural concepts. He explains that with 'age and the effect of instruction … the fusion between the figural and the conceptual facets improve'.

Freudenthal (1981) offers a suggestion for how a familiar environment may lead to children's understanding of geometry. From a very young age, before children are able to articulate their thinking, they are able to grasp space and relations in space by 'seeing, listening and moving in space'. Children undertake the process of becoming conscious about their intuitive grasp of space and during this time verbalisation also occurs leading to definitions, theorems and proofs.

## Case Study 4: 'It's a square. 'No, it's a diamond!' (Y1)

### Context

Melissa, a trainee teacher, is working with her focus group, who are working in pairs to sort shapes into two sets: those that are square and those that are not square.

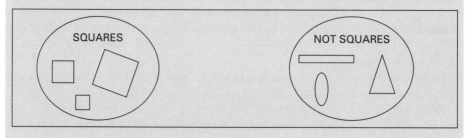

She listens to two children sitting perpendicular to each other at the corner of the table.

## Curriculum links

| | |
|---|---|
| NC | **KS1 Ma3:** Pupils should be taught to:<br>**2a** try different approaches and find ways of overcoming difficulties when solving problems<br>**2b** observe, handle and describe common 2D shapes; name and describe the mathematical features |
| 2006<br>PNS Framework | **Y1** Visualise and name common 2D shapes and 3D solids and describe their features; use them to make patterns, pictures and models |
| 1999<br>NNS Framework | **Y1** Investigate a general statement about familiar shapes by finding examples that falsify it |

| | |
|---|---|
| **Sam:** | You can't put that there – it isn't a square! |
| **Kim:** | Yes it is! |
| **Sam:** | No, it is a diamond |
| **Kim:** | No, it is a square – look |
| **Sam:** | What are you talking about? It isn't a square! It is a diamond!<br>*[Melissa makes her way around the table to the two children]* |
| **Melissa:** | What are you two talking about? |
| **Sam:** | Kim put that in the wrong one but he won't take it out! |
| **Melissa:** | Why do you think it is in the wrong set? |
| **Sam:** | Because it is a diamond<br>*[At this point Melissa realises why the children are confused]* |
| **Melissa:** | Sam, I'd like you to hop off your chair for a moment and come and stand next to Kim. What do you see? |
| **Sam:** | *[Silence]* |
| **Kim:** | It is a square! |
| **Sam:** | *[Moves to where he had been sitting]*<br>It's a diamond … [mumbles] but it is square if you go over there |
| **Melissa:** | You are right, Sam. Kim, you come and stand here. Can you see why Sam thought that the shape was a diamond? |
| **Kim:** | *[Moves to stand next to Sam]*<br>*[Laughs]* That's funny! |
| **Melissa:** | So who was right? |
| **Kim:** | I was right and Sam was right! |
| **Melissa:** | Yes, Kim, you were both right in naming the shape. This is a square and a diamond. Why do you think you were confused? |
| **Sam:** | Because I saw it and it looked like a diamond and Kim saw it and it looked like a square. But it is both |
| **Melissa:** | That's spot on, Sam *[Places two shapes next to each other like this:]* |

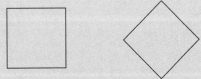

I'd like you both to think about what these shapes have in common. How are they the same? What is different about them?

45

### How was the resource used effectively?

By actually handling the shapes, the children were able to consider their representations and sort them into two sets: squares and not squares, developing their logical thinking. (For further discussion on using sorting to develop logical thinking, see Chapter 4.) Not all the children knew the names of all the shapes, but this was not necessary. They could use their visual understanding (van Hiele's level 1) to reason whether a shape was a square or not. By working in pairs, the children were able to further their reasoning through discussion.

Providing shapes for the children was important for the children to help them begin to generalise about squares. They had a number of squares that varied in size and colour. By asking the children to identify attributes of the two shapes that were the same and different, Melissa was helping the children to begin to think explicitly about properties of shapes. The children were able to consider the number of sides and corners that they had in common by touching them and rotating them. They saw that the size, colour and orientation of the shapes were different. All of these attributes are irrelevant to the properties of shape, but it takes many years for children to develop this understanding.

# Using models and images to solve problems

## 'Realistic' problems

By putting a problem into a 'realistic' context, it can provide meaning and motivation for the children. In addition to this, being able to return to the problem context throughout the problem solving process helps children to remain focused on the problem to be solved. English (2000) identified that children who could work through a modelling problem (for example, starting up a lawn-mowing company) were able to describe, construct, explain, justify, check and communicate their ideas; all of this to an appropriate level without teacher intervention.

### Case Study 5: The snake problem (Y6)

#### Context

In this case study, the children are asked to work in self-selected groups to solve a problem. This predominantly results in similar-attainment groupings; however, there are also two mixed-attainment groups. It is one of these we follow. The group is made up of a friendship group of four boys. James and Chris are working at level 5 in all areas of mathematics. Vinny is working at level 4 in all areas. Aron works consistently at level 2 in number, although he usually works at level 3 in using and applying. In this lesson the teacher and teaching assistant have decided to move around all the groups to offer support as required. It is the problem itself that is the model used by the children to develop their mathematical thinking.

#### Curriculum links

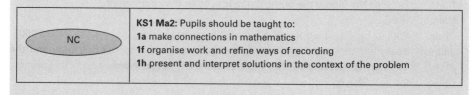

KS1 Ma2: Pupils should be taught to:
1a make connections in mathematics
1f organise work and refine ways of recording
1h present and interpret solutions in the context of the problem

| | |
|---|---|
| **2006 PNS Framework** | **Y6** Represent and interpret sequences, patterns and relationships involving numbers and shapes; suggest and test hypotheses; construct and use simple expressions and formulae in words then symbols<br>**Using and applying mathematics**<br>Tabulate systematically the information in a problem or puzzle; identify and record the steps or calculations needed to solve it, using symbols where appropriate; interpret solutions in the original context and check their accuracy<br>Suggest, plan and develop lines of enquiry; collect, organise and represent information, interpret results and review methods; identify and answer related questions<br>Explain reasoning and conclusions, using words, symbols or diagrams as appropriate |
| **1999 NNS Framework** | **Y6** Explain methods and reasoning orally and in writing<br>Solve mathematical problems or puzzles, recognise and explain patterns and relationships, generalise and predict |

The class have been presented with a story to solve:

*There are 100 dangerous snakes in separate boxes about to be transported to a zoo. Because they were rare breeds, there were 100 snake specialists looking after them. The first specialist went along and checked that every box was unlocked as they were due to be fed. The second specialist visited every second box, but accidentally locked them. The third specialist visited every third box and turned the key: this locked the third box, unlocked the sixth box, locked the ninth box and so on. The fourth specialist came along and turned the key in every fourth box: this unlocked the fourth box, unlocked the eighth box, locked the twelfth box and so on. This went on until all 100 snake specialists had completing their key turning, so the one hundredth specialist turned the key in the one hundredth box. The question is ... after this happened, which dangerous snakes were free to escape and which remained locked in their boxes?*

**James:** What are we going to write on?

**Vinny:** Let's use a large sheet so we can see. Can you get the felts, Aron?

**Aron:** Yup

[*The group get organised on the carpet around the paper*]

**Aron:** Shall I draw the snake boxes?

[*General agreement. Aron gets to the end of the row at 14*]

| 1 | 2 | 3 | 4 | 5 | 6 | 7 | 8 | 9 | 10 | 11 | 12 | 13 | 14 |
|---|---|---|---|---|---|---|---|---|----|----|----|----|----|

**Aron:** How much space shall I leave?

**Chris:** Why don't we lock and unlock these and see how much space for the others?

**James:** But the others are bigger numbers so they'll be visited more

[*Pause*]

**Chris:** No, 'cos the bigger the number, the less often they get visited

**Vinny:** Huh?

**Chris:** Well its like the multiples. If it is the 50th zoo keeper, he only goes to 50 and 100

**James:** Yeah, but the hundredth one has also been visited by the first one, and the second, and the fourth, fifth, tenth, twentieth, and way more

**Chris:** OK, well just try it then

[*Aron hands the pens to Vinny*]

| Vinny: | What shall we do? |
|---|---|
| Aron: | They are all locked but they need to be fed so they get unlocked |
| Vinny: | OK. [*Writes 'U' for 'unlocked' under each box*] Now they're unlocked |
| Chris: | Now the second zoo keeper goes and locks the multiples of two |
| Vinny: | Huh? |
| James: | The even numbers |
| Vinny: | Oh yeah. [*Crosses out 'U' and writes 'L' for 'locked'*] |
| Aron: | Then the third one does it in threes |
| Vinny: | [*Crosses out 'U' under 3 and writes 'L'. Crosses out 'L' under 6 and writes 'U'. Continues to 12*] |
| Chris: | Now four |
| | [*They continue until they get to the 14th box*] |
| Aron: | Now I'll draw more boxes ... to 28 |
| James: | Oh no! |
| Aron: | What? |
| James: | We should do all 100 at once |
| Aron: | Why? |
| James: | Cos we'll forget which snake has been visited ... it is easier to do all the ones that each specialist visits all at once |
| Vinny: | Yeah |
| Chris: | We should do it on squared paper and write one to 100 in the margin. |
| James: | Will it be wide enough to do all the Us and Ls? |
| Chris: | Should be. Those numbers are fine and they'll never be visited again. We could do it landscape just to make sure |
| James: | OK |

| 1 | U | | | | | |
|---|---|---|---|---|---|---|
| 2 | ~~U~~ | L | | | | |
| 3 | ~~U~~ | L | | | | |
| 4 | ~~U~~ | ~~L~~ | ~~U~~ | L | | |
| 5 | ~~U~~ | L | | | | |
| 6 | ~~U~~ | ~~L~~ | ~~U~~ | L | | |
| 7 | ~~U~~ | L | | | | |
| 8 | ~~U~~ | ~~L~~ | ~~U~~ | L | | |
| 9 | ~~U~~ | ~~L~~ | U | | | |
| 10 | ~~U~~ | ~~L~~ | ~~U~~ | L | | |
| 11 | ~~U~~ | L | | | | |
| 12 | ~~U~~ | ~~L~~ | ~~U~~ | ~~L~~ | ~~U~~ | L |
| 13 | ~~U~~ | L | | | | |
| 14 | ~~U~~ | ~~L~~ | ~~U~~ | L | | |

[*After they have completed all 100 ...*]

| Aron: | Which ones are unlocked? |
|---|---|
| Vinny: | [*Circles the 'U's*] |
| | 1, 4, 9, 16, 25, 36 ... |
| James and Chris: | The square numbers! |
| Aron: | The what? |
| James: | You know: one one, two twos, three threes |
| Aron: | Huh? |
| James: | [*Sighs*] One times one is one, two times two is four, three times... |
| Aron | [*interrupts*] Oh, yeah, yup, OK, I get it |

| Teacher: | I see you have found which snakes can roam free |
|---|---|
| Aron: | [*Loudly*] It's the square numbers! |
| **James, Chris and Vinny:** | Shhhhh! |
| Teacher: | [*Laughs*] OK, well done. My next question for you now is, why are those the boxes that are left unlocked? |

## How was the resource used effectively?

Lesh and Clarke (2000: 143) warn us that 'the results that students are requested to produce seldom include descriptions, explanations, or justifications in which they must reveal and test explicitly how they interpret problem solving situations and, even in cases where a mathematical interpretation needs to be generated, the kinds of quantification that are involved rarely go beyond simple counts and measures'. In this lesson, the children did go on to consider why the square numbers were left unlocked and saw that each of those boxes had been visited an odd number of times whereas all the others had been visited an even number of times. In the plenary the teacher drew together the work of all the groups, considering how they developed and represented their work. They all listened to the ways others solved the problem and they were required to justify their processes. They were also expected to explain their solution in mathematical terms. The teacher drew to the children's attention that square numbers have an odd number of factors and she also considered the even number of factors that prime and rectangular numbers have.

This case study demonstrates how the story provided a 'meaningful' context in which the children could frame their work. The story immediately captured all the children's interest. Although they were mature enough to know that the story was unlikely to happen in reality, they were able to 'buy into' the scenario sufficiently to want to solve it.

The problem itself was a worthwhile choice because it used and applied the mathematical knowledge that the teacher aimed for the children to gain: that square numbers have an odd number of factors. This was something that with guidance all the children discovered throughout the lesson.

It is interesting to note that although the children in the group were of mixed levels of attainment, all of them undertook integral roles within their group in solving the problem. They challenged each other's thinking, asked questions and explained things in alternative ways when they were not understood by their friends. They made links with prior understanding and applied it in this problem-solving context. One example of this is when James connected the multiples of 2 and the even numbers to help Vinny make sense of the boxes that the second snake specialist visits. Tasks that encourage collaborative learning need careful planning (see, for example, Lyle, 1996). In addition to this, it is necessary to ensure that children have the appropriate skills for undertaking this interaction (Blatchford *et al.*, 2005).

The group's recording became more systematic through the 30-minute activity. Aron was keen to draw each of the boxes that the snakes were in: this is an iconic representation of the problem (Bruner, 1966). It was reasonable to start with a small number of boxes as he did, either to see if they could identify a pattern early or, as Aron suggested, to identify the amount of space they needed to solve the problem. Later, this became more symbolically or abstractly represented with Chris's idea of using squared paper, although they did not think through the amount of space actually required as effectively as they could have.

## SUMMARY OF **KEY POINTS**

This chapter has explored how models and images can develop children's mathematical thinking. It has discussed how physical and virtual models and images can be used in the classroom to enable children to solve problems, communicate and reason about mathematics. It has also identified the need for teachers to consider how they might support their children to create and develop their own, powerful, mental models and images to support their mathematical development. Thirdly, it has considered how models can be used to help children to make connections within mathematics and between mathematics out of the classroom, and to solve problems.

We have seen how using and creating models allows children to see mathematics as a creative endeavour, allowing them to use evolve creative strategies and solutions to problems. In each of the case studies presented, the models have provided a context that allows us to make connections. English and Halford (1995: 57) remind us: 'The important thing about mental models, especially in the context of mathematics, is the relations they represent.'

Throughout the other chapters in this book there are further opportunities for you to explore many more models and images that support children's development of mathematical thinking through using resources effectively in mathematics lessons.

## REFLECTIONS ON PRACTICE

1. Think how you currently use resources in your teaching. Which ones have created the context for the children to *discuss* mathematics, in order to develop their mathematical thinking?
2. Think about a lesson you have taught that used a limited number of resources with one group, or no resources at all. In that lesson, how did you support the children to develop their own models for helping their mathematical thinking? How could you have improved this through using models and images?
3. Think about a lesson that you have taught that has delivered some curriculum content, but hasn't explicitly developed your pupils' mathematical thinking. How might you have done this differently, using a problem to solve as the basis, to develop your pupils' problem solving techniques as well as the mathematical content knowledge?

## REFERENCES REFERENCES REFERENCES REFERENCES REFERENCES REFERENCES

Anghileri, J. (ed.) (2003) *Children's mathematical thinking in the primary years*. Continuum: London.

Arnold, S. (1996) Algebraic thinking within a technology-rich learning environment, in Clarkson, P. (ed.) *Technology in mathematics education. Proceedings of the 19th annual conference of the Mathematics Education Research Group of Australasia*. Melbourne: MERGA, pp49–56.

Asp, G. and McCrae, B. (2000) Technology-assisted mathematics education, in Owens, K. and Mousley, J. (eds) *Research in mathematics education in Australasia*. Sydney: MERGA, pp181–214.

Bishop, J. (2000) Linear geometric number patterns: Middle school students' strategies. *Mathematics Education Research Journal*, 12(2): 107–126.

Blatchford, P., Galton, M., Kutnick, P. and Baines, E. (2005) Improving the effectiveness of pupil groups in classrooms. Final Report to ESRC (L139 25 1046).

Bruner, J. (1966) *Toward a theory of instruction*. Cambridge, MA: Harvard University Press.

Department for Education and Employment (1999) *The National Numeracy Strategy. Framework for Teaching Mathematics from Reception to Year 6*. London: DfEE Publications.

Department for Education and Skills (2003) *Models and images*. London: DfES.

English, L.D. (2000) Development of 10-year-olds' mathematical modeling, in Cockburn, A.D. and Nardi, E. (eds) *Proceedings of the Twenty-sixth Annual Conference of the International Group for the Psychology of Mathematics Education Conference*, Volume 3. Norwich: University of East Anglia, pp329–335.

English, L.D. and Halford, G.S. (1995) *Mathematics education: models and processes*. Mahwah, NJ: Lawrence Erlbaum Associates.

Fischbein, E. (1993) The theory of figural concepts. *Educational Studies in Mathematics*, 24: 139–162.

Freudenthal, H. (1979) New maths or new education? *Prospects*, 9(3): 321–331.

Freudenthal, H. (1981) Major problems of mathematical education. *Educational Studies in Mathematics*, 12: 133–150.

Fusion, C.K. (1998) *Children's counting and concept of number*. New York: Springer Verlag.

Gravemeijer, K. and Doorman, M. (1999) Context problems in realistic mathematics education: a calculus course as an example. *Educational Studies in Mathematics*, 39: 111–129.

Gray, E.M. and Pitta, D. (1997) Changing Emily's images. *Mathematics Teaching*, 161: 38–51.

Gray, E., Pinto, M., Pitta, D. and Tall, D. (1999) Knowledge construction and diverging thinking in elementary and advanced mathematics. *Educational Studies in Mathematics*, 38(1–3): 111–133.

Handscombe, K. (2005) *Image-based reasoning in geometry*. Thesis submitted for the partial fulfilment of the requirements for the degree of master of science. Simon Fraser University, Canada. **http://ir.lib.sfu.ca/retrieve/2201/etd1863.pdf** (accessed 19/09/06).

Kieran, C. and Sfard, A. (1999). Seeing through symbols: The case of equivalent expressions. *Focus on Learning Problems in Mathematics*, 21(1): 1–17.

Lesh, R. and Clarke, D. (2000) Formulating operational definitions of desired outcomes of instruction in mathematics and science education, in Kelly, A. and Lesh, R. (eds) *Handbook of research design in mathematics and science education*. Mahwah, NJ: Lawrence Erlbaum, pp113–150.

Lesh, R. and Kelly, A. (2000) Multitiered teaching experiments, in Kelly, A. and Lesh, R. (eds) *Handbook of research design in mathematics and science education*. Mahwah, NJ: Lawrence Erlbaum, pp197–230.

Lesh, R., Hoover, M., Hole, B., Kelly, A. and Post, T. (2000) Principles for developing thought-revealing activities for students and teachers, in Kelly, A. and Lesh, R. (eds) *Handbook of research design in mathematics and science education*. Mahwah, NJ: Lawrence Erlbaum, pp591–645.

Lyle, S. (1996) An analysis of collaborative group work in the primary school and the factors relevant to its success. *Language and Education*, 10(1): 13–32.

Mason, M.M. (1998) The van Hiele levels of geometric understanding, in *The professional handbook for teachers: geometry*. Boston: McDougal-Littell/Houghton-Mifflin, pp4–8.

Nelson-Herber, J. (1986). Expanding and refining vocabulary in content areas. *Journal of Reading*, 29: 626–633.

Oldknow, A. (2003) Geometric and algebraic modeling with dynamic geometry software. *Association of Teachers Micromath Journal*, 19(2): 16–19.

Resnick, L.B. and Collins, A. (1996) Cognition in learning, in Plomp, T. and Ely, D.P. (eds) *International encyclopedia of educational technology* (2nd ed.). Oxford: Elsevier Science, pp48–51.

Sfard, A. (2001) There is more to discourse than meets the ears: Looking at thinking as communicating to learn more about mathematical learning. *Educational Studies in Mathematics*, 46(1–3): 13–57.

Skemp, R.R. (1971) *The psychology of learning mathematics*. Harmondsworth: Penguin.

Thompson, I. (1998) The influence of structural aspects of the English counting word system on the teaching and learning of place value. *Research in Education*, May 1998.

Treffers, A. (1987) *Three dimensions. a model of goal and theory description in mathematics instruction: the Wiskobas project*. Dordrecht: Reidel.

van den Heuvel-Panhuizen, M. (2000) Mathematics education in the Netherlands: A guided tour, in *Freudenthal Institute CD-ROM for ICME9*. Utrecht: Utrecht University.

van Hiele, P.M. (1986) *Structure and insight: a theory of mathematics education*. London: Academic Press.

Whiteley, W. (2006) *Exploring the parallelogram through symmetry*. Presentation to the Geometers Sketchpad Users Group, York University, January 2006. Available at: **http: //keycurriculumpress.com/sketchpad/general_resources/ user_groups/jmm_2006/download/ExploringParallelorams.doc** (accessed 31/07/06).

Yackel, E. and Cobb, P. (1996) Sociomathematical norms, argumentation, and autonomy in mathematics. *Journal for Research in Mathematics Education*, 27(4): 458–477.

# 4

# Designing resources and selecting games to develop logic and reasoning

Doreen Drews

The need for teachers to develop and support children's ability to reason mathematically is clearly identified in the National Curriculum for Mathematics (NC) as one of the three strands involved in using and applying mathematics (DfEE, 1999a). Being able to reason mathematically involves an ability to search for patterns and relationships within set tasks, make connections with previous learning, generalise mathematical relationships and think logically. In many ways, the other two strands – decision-making and communicating in mathematics – support the development of reasoning through encouraging the notion that there may be alternative decisions/solutions to solving a problem and a need to explain those ideas to others. Despite its importance, many teachers, newly qualified and experienced alike, find the development of children's mathematical reasoning one of the most difficult aspects of their mathematics planning, assessment and teaching.

## Chapter focus

This chapter will explore how the use of specific resources and choice of activity can support primary teachers and other practitioners in creating mathematical situations in which children's reasoning skills can be developed. It will focus on:

- **the design and effective use of specific resources to develop reasoning skills in the Foundation Stage, Key Stage 1 and Key Stage 2;**
- **the selection and use of mathematical games to encourage mathematical thinking;**
- **the need for logical and reasoning activities to be given a higher profile within primary mathematics curricula.**

# Designing and using specific resources to develop mathematical reasoning

Burton (1994: 13) finds it 'impossible to think about learning or using mathematics in any other way than by patterning or looking for relationships'. Fundamental to searching for patterns and relationships is the ability to note similarities and differences between the numbers, objects or images involved. In order to do this, children need to be able to acquire and develop a range of skills: they need to:

- recognise an attribute that the object/image possesses (e.g. it is red);
- compare that to other objects/images to notice if they have the same attribute;
- determine attributes that the objects/images do not possess;

- use reasoning to distinguish between what must therefore be the same and be different about the objects/images compared.

These skills should not be undervalued. Greater emphasis needs to be placed on the development of these skills throughout the primary years with the focus on equipping children with the appropriate language to demonstrate their thought processes.

## What's the same and what's different?

Comparing the similarities and differences initially between only two objects or images is helpful in allowing young children to focus their attention and remember the attributes under discussion. While such an activity could be undertaken with any two objects, it is only likely to hold children's interest if they find the resources provided stimulating. An example of such a resource would be two specifically designed dolls, henceforth referred to as 'difference dolls'.

**Figure 4.1: Difference dolls**

As can be seen in Figure 4.1, difference dolls can be made to reflect a range of cultural contexts and include tactile attributes to match the needs of the age range or specific learning needs of individual children. When designing the dolls, consideration should be given to the following:

- The dolls need to be sufficiently similar to another for young children to immediately spot that they 'belong together'.
- The differences between the dolls may be linked to colour (e.g. one has red shoes, the other blue shoes); shape (e.g. one has circular buttons, the other triangular buttons); pattern (e.g. stripes on the trousers are horizontal for one but vertical for the other); style (e.g. one has plaited hair, the other straight hair); or texture (e.g. one jacket is wool, the other cotton).
- There should be a balance between characteristics which are the same and those which are different.
- The greater the number of characteristics, the greater the scope for development of language and use of the dolls throughout the Foundation Stage or with children with specific needs.

# Case Study 1: Using difference dolls in the Foundation Stage

## Context

A 'toy shop' in a Reception class. In the shop are a variety of toys including two pairs of difference dolls. Habiba and James (both 5) are 'managing' the shop this afternoon and have been busy arranging and checking their 'stock'. Their teacher joins them and discusses what they have for sale. She notices that the children have placed the pairs of difference dolls together: she shows interest in one pair of the dolls and asks the children to tell her about them as she may be interested in buying them.

During the conversation, the children state that the two dolls will cost a lot of money as they have to be bought together 'because they are sisters'. Their teacher initiates further discussion.

## Curriculum links

| | |
|---|---|
| NC | **KS1 Ma3:** Pupils should be taught to:<br>**1d** use the correct language and vocabulary for shape, space and measures<br>**1f** use mathematical communication and explanation skills |
| CGfFS | **ELG** Use everyday words to describe position<br>**Stepping Stone (Green)** Show curiosity and observation by talking about shapes, how they are the same or why some are different<br>Use developing mathematical ideas and methods to solve practical problems |
| 2006 PNS Framework | **FS Using and applying mathematics**<br>Sort objects, making choices and justifying decisions<br>Use developing mathematical ideas and methods to solve practical problems<br>Describe solutions to practical problems, drawing on experience, talking about their own ideas, methods and choices |
| 1999 NNS Framework | **Reception:** Use developing mathematical ideas and methods to solve practical problems involving counting and comparing in a real or role play context |

**Teacher:** What makes you think that they're sisters?

**J:** Cause they're the same [*holding both and looking at the dolls' faces*]

**Teacher:** Oh ... are they? How are they the same?

**H:** [*Taking one of the dolls off James*] Look, look at the ribbons ... and they've both got hats and skirts

**J:** And buttons

**Teacher:** Oh yes, they both have lovely buttons and I can see that they both have laces in their shoes

**J:** And both are big [*placing them together*]

**H:** The same [*tapping the heads and feet of both dolls which are the same length*]

**Teacher:** Yes the same height ... I see why you think they're sisters. But I can see some different colours on this one, though

**H:** Yeah, red shoes on this one and that one has green shoes

**Teacher:** I can see some other things that are different between them ... can you?

**J:** These are round [*handling the buttons on one doll*] and these are ... mmm ... squares [*indicating the buttons on the other doll*]

**H:** She has her hair all twisted and hers is just down like yours

| | |
|---|---|
| **Teacher:** | Mmm ... straight hair, like mine. I like the pattern on this one's skirt |
| **J:** | Lots of colours ... that way [*using his finger to indicate stripes going horizontally*] |
| **Teacher:** | And this one? |
| **H and J:** | Down, going down, lines, green, red and blue |
| **Teacher:** | I think that I'd like to buy them because they are special dolls ... but they might be too expensive |
| **J:** | You can buy one and get one free! |

### How was the resource used effectively?

By placing the difference dolls within this role-play area, the teacher provided a context for the children which was meaningful to them and, therefore, a context which is much more likely to promote and encourage use of language and logical thinking. As Pound (1999: 34) points out, 'we provide activities not only to promote mathematical learning but also because they are rich learning contexts where children can reflect on previous experiences and consolidate their current understanding'.

While the teacher instigated the conversation, she has listened respectfully to what the children had to say, used their own ideas to develop the dialogue, and helped them make links between their informal language and specialist mathematical language.

Through asking questions related to the similarities in the dolls, the teacher is encouraging the children to notice a relationship between the objects and to move towards making simple, but general, statements: 'and both are big'. Key questions, such as 'what makes you think that...', encourage logical thinking as they place children in situations where they want to make their thinking explicit to others.

Drawing attention to, and encouraging thinking about, the differences in the dolls presents further challenges for the children: they have to focus on an attribute which one doll possesses, compare that to the other doll, consider what is different in terms of colour/shape, etc., and then use appropriate language to share their thoughts. Further activities with the dolls could provide opportunities for the children to start to use, and practise, the language of negation (i.e. this has/this has not); the mastery of such language is essential for developing children's reasoning skills. Atkinson (1992) takes this further by defining language as the main tool for teachers and children to employ in the mastery of mathematical concepts.

## Structured sets

An example of a resource which builds upon concepts of sameness and difference and which encourages the development of classification skills is a structured set. These sets could be three-dimensional or images on card, have characteristics and attributes which could be identified as the same or different, can be made complex enough to challenge the thinking of Year 6 children (or even adults), and are versatile enough to be used in a wide range of mathematical activities. There are commercially produced structured sets, perhaps the most well known being Logicblocs.

When children are engaged in classification activities, they focus on one particular property the objects possess. The articulation of that attribute provides a 'label' for the group of objects which have been placed together. These types of activities have been criticised where they have been viewed as necessary precursors to learning to count or understand the cardinal value of a given number (Merttens, 1997; Askew, 1998). Jared and Thwaites (1995) also suggest that there is a danger that sorting/classification activities with materials such as Logicblocs may have no relevance to other mathematical or cross-curricular activities going on in the classroom.

The argument for promoting the use of structured sets is based not on the notion that they are necessary as pre-counting tasks, but rather that through engaging in classification activities children can learn to think analytically, express their ideas clearly and that such processes encourage the growth of clear and logical thinking. Identifying attributes, and establishing the relevant from the irrelevant, holds importance not only for mathematics but also across the range of human activity.

The advantage of designing and constructing structured sets for a particular class or group of children is that the set(s) can be 'tailor-made' to suit the children's interests and learning needs. Structured sets can also be designed around specific cross-curricular themes or stories which the class or groups are using within a planned scheme of work.

When designing a structured set, consideration should be given to the following:

- The total number of objects/images in the set should be a number with a high level of factors, in order to enable a wide range of classification groupings: e.g. a set with 18 objects/images could be rearranged and grouped in subsets of two, three, six and nine as well as looking at the items as 18 individuals or one whole group of 18.
- The greater the number of attributes in the set, the greater the challenge.
- The number of objects/images with a particular attribute should be connected to one of the factors, e.g. in a set of 18, six of the objects may be the only ones with a particular attribute.
- Each individual object/image is unique.

The design in Table 4.1 would produce a structured set of snakes which had 3 sizes × 3 body colours × 2 snake widths, which gives a total of 18 snakes. To make the set more challenging, the following additional attributes have been added:

- shape of eyes (three shapes);
- colour of eyes (three colours);
- types of 'stuffing' for the snakes, which will be made up as toys (three types of stuffing);
- number of stripes on the body (two or three);
- type of tongue (two types).

The use of a grid is very helpful for designing structured sets (see Table 4.1). Note that within this grid, the number of snakes which have any particular attribute (e.g. a specific eye shape) is always a factor of 18. The advantage of the grid is that additional attributes can be randomly placed so that, for example, not all the red snakes have orange eyes or forked tongues. This presents greater challenge in terms of logical thinking, classification skills and using reasoning to establish which subset(s) a particular object/image can or cannot belong to. When used within group activities, structured sets place children in situations where they want to and need to demonstrate their thinking.

**Table 4.1  Designing a structured set**

|  | LARGE | MEDIUM | SMALL |
|---|---|---|---|
| RED | · fat snake · square eyes<br>· orange eyes · 2 stripes<br>· forked tongue<br>· plastic bag stuffing | · fat snake · square eyes<br>· black eyes · 2 stripes<br>· forked tongue<br>· cotton wool stuffing | · fat snake · triangular eyes<br>· pink eyes · 3 stripes<br>· forked tongue<br>· beans stuffing |
| RED | · thin snake ·triangular eyes<br>· pink eyes · 2 stripes<br>· forked tongue<br>· beans stuffing | · thin snake · circular eyes<br>· black eyes ·3 stripes<br>· forked tongue<br>· plastic bag stuffing | · thin snake · circular eyes<br>· orange eyes · 3 stripes<br>· round tongue<br>· cotton wool stuffing |
| GREEN | · fat snake · circular eyes<br>· pink eyes · 2 stripes<br>· round tongue<br>· cotton wool stuffing | · fat snake · square eyes<br>· black eyes · 3 stripes<br>· round tongue<br>· plastic bag stuffing | · fat snake · triangular eyes<br>· orange eyes · 2 stripes<br>· round tongue<br>· cotton wool stuffing |
| GREEN | · thin snake · square eyes<br>· pink eyes · 2 stripes<br>· forked tongue<br>· beans stuffing | · thin snake ·triangular eyes<br>· orange eyes · 3 stripes<br>· round tongue<br>· beans stuffing | · thin snake · circular eyes<br>· black eyes · 2 stripes<br>· round tongue<br>· beans stuffing |
| BLUE | · fat snake · square eyes<br>· orange eyes · 3 stripes<br>· round tongue<br>· plastic bag stuffing | · fat snake · triangular eyes<br>· black eyes ·2 stripes<br>· forked tongue<br>· cotton wool stuffing | · fat snake · square eyes<br>· orange eyes · 3 stripes<br>· forked tongue<br>· beans stuffing |
| BLUE | · thin snake ·triangular eyes<br>· black eyes · 2 stripes<br>· round tongue<br>· plastic bag stuffing | · thin snake · circular eyes<br>· pink eyes · 3 stripes<br>· round tongue<br>· cotton wool stuffing | · thin snake · circular eyes<br>· pink eyes · 3 stripes<br>· forked tongue<br>· plastic bag stuffing |

## Case Study 2: Using a structured set in a Y2 classroom

### Context

The class teacher was working on developing the children's listening skills and ability to realise that there were often alternative ways to achieve a 'correct' answer. Over several weeks the children had familiarised themselves with a structured set of 18 snakes and had used them to aid counting and 'number stories'. In small groups the children began to further explore and discuss the attributes of the snakes.

### Curriculum Links

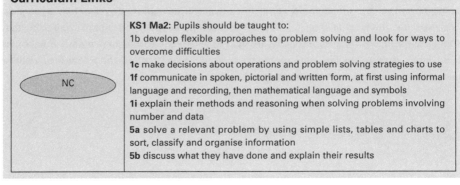

**KS1 Ma2:** Pupils should be taught to:
**1b** develop flexible approaches to problem solving and look for ways to overcome difficulties
**1c** make decisions about operations and problem solving strategies to use
**1f** communicate in spoken, pictorial and written form, at first using informal language and recording, then mathematical language and symbols
**1i** explain their methods and reasoning when solving problems involving number and data
**5a** solve a relevant problem by using simple lists, tables and charts to sort, classify and organise information
**5b** discuss what they have done and explain their results

| 2006 PNS Framework | **Y2 Using and applying mathematics** Follow a line of enquiry; answer questions by choosing and using suitable equipment and selecting, organising and presenting information in lists, tables and simple diagrams |
|---|---|
| 1999 NNS Framework | **Y2** Explain how a problem was solved orally and, where appropriate, in writing. Solve a given problem by sorting, classifying and organising information in a simple way |

Katy, Mehmet, Peter, Daniel, Sarah and Veena were given the scenario that they were packing up the snakes into boxes with the rule that *snakes in the same box have to be the same in some way*. The children were provided with a large quantity of boxes, tape, pencils, pens and paper. Katy immediately picked up three boxes. The teacher encouraged the group to question each other's choices and decisions: Katy explained that she had chosen three boxes because she wanted to put the snakes into 'colour' boxes – a green, red and blue box. The group agreed that was a good way and also noted that each box would have six snakes.

The teacher wondered (aloud) if that was the only way that the snakes could be packaged.

After a pause, the children started to handle the snakes and move them around. Sarah said that they could be put into 'eye boxes'. The teacher said nothing. Mehmet said that he didn't know: Sarah responded by moving the snakes into two distinct groups and saying 'all these have round eyes and all these have triangle eyes'. The group agreed that this way of packing up the snakes was also a good way: they also noted that there would be only two boxes required for packaging and that each box would hold nine snakes.

Peter, a child who was normally hesitant in offering suggestions, began to move the snakes in a different arrangement and said 'there's another way'. The teacher asked him not to give any more clues but to see if the group could find out 'what must Peter be thinking?' After much discussion the group decided that Peter had been looking at the number of stripes on the back of each snake and that the snakes either had one, two or three stripes. Peter, very proudly, told them that they were correct.

The teacher put the children into pairs and asked them to put something on paper to show a way in which the snakes could be packaged: these 'drawings' would be used later on in the week to play a game with the rest of the class. During the course of the week the teacher 'repeated' the activity with the remaining groups until all the children had, in pairs, represented on paper an attribute of the snakes. Using a digital camera and an interactive whiteboard, the teacher was able to illustrate each pair's choice. In a whole-class situation the children were asked to discuss what the representation showed, to 'work out' how the boxes must therefore have been labelled, and the relevant pair of children had to explain how they knew how many snakes had to be in each box.

## How was the resource used effectively?

The children were allowed to gain familiarity with the resource through play-related activities, structured and unstructured, prior to being asked to focus on specific attributes inherent in the structured set. This allowed the children an opportunity to develop their logic and reasoning through use of resources which they had already engaged with and enjoyed. Delaney (2001: 139) highlights that the value of engagement with resources lies in the feelings that this gives to children of 'personal involvement in making choices and decisions'.

The children were set a problem to resolve which had a range of different solutions. This put them in a situation where they had to listen to possible outcomes, recognise that different solutions may also be correct, agree or disagree with those outcomes and demonstrate how their solution must be viable.

The teacher chose a context for these skills to be developed: while the context may not have been a real-life situation, it was one that held meaning for the children. By engaging a child's imagination, an activity becomes real in the mind of the child and can, therefore, be a productive situation in which the child's logic and reasoning can be developed.

Significantly, the teacher chose to make few comments on the children's responses but, instead, encouraged a discussion/questioning culture. This tactic put the children into a situation where they could offer alternative suggestions, had to justify their ideas and recognise that their solution might not be the only solution to the set problem. Anghileri (1995: 7) recognises the benefit that such skills can have across the curriculum:

> *Explaining what they are doing and justifying their decisions helps children to develop skills in reasoning and clarity in communication that will have benefits across many aspects of learning.*

The children's representations of their packaged snakes were given value and purpose in the whole-class activity. The children had to interpret the images shown, relate them to the actual structured set, notice the number of packages and offer suggestions on what the box labels could say/couldn't say. For example, when discussing Sarah and Veena's picture (Figure 4.2), the children stated that the labels couldn't relate to either colour or number of stripes or thin snakes because both boxes held snakes with those characteristics. The role of the pair of children who had made the representation was to listen and offer clues if needed: Veena said 'our labels would have some shapes on'. The children's representations were all displayed and provoked much discussion and interest in the children over further weeks. The teacher noted that the children enjoyed placing the actual set of snakes into boxes to match particular representations: this allowed further exploration of some of the more challenging attributes such as the type of stuffing.

The teacher saw her role here as helping the children realise that

- they could make decisions and choices which may be different from others but equally as valid;
- listening to other children's ideas was useful;
- reflecting, thinking and talking about their ideas helped their understanding;
- pictorial images could show information but needed to be interpreted.

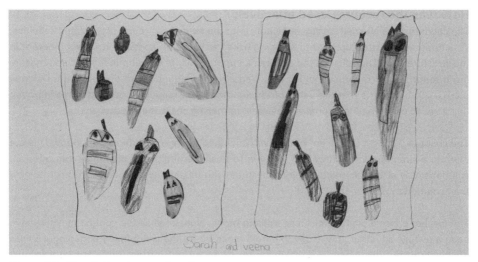

**Figure 4.2: Classifying the set of snakes**

## Using structured sets in Key Stage 2

If children have been introduced to structured sets in Key Stage 1, they can be used in Key Stage 2 to further develop children's abilities to use reasoning to establish the attributes/properties of an object/image or number. This can be especially challenging where the children are not given all the items in a particular set.

## Case Study 3: One of our spoon people is missing! (Y4)

### Context

A Year 4 classroom during a design and technology focus week. The task for the week was for the children, in small groups, to design and construct toys or games for Key Stage 1 children: the toys/games had to help the children's use of mathematics and/or literacy.

Daniel, a trainee teacher, had shown and discussed a range of toys and games as starting points for the children's thinking. He brought in a structured set which he named 'spoon people'. This set consisted of 24 spoon people made from three sizes of wooden spoons: other attributes were linked to hair colour, hair style, eye colour, facial expression, colour of cape, position of a bow, painted tip of the spoon and stripes on the cape.

### Curriculum links

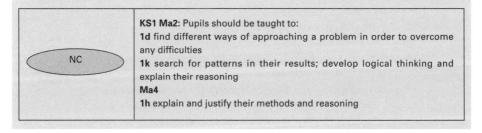

| NC | **KS1 Ma2:** Pupils should be taught to:<br>**1d** find different ways of approaching a problem in order to overcome any difficulties<br>**1k** search for patterns in their results; develop logical thinking and explain their reasoning<br>**Ma4**<br>**1h** explain and justify their methods and reasoning |
| --- | --- |

| 2006 PNS Framework | **Y4 Using and applying mathematics** Suggest a line of enquiry and the strategy needed to follow it; collect, organise and interpret selected information to find answers Report solutions to puzzles and problems, giving explanations and reasoning orally and in writing, using diagrams and symbols |
|---|---|
| 1999 NNS Framework | **Y4** Explain methods and reasoning, orally and in writing Solve mathematical problems or puzzles, recognise and explain patterns and relationships, generalise and predict |

Daniel hid one of the spoons and challenged the children to describe all the attributes of the missing spoon. This task was undertaken in small groups, with each group recording their thoughts for discussion later in the day.

Megan, Leila, Rani and Nazma decided to divide the set randomly between them, reasoning that one of them would have one less than the others and this would help with identifying something about the missing spoon. The girls realised that this approach was not particularly helpful as all they had noted was that Leila had one less spoon than anyone else. Rani started counting and spotted that there was one less large spoon than the number of medium and small spoons: she announced that the missing spoon was large.

Daniel joined them. The girls explained that they had looked at collections like this before when they were younger, although they had never had to find a 'missing one' before.

| | |
|---|---|
| **L:** | If you put them into groups it helps |
| **Daniel:** | I see ... what have you found out so far? |
| **R:** | It has to be a large spoon 'cause there are only seven of them ... there's eight in the other sizes |
| **Daniel:** | So counting and checking helps ... good thinking ... anything else you've found out so far? [*The girls moved the spoons around but without any discussion with each other*] |
| **N:** | I think that it might have brown eyes ... oh no, maybe green. We need to move them [*She starts to move the spoons into four groups to show the four eye colours in the set*] |
| **Daniel:** | Can you explain why you moved them, Nazma? |
| **N:** | Well, we need to count them in their eye colour so we can see what's missing. It's easier if you put them into the right groups. Look, it has to have brown eyes, there's only five here but six in those three groups |
| **Daniel:** | What do you think about Nazma's method? |
| **M:** | Yeah it's good: we can work out what the spoon must have from what's missing in the groups |
| **Daniel:** | OK. Can you suggest what you could do next? |
| **R:** | We could look at the capes ... there's different colours and stripes |
| **L:** | Yeah, but we'll need to move them twice then ... the colour of the capes doesn't match the number of stripes ... they're different ... see, these both have blue capes but one's got three stripes and one's got two stripes |
| **Daniel:** | So what will you all need to think about and decide if you want to find out all details about the missing spoon? |
| **M:** | We'll need to work together |
| **N:** | And decide which bit we want to look at each time and then move the spoons into those groups |

## How was the resource used effectively?

The presentation of the resource in the context of the design and technology week gave relevance to the activity as it assisted the children in their decision-making with the task they were set to make a toy/game for Key Stage 1. The resource, and the associated challenge, placed the children in a problem-solving context where they had to think logically in a mathematical situation.

The children had to hypothesise about the missing spoon person based on the evidence of the attributes of the set which they could see: 'I think that it might have brown eyes.' They had to construct a method/system whereby they could test out their ideas to check if they were likely to be correct. By testing out their ideas and using logical statements, the children moved towards proving that their hypothesis was correct: 'Look it has to have brown eyes, there's only five here but six in those three groups.'

The trainee teacher was careful in assisting the children's thinking rather than doing the thinking for them. As Hopkins *et al.* suggest (1999: 7), a 'teacher's interventions serve to keep the children's thinking momentum going rather than interfering with it or stifling it'.

Whole-class discussion and comparison of results took place in a plenary later the same day. The four girls, along with the rest of the class, were asked to justify their results and explain methods used. The children agreed that the task had made them think, change ideas, make connections between the spoon people, count and compare, talk about sameness and differences and find a system to solve the problem.

Two groups of the children decided to work together to produce a structured set for Key Stage 1 children. They chose teddy bears as the theme and, with support from Daniel, designed a grid to show the attributes of a set of 12 bears with attributes of size, colour, types of filling, number of buttons, facial expression and position of a bow. During the week the children drew out each bear and, with some adult support, constructed their structured set toy collection. Along with the other toys and games produced, the children presented their designs and structured set in an assembly, where they explained what they had to think about in the design.

# Fraction bags

The final resource for discussion in this section is a collection of materials placed together in a bag and linked specifically to the mathematical topic of fractions.

As Frobisher *et al.* (1999) point out, textbook fraction activities which children are asked to undertake tend to be very limiting and often involve shading in parts of a given shape. Lawton (2005) suggests that children find fractions difficult due to a lack of understanding of the need for fractions. What appears to be needed, therefore, are more problem-solving activities which allow children to explore the use of fractions, and form a better understanding of the purpose of these 'different kinds of numbers'.

A 'fraction bag' is relatively easy to create and provides opportunities for children to use and apply their understanding of unit fractions, parts of a whole, to make decisions, consider appropriate strategies, hypothesise, test out ideas and work collaboratively in a problem-solving situation.

A fraction bag could consist of the following items:

- a length of string;
- a ball of plasticine/soft stuff;

- an amount of dried peas;
- a quantity of counters (24);
- a paper shape (circle);
- an amount of Cuisenaire/number rods (measuring 144cm in total).

## Case Study 4: Using fraction bags in a Y6 classroom

### Context
A sequence of lessons planned by the class teacher to enable the children to use and apply their knowledge of fractions to a practical situation: various activities were planned for small group collaboration. The teacher was particularly interested in the children finding ways in which to present their solutions to the problems so that their ideas and thinking could be understood by all in the class.

### Curriculum links

| | |
|---|---|
| NC | **KS2 Ma2:** Pupils should be taught to:<br>**1a** make connections in mathematics and appreciate the need to use numerical skills and knowledge when solving problems in other parts of the mathematics curriculum<br>**1d** find different ways of approaching a problem in order to overcome any difficulties<br>**1h** present and interpret solutions in the context of the problem<br>**1i** communicate mathematically, including the use of precise mathematical language<br>**2d** understand unit fractions and use them to find fractions of shapes and quantities<br>**4b** choose and use an appropriate way to calculate and explain their methods and reasoning |
| 2006 PNS Framework | **Y6** Solve multi-step problems, and problems involving fractions, decimals and percentages; choose and use appropriate calculation strategies at each stage, including calculator use<br>**Using and applying mathematics**<br>Explain reasoning and conclusions, using words, symbols or diagrams as appropriate |
| 1999 NNS Framework | **Y6** Explain how a problem was solved orally and, where appropriate, in writing. Solve a given problem by sorting, classifying and organising information in a simple way |

Robert, Aaron and Tina were given a fraction bag and asked to each end up with a third of each item in the bag. They were told that they could use anything in the room to assist their problem-solving. They were advised that any one of them could be asked to explain the methods used so they had to ensure that all three of them were involved in the decision-making.

- After checking the contents of the bag the children decided to start with the small bag of 24 counters. After an initial discussion they decided that the counters could not be distributed by colour as the six colours did not have the same amount of counters in each colour set. Having established that there were 24 counters, they agreed to form three groups with eight counters in each. They chose a large sheet of paper to record their ideas and placed the counters in three small groups, recording 24 ÷ 3 = 8.

- The length of string provoked more discussion: Robert suggested that they measured it with a metre stick and then divided that amount by three. Aaron hypothesised that a quicker way was to fold the string and demonstrated this by folding the string into two (halving), and then halved it again. Tina pointed out that this produced four quarters and not three thirds. They all agreed, however, that Aaron's strategy was more useful and refolded the string into three approximately equal lengths.
- All three children agreed that the ball of soft stuff had to change its shape. Robert rolled it into a cylinder. Aaron said 'ah yeah, just like the string, we need three pieces', and cut it into three pieces of approximately equal lengths. He recorded that the sphere had been changed into a cylinder.
- Robert attempted to fold the paper circle into three 'equal' pieces but gave up. Aaron suggested that the paper circle could be transformed into another shape so that they could cut it into three equal pieces. Tina suggested that a protractor might help them measure the circle into three equal pieces: she brought a semicircular protractor to the table but the children could not work out how to use it to help solve the particular problem. They asked for help from their teacher, showing her the attempt to fold the paper into three sections. The teacher indicated a wall poster which illustrated fraction equivalences and focused their attention on relationships between thirds, sixths and ninths. After further trial and improvement, the children folded the circle into sixths and cut this up to give each of them two-sixths of the circle. Tina recorded 'two sixths is the same as each of us having one third of the circle'.
- Tina suggested that the peas could be counted and then that number divided between the three of them. Robert pointed out that that approach would take a long time and, without counting, moved the peas into three identical pots. Aaron asked 'how do we know we've all got the same?' Robert picked up a balance scale and suggested 'if we weigh them we can move the peas about'. This was agreed and peas moved around the three pots until each pot recorded approximately the same when placed on the scale.
- After initial attempts to divide the Cuisenaire rods by size and colour, the children realised that the strategy would not work as they did not have sufficient quantities of each. Tina started to move some of the rods against each other and suggested that 'we can swap the rods for other coloured rods worth the same'. She demonstrated this by showing that an orange rod (10cm in length) matched a yellow (5cm), a light green (3cm) and a red (2cm) when they were placed alongside each other. Using this idea, the children formed columns of rods which measured 10cm in length (14 columns in total plus 4cm of length remaining). They divided between them 12 of the columns, repeating this process with the remaining two columns and 4cm lengths, substituting and exchanging colour rods where needed. Each child ended up with rods equivalent in total length to 48cm.

When presenting their solutions to the rest of the class, the children used a poster display and the actual items from the fraction bag. Their poster, and explanations, made it clear that their first ideas had not always been the most useful, that testing out their ideas had been useful and had led them to seeking out alternative solutions, and that working together had helped their thinking.

## How was the resource used effectively?

The items in the bag presented the children with specific challenges linked to using knowledge, effective strategies and reasoning to determine one-third or two-thirds of each item. Unlike many textbook activities, the children had to think beyond shading in a given shape or finding a fractional quantity of a given number. Interestingly, it was the shape activity which caused the most difficulty: the teacher's choice of a circle for this task allowed her to assess the children's ability to make connections with measurement of angles, understanding the properties of a circle and equivalence of fractions.

While some of the materials could not be described as 'everyday' items, the children were given no clues as to how to obtain the desired fractional value of each item. This placed the children in the situation that they had to think about how they could find one-third of each item. Through testing out their ideas, and overcoming difficulties encountered, the children realised that one-third of an item could not be found by halving and halving again, and that finding one-third often involved more than simply dividing between three. Some of their solutions involved estimations and approximations as measurement was implicitly linked to the nature of the task.

Specific choices were made by the teacher to encourage the use of logic, reasoning and collaborative practices. She actively encouraged:

- flexible thinking by suggesting that the children could use anything in the room to assist them;
- use of reasoning by providing materials which were familiar to the children but not within the context of 'fractions': this allowed the children to have a starting point for their strategies;
- discussion and questioning between the children as all three had to understand why a particular strategy worked/didn't work in order to present their solutions.

In addition, resources such as fraction bags allow children to make connections between and across different 'aspects' of mathematics: in this case there were direct connections between finding a fractional quantity, division, conservation of number, measurement and the use of appropriate measuring tools. The need for children to have a good knowledge of links and connections between the different parts of the mathematics curriculum has been highlighted by Her Majesty's Chief Inspector of Schools (OFSTED, 2005a).

# Whole-class games to encourage mathematical thinking

This section will revisit the value of mathematical games previously discussed in Chapter 2. The focus here is on identifying the type of mathematical games which are more likely to encourage the children's use of logic and reasoning, and how such games can be used effectively in whole-class contexts. Games can offer opportunities for children to use mathematical processes and think in a mathematical way (Ainley, 1988: 243). In order for this to happen, the game needs to allow children to make predictions, hypothesise solutions and justify ideas. The four games discussed in this section provide opportunities for children to develop and use these mathematical processes in whole-class situations.

# Case Study 5: 'I'm thinking of a number' in a Y5 classroom

## Context

Sobia, a trainee teacher, wanted her Year 5 placement class to use and develop their reasoning skills to solve problems beyond 'word problems'. She introduced the children to a game called 'I'm thinking of a number'.

## Curriculum links

| | |
|---|---|
| NC | **KS2 Ma2**: Pupils should be taught to:<br>**1d** find different ways of approaching a problem in order to overcome any difficulties<br>**1h** present and interpret solutions in the context of the problem<br>**1k** search for patterns in their results; develop logical thinking and explain their reasoning |
| 2006 PNS Framework | **Y5 Using and applying mathematics**<br>Explore patterns, properties and relationships and propose a general statement involving numbers or shapes; identify examples for which the statement is true or false |
| 1999 NNS Framework | **Y5** Explain methods and reasoning, orally and in writing<br>Solve mathematical problems or puzzles, recognise and explain patterns and relationships, generalise and predict |

## The rules

One individual thinks of a number and gives all the players certain clues; e.g. 'It's a whole number between 1 and 40.' From this point on the individual only responds 'yes' or 'no' to any questions. The players ask questions to help determine information about the number. The players are not allowed to directly name the number until the end of the game.

Sobia assisted the children's thinking in two ways:

1. she allowed the children to use mini-whiteboards in order for them to check their thinking and to compare that thinking with others near them;
2. she recorded on the class board the type of vocabulary which could be useful: 'multiple', 'factor', 'divisible by'.

*I'm thinking of a positive whole number between 1 and 100 – what could it be?*
Examples of the children's questions:

| | |
|---|---|
| Is it an odd number? | *yes* |
| Is it a multiple of 5? | *no* |
| Is it less than 50? | *no* |
| Is it divisible by 3? | *yes* |
| Is it less than 70? | *yes* |

Sobia called a 'time-out' at this point to allow groups and pairs to compare/discuss their thinking: points were offered for suggestions as to what the number couldn't be and why. Further points were then offered for questions using different vocabulary.

Has it got 6 as one of its factors?   *no*
Is it in between 51 and 59?             *yes*

Finally, after reviewing all their evidence, the children were asked to provide statements to justify how they knew that they had found the correct number.

The following week Sobia took the children into the hall to play a variation of this game called 'What am I?' On the back of each child was attached a unique number card. The same rules applied, although this time each child had to ask questions to determine the number on his/her back. They had the advantage of being able to see everyone else's number and could use this information to determine, therefore, what number they could not be. The game proved so successful that Sobia planned to use it again as part of work on fractions and decimal fractions: to challenge the children's thinking further, she planned to use a mixture of whole numbers, mixed numbers, proper fractions and decimal fractions.

## How was the game used effectively?

The children had to draw upon their existing knowledge of number and to focus on the properties of number in order to formulate appropriate questions and 'make sense' of the answer given. They were placed in a position where they had to use the information gleaned to reason what the number could or couldn't be. By using the mini-whiteboards to organise their thinking, the children understood the usefulness of recording for a purpose. Sobia's 'time-out' allowed the children to clarify their thinking, listen to others, hypothesise on what it could be and justify ideas.

With practice, children improve on their choice of questions, use of reasoning and speed of result. Using the same set of numbers for a period of time allows the children to challenge themselves by 'beating' their previous time.

As well as developing skills in asking and answering questions using mathematical language, these types of games 'stimulate children to reflect on numerical relationships in a way that encourages them to seek results and relationships that will be advantageous in their game strategy' (Anghileri, 2000: 13).

The search for pattern and relationships is even more clearly the objective in the game 'What's the rule?'.

## Case Study 6: 'What's the rule' in a Y6 classroom

### Context

A sequence of lessons on number patterns. Megan, the Year 6 teacher, planned for the final lesson to be an opportunity for the children to demonstrate their understanding in a different context, with the emphasis on explanation of thinking. The essence of the game was for mixed attainment teams of children to predict, and prove, the next few parts of a given sequence. Each team had large sheets of paper, pens and interlocking cubes such as Multilink.

## Curriculum links

| | |
|---|---|
| NC | **KS2 Ma2:** Pupils should be taught to:<br>**1d** find different ways of approaching a problem in order to overcome any difficulties<br>**1i** communicate mathematically, including the use of precise mathematical language<br>**1k** search for patterns in their results; develop logical thinking and explain their reasoning<br>**2b** recognise and describe number patterns |
| 2006<br>PNS Framework | **Y6** Represent and interpret sequences, patterns and relationships involving numbers and shapes; suggest and test hypotheses; construct and use simple expressions and formulae in words and then symbols |
| 1999<br>NNS Framework | **Y6** Recognise and extend number sequences<br>Explain methods and reasoning, orally and in writing<br>Solve mathematical problems or puzzles, recognise and explain patterns and relationships, generalise and predict |

## The rules

The teacher shows the first two numbers in a number sequence and the teams have to:

- discuss how the sequence could be continued up to the fourth/fifth part of the pattern;
- select one way and record the sequence on the paper;
- model the sequence with the cubes to show pattern in the shape as well as number.

After an amount of time, Megan asked each team to simultaneously hold up their results. She selected team members to justify their predictions and explain the rule by which the pattern works: all the other teams had to agree that the named sequence 'worked'. A point was awarded to each team that justified a solution and a second point was given for illustrating the sequence as a shape pattern.

To challenge their thinking further, Megan awarded extra points to teams that presented a solution that no other team had suggested. Each team was then allowed a further amount of time to consider alternative solutions, for which they could gain further points.

Each time a new sequence was presented, Megan selected a different team member to explain the predictions, thereby ensuring that all team members had to understand the pattern and relationship involved. As the game progressed, Megan challenged the children to predict ahead to the tenth part of the pattern and win additional points for explanations using either word sentences or use of symbols/letters.

## How was the game used effectively?

This team game allowed all the children to collaborate in order to recognise and extend number sequences. The focus of the game was on the search for pattern, predicting, and the use of reasoning to justify ideas. Megan catered for the learning needs of all the children by providing for concrete, visual, pictorial, written and symbolic recording/presentation of the patterns. (Chapter 3 provides further detail on these forms of representation.) This provision ensured that all the children could participate, and be challenged, at appropriate levels. The awarding of points for alternative solutions encouraged the children to explore the patterns in greater depth, and extend their thinking beyond their first ideas. By allowing the children to discuss their ideas in teams first, Megan built up their confidence: this ensured that all the children were willing to explain and rationalise their team's solutions as they had been compiled through peer support and collaboration.

This team game approach can be applied to the final game that is discussed in this chapter, 'What's the same and what's different?'. The game returns us to the starting point for the chapter and illustrates that the concepts of sameness and difference underpin children's ability to develop their mathematical reasoning skills.

## Case Study 7: 'What's the same and what's different' in a small school (Key Stage 1 and Key Stage 2)

### Context
A focused 'mathematics week' in a small school with the emphasis on using and applying mathematical knowledge and skills. Jason (Key Stage 1 teacher), and Helen (Key Stage 2 teacher) planned many of the activities together, including the two variations of the same game described below.

### Curriculum links

| | |
|---|---|
| NC | KS1 Ma2: Pupils should be taught to:<br>**1b** develop flexible approaches to problem solving and look for ways to overcome difficulties<br>**1c** make decisions about operations and problem solving strategies to use<br>**1f** communicate in spoken, pictorial and written form<br>**4b** check that their answers are reasonable and explain their methods or reasoning |
| 2006 PNS Framework | **Y1** Describe simple patterns and relationships involving numbers or shapes; decide whether examples satisfy given conditions<br>**Using and applying mathematics**<br>Describe ways of solving puzzles and problems, explaining choices and decisions orally or using pictures<br>**Y2** Describe patterns and relationships involving numbers or shapes, make predictions and test these with examples<br>**Using and applying mathematics**<br>Present solutions to puzzles and problems in an organised way; explain decisions, methods and results in pictorial, spoken or written form, using mathematical language and number sentences |
| 1999 NNS Framework | **Y1 and Y2** Solve mathematical problems or puzzles, recognise simple patterns and relationships, generalise and predict |

| | |
|---|---|
| NC | **KS2 Ma3:** Pupils should be taught to:<br>**1d** use checking procedures to confirm that their results of geometric problems are reasonable<br>**1g** present and interpret solutions to problems<br>**1h** use mathematical reasoning to explain features of shape and space<br>**2b** visualise and describe 2D and 3D shapes |
| 2006<br>PNS Framework | **Y3/4** Describe patterns and relationships involving numbers or shapes, make predictions and test these with examples<br>**Y5/6 Using and applying mathematics**<br>Explore patterns, properties and relationships and propose a general statement involving numbers or shapes; identify examples for which the statement is true or false |
| 1999<br>NNS Framework | **Y3, 4, 5 and 6** Explain methods and reasoning<br>Solve mathematical problems or puzzles, recognise and explain patterns and relationships, generalise and predict<br>Classify/describe/visualise 3D and 2D shapes |

Jason arranged the children into mixed age and mixed attainment teams. He presented each team of children with the same set of numbers. Each team had a period of time to make statements regarding what could be the same and what could be different about all the numbers. Jason and his teaching assistant acted as scribes for the children's ideas where necessary. All teams shared their ideas at the same time and gained points for justification and originality.

The following example shows samples of the children's responses:

- a set of numbers: 1, 3, 6, 10, 15
  - 'they are different because some of the numbers are curvy and some are straight' (Y1)
  - 'they are the same because they are all less than 20' (Y1)
  - 'they are different because some are odd and some are even' (Y2)
  - 'they're the same because they've all got numbers missing from the last number' (Y2)
  - 'they are the same because they are in a pattern … two odd numbers followed by two even numbers … the next number will be odd' (Y2) [*This statement provoked much discussion and Jason invited all the teams to find a way to check the statement. Within a short space of time the team that had made the original statement demonstrated it was correct by showing how the next consecutive whole number was being added on each time.*]

Helen gave each of her teams pictures of a specific set of shapes:

- a set of shapes: a square, an oblong, a rhombus and a parallelogram
  - 'they're the same because they've all got four corners' (Y3)
  - 'they're different because only two of them have got right angles' (Y4)
  - 'they're the same because they're all quadrilaterals' (Y5)
  - 'they are the same because they all have two sets of parallel sides' (Y6)
  - 'they're different because they don't all have reflective symmetry' (Y6). [*Most of the class didn't agree with this statement so were invited to 'prove/disprove' by cutting out the shapes in paper and folding or checking with mirrors.*]

## How was the game used effectively?

These team games are at their most productive when played in mixed attainment or mixed age groupings: the 'ethos' needs to be one in which all understand that each team member has to participate, contribute, listen and be able to demonstrate/explain their ideas in some way. While team games are viewed as competitive, these games put much more emphasis on co-operation as more points are accrued for alternative suggestions and creativity of thinking. Hatch (1998: 33) notes further benefits in such mathematical game situations by suggesting that in co-operative games there is 'time and opportunity for peer tuition as the task is being completed, mental methods can be compared and discussed'.

Significant to all these games is the encouragement and 'reward' for 'thinking aloud', the use of mathematical language, and the value in conjecturing, predicting, checking and justifying ideas – the very skills inherent in logic and reasoning. While children need to draw upon their mathematical knowledge as part of these games, they are using what Skemp (1989) describes as 'intelligent learning' rather than relying on memorising known facts, or rote learning. Children who have the opportunity to develop their mathematical thinking skills through the inclusion of these types of games within their curriculum, are more likely to gain the benefits of intelligent learning and develop relational understanding of mathematics.

# The need for logical and reasoning activities to be given a higher profile

The case studies and discussion in the previous two sections exemplify the benefits of teachers, and trainee teachers, planning lessons/activities which give high status to children communicating mathematical ideas and developing mathematical reasoning.

The National Numeracy Strategy Framework (NNS) (DfEE, 1999b) includes objectives linked to 'Reasoning about numbers or shapes, number puzzles and making general statements' within the solving problems strand for each year group teaching programme. There is evidence (OFSTED, 2005b) that these limited objectives have not supported primary teachers in providing sufficient opportunities for collaborative work during which pupils have time to discuss ideas and clarify thinking. One factor in this appears to be an over-emphasis on the need for pupil recording:

> In mathematics, teachers sometimes place too much emphasis on pupils' recording and presentation of their calculations, deflecting their attention from the necessary mathematical reasoning.
> (OFSTED, 2005b: para 64)

As described in this chapter's opening paragraph, the NC gives greater credence to the need for the development of process skills by embedding them within the using and applying strands in each of the mathematics programmes of study. The rationale here is the need for the development of problem-solving, communication and reasoning skills to permeate through the curriculum content. However, HMI evaluations have consistently noted that too few pupils are able to use and apply their mathematics to solve problems in unfamiliar contexts. (OFSTED, 2002, 2003, 2005b). This would suggest that teachers are basing their curriculum solely on the content/objectives within the NNS Framework and continue to have difficulty in finding ways, and sufficient time, to allow for the development of children's mathematical thinking.

The changes brought about in the Primary Framework for mathematics (2006) suggests a recognition that the 1999 Framework, with its many objectives, has led to insufficient time for consolidation and depth of pupil understanding (DfES, 2005). One significant change in the new framework is the inclusion of using and applying objectives within all blocks and units of work.

While these changes, and attempts to encourage schools to employ greater flexibility and creativity within mathematics planning and teaching approaches, are to be welcomed, in itself this will not necessarily lead to a greater emphasis on the development of children's communication and reasoning skills within mathematics schemes of work. Greater guidance and support are needed to encourage teachers to build for the development of these skills within their planning and to recognise that the 'development of reasoning skills is closely bound with the development of communication skills' (Jones, 2003: 92).

Central to this change of emphasis within mathematics schemes of work needs to be an understanding of the importance of the processes of social interaction and dialogue to the development of children's logic and reasoning. Vygotsky's research (Moll, 1990) suggested that it is through engagement of these processes with more experienced learners (adults or peers) that children learn to be reflective upon their own thought processes. These reflections lead to 'meta-cognitive' developments in which children can better learn how to learn (Whitebread, 1995: 37).

In order for the development of children's logic and reasoning to be given higher profile within mathematics curricula, therefore, greater time needs to be allowed for the types of lessons/activities which:

- use resources and games/tasks in flexible, creative, open and collaborative ways as described throughout this chapter;
- allow children to engage with such resources in order to encourage discussion questioning, hypothesising and justification of ideas;
- promote the involvement of all children in child–child, adult–child dialogues which encourage awareness of, and reflection upon, mathematical processes;
- 'reward' children for doing their own thinking.

## SUMMARY OF **KEY POINTS**

This chapter has been concerned with the need for greater emphasis to be placed on the development of children's mathematical reasoning within planned curricula/units of work, and how the use of specific resources and games can actively support that development. By using the resources and games in discussion-based, collaborative activities, children learn to think logically, develop the ability to explain their thinking, use existing knowledge, note how things are related and draw conclusions. The development of these 'thinking skills' will be beneficial beyond discrete mathematical lessons. Enjoyment and challenge underpin the ways in which these resources and games have been used: such activities enrich the mathematics curriculum and allow scope for creative thinking.

The role of talk, dialogue and debate has been emphasised alongside the use of these resources and games as significant to the promotion of mathematical thinking. Greater time is advocated for pupil–pupil and adult–pupil dialogues to test out ideas, listen to alternative explanations and present reasoned arguments. This does not mean a diminished role for teachers or other practitioners, but rather one that attaches great importance to creative use of resources, collaborative learning, challenging tasks to use and develop thinking, and effective interactions. A mathematics curriculum based on an uncritical adherence to a model which overly focuses on the learning of knowledge and facts, encourages children to sit passively for excessively long periods of time, is dominated by teacher talk and demonstration, and views the purpose of children's activities as mainly practice/reinforcement, can no longer be sustained (OFSTED, 2005a).

REFLECTIONS ON PRACTICE

1. Do the resources which you use have potential for encouraging purposeful talk and aspects of mathematical thinking?
2. Is there scope in your existing plans to allow sufficient time for children to reflect upon their learning and/or make statements to justify their thinking?
3. What activities could you plan within your mathematics unit of work which allow children to apply logic, identify sameness and difference, and look for relationships involved?
4. How can you encourage all children within the class to share/discuss their mathematical ideas, participate in collaborative tasks and accept alternative solutions?

**REFERENCES** REFERENCES **REFERENCES** REFERENCES **REFERENCES** REFERENCES

Ainley, J. (1988) Playing games and real mathematics, in Pimm, D. (ed.) *Mathematics, teachers and children*. London: Hodder and Stoughton/Open University Press, pp239–248.

Anghileri, J. (2000) *Teaching number sense*. London: Continuum.

Askew, M. (1998) *Teaching primary mathematics. A guide for newly qualified and student teachers*. London: Hodder and Stoughton Educational.

Atkinson, S. (ed.) (1992) *Mathematics with reason. The emergent approach to primary maths*. London: Hodder and Stoughton.

Burton, L. (1994) *Children learning mathematics: patterns and relationships*. Hemel Hempstead: Simon and Schuster Education.

Delaney, K. (2001) Teaching mathematics resourcefully, in Gates, P. (ed.) *Issues in mathematics teaching*. London: Routledge Falmer, pp123–145.

Department for Education and Employment (1999a) *Mathematics. The National Curriculum for England: Key Stages 1–4*. London: DfEE Publications.

Department for Education and Employment (1999b) *The National Numeracy Strategy. Framework for Teaching Mathematics from Reception to Year 6*. London: DfEE Publications.

Department for Education and Employment (2000) *Curriculum Guidance for the Foundation Stage*. London: QCA.

Department for Education and Skills (2005) *Primary National Strategy. Reviewing the Frameworks for teaching literacy and mathematics*. London: DfES Publications. Ref. 1786–2005DOC-EN.

Department for Education and Skills (2006) Primary Framework for literacy and mathematics. **www.standards.gov.uk/primaryframeworks**.

Frobisher, L., Monaghan, J., Orton, A., Orton, J., Roper, T. and Threlfall, J. (1999) *Learning to teach number*. Cheltenham: Stanley Thornes.

Hatch, G. (1998) Replace your mental arithmetic test with a game. *Mathematics in School*, 27(1): 32–35.

Hopkins, C., Gifford, S. and Pepperell, S. (1999) *Mathematics in the primary school. A sense of progression* (2nd ed.). London: David Fulton.

Jared, L. and Thwaites, A. (1995) What is your favourite colour?, in Anghileri, J. (ed.) *Children's mathematical thinking in the primary years: perspectives on children's learning.* London: Cassell, pp110–123.

Jones, L. (2003) The problem with problem-solving, in Thompson, I. (ed.) *Enhancing primary mathematics teaching.* Berkshire: Open University Press, pp86–96.

Lawton, F. (2005) Section 4. Fractions, in Hansen, A. (ed.) *Children's errors in mathematics. Understanding common misconceptions in primary schools.* Exeter: Learning Matters, pp37–42.

Merttens, R. (ed.) (1997) *Teaching numeracy: maths in the primary classroom.* Leamington Spa: Scholastic.

Moll, C. (ed.) (1990) *Vygotsky and education.* Cambridge: Cambridge University Press.

OFSTED (2002) *The National Numeracy Strategy: the first three years 1999–2002.* OFSTED Publications. Ref. HMI 554.

OFSTED (2003) *The national literacy and numeracy strategies and the primary curriculum.* OFSTED Publications. Ref. HMI 1973.

OFSTED (2005a) *The Annual Report of Her Majesty's Chief Inspector of School 2004/5. Mathematics in primary schools.* OFSTED Publications.

OFSTED (2005b) *The national literacy and numeracy strategies and the primary curriculum. OFSTED Publications.* Ref. HMI 2395.

Pound, L. (1999) *Supporting mathematical development in the early years.* Buckingham: Open University Press.

Skemp, R. (1989) *Mathematics in the primary school.* London: Routledge.

Whitebread, D. (1995) Emergent mathematics or how to help young children become confident mathematicians, in Anghileri, J. (ed.) *Children's mathematical thinking in the primary years: perspectives on children's learning.* London: Cassell, pp11–39.

# 5

# Adapting resources for children with specific needs

## Anne Gager

In any classroom a teacher will be faced with a number of children with diverse learning needs. This can often be a daunting prospect for a trainee teacher. It is important to remember, however, that many teachers often feel inexperienced and unprepared for this task. Teaching children with additional needs is merely an extension of teaching all children. It is important to recognise that 'students with and without disabilities are more alike than they are different from one another' (Westwood, 2003: xv). Teaching children with additional needs, while challenging, actually refines and hones the practitioner's teaching skills, as 'the heart of the matter is trying to teach a child who is hard to teach – and learning from the experience' (Gulliford, 1985: 32, cited in Daniels, 2006: 4). This chapter will explore the use of resources that promote inclusive practices within primary mathematics teaching. It will identify the diversity of learners in a classroom and the issues that this raises in delivering an inclusive mathematics lesson that develops children's mathematical thinking.

## Chapter focus

The chapter will explore how the use of specific resources can help children develop their mathematical thinking while enabling them to be part of a class. It will focus on:

- the general principles for inclusion;
- resources for children experiencing barriers to learning in mathematics;
- resources for children who are more able at mathematics;
- resources for children who are learning mathematics with English as an additional language;
- the significance of the teaching assistant (TA) as an important resource.

## The general principles for inclusion

The barriers to learning that children experience can be extremely diverse, because each child is an individual with their own skills, traits and needs. The Special Educational Needs (SEN) Code of Practice notes this: 'this guidance does not assume that there are hard and fast categories of SEN. It recognizes … that each child is unique' (DfES, 2001a: 85). For the purposes of this chapter, three groups of children will be addressed. While there is understandable reluctance and caution over labelling children (Norwich, 1999), grouping children can serve practical purposes. The purpose of grouping children in this context is to identify children who may need extra or different resources in order for them to develop their mathematical thinking. The chapter will consider issues surrounding how resources can support the mathematical development of children with SEN, children with English as an additional language (EAL), and children who are more able in mathematics.

The National Curriculum (NC) (DfEE, 1999) has given three important principles to aid effective inclusion in lessons:

1. setting suitable learning challenges for all pupils;
2. responding to pupils' diverse learning needs;
3. overcoming potential barriers to learning.

These have been adapted by the Primary National Strategy and translated into good classroom practice as 'circles of inclusion' (see Figure 5.1).

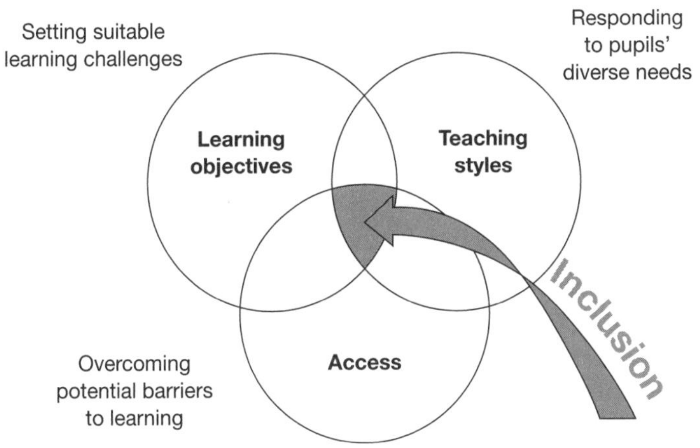

Figure 5.1: Including all children in literacy and mathematics (Ref. DfES 0465/2002)

The circles of inclusion act as a useful guide when preparing lessons. If it is proving difficult to include a child in a lesson, the circles can help to address an area of planning which might have been overlooked. The circles of inclusion will be referred to in the case studies that follow.

# Resources for children experiencing barriers to learning in mathematics

Mathematics is much more than number work, but for some children the difficulties they experience with numbers may mean they can be excluded from many of the class mathematics activities. There can be the tendency for teachers to focus on procedure and techniques for such children rather than challenging their mathematical thinking (Watson *et al.*, 2005: 19). This is particularly true towards the end of Key Stage 2. Simple number resources can be used to overcome this and to help children to participate more fully in lessons. At the end of Key Stage 2 the resources must be considered carefully since the presentation of resources such as Unifix, as valuable as it is, will not be welcomed by a Year 6 child who will recognise this as a resource used by younger children.

This section contains two case studies from two key stages. The first makes use of a selection of 'home-made' laminated 100 squares. There are nine 100 squares and each one is coloured for an appropriate times table. The squares are joined together with a treasury tag. The squares have been customised for Robert, a Year 5 child.

## Case Study 1: A set of 100 squares helps Robert to participate fully in the lesson (Y5)

### Context

Robert is a Year 5 boy with SEN. He is at the stage of School Action Plus on the SEN Code of Practice (DfES, 2001a). Robert is working at level 2 in Ma2: Number. He is very conscious of his inability in this area of mathematics, particularly with mental calculations. He may have a specific number problem, dyscalculia (see further information at the end of the chapter). He is depressed by having to repeat what he considers 'work sheets for babies' and longs to be able to participate with his peers. It is thought that he may be better at Ma1: Using and applying than he is at Ma2: Number, since he often has good ideas about how to solve a problem, but does not then have the number skills to implement his idea. (Chapter 1 discusses this issue further.) Despite great efforts by Robert, his teachers and his parents, he has not been able to memorise tables other than 2, 10 and, on a good day, 5.

### Curriculum links

| | |
|---|---|
| NC | **KS2 Ma2:** Pupils should be taught to:<br>**3f** recall multiplication facts to 10 × 10 |
| 2006 PNS Framework | **Y5** Recall quickly multiplication facts up to 10 and use them to multiply pairs of multiples of 10 and 100; derive quickly corresponding division facts<br>**Using and applying mathematics**<br>Explore patterns, properties and relationships and propose a general statement involving numbers or shapes; identify examples for which the statement is true or false |
| 1999 NNS Framework | **Y5** Consolidate knowing by heart number facts up to 10 × 10<br>Choose and use appropriate number operations to solve problems and appropriate ways of calculating mental with jottings written methods, calculator |

Robert's teacher has used the first principle of inclusion: 'Setting suitable learning challenges', and ensured that the objectives of the lesson are appropriate for him. Since Robert has barriers to learning in areas of number, the teacher has tracked back through the NNS framework (DfES, 2002) and selected objectives from previous year groups in order to make it relevant. She has ensured that her teaching style is appropriate, thus incorporating the second principle of inclusion. The third strand of the inclusion principles is 'overcoming barriers to learning' or 'access'. This is the most crucial part of the principles when thinking about resources. It is the provision of the appropriate resources that will enable Robert to be able to access and be included in this lesson.

For support during the oral/mental starter, Robert has been provided with a number of table squares (see Figure 5.2). Robert has used these over the years but the teaching assistant (TA) has now developed them so that he can hold them in the palm of his hand. During the oral/mental starter, Robert sits with the rest of the class. The teacher begins with some straightforward multiplication calculations. Because the teacher has considered her teaching style as a principle of inclusion, she is not looking for the fastest answer. She is aware that Robert's use of table squares will restrict his speed of answering, but there is also a child in the class with an auditory processing disorder. The use of thinking time is important for this girl as well as for Robert.

**Figure 5.2: Robert's table squares**

Robert is able to look up the answers quickly on his cards and is able to join in with the rest of the class. This has given him the opportunity to feel included in the lesson. This helps Robert's self-esteem and also allows him to develop his mathematical thinking by overcoming the barrier he has in number. While Robert is answering questions he notices that Tamsin moves nearer to him. She has been unable to answer any of the questions that have been posed so far. Robert generously shares his squares with Tamsin and shows her how the cards work. The teacher notices that Tamsin is now putting her hand up too and is able to answer the question and provides the appropriate praise. As the class begins to move into groups for their focused work, Tamsin and Robert begin to talk.

**Tamsin:** They're pretty those cards

**Robert:** How can maths cards be pretty?

**Tamsin:** Well I mean like the pattern. Don't look at the numbers, just look at the colours shaded in. I like how on that 3× one, it goes in diagonal lines

**Robert:** Yeah, but it's orange, I like red best

**Tamsin:** Well you could make it whatever colour you want, but I like the stripes, like steps

**Robert:** Oh yeah, I'd not noticed that. Hey, this one is a pretty boring pattern.
    [*Robert has selected the ×5 square*]

**Tamsin:** Just two stripes, but at least they're red

**Robert:** That's why I can do my 5 times table

**Tamsin:** What, because it's red?

**Robert:** No, because it's boring and it's just a five or a nought

**Tamsin:** Are there any other nice patterns; what about ×4?

**Robert:** Purple
    [*The teacher has been allowing this conversation to develop but has so far not intervened. She now decides to direct the children's mathematical thinking a little further*]

**Teacher:** If you compare the ×2 with the ×4 do you notice anything?

**Tamsin:** One's purple one's blue

**Robert:** They're the same

**Tamsin:** No they're not

**Robert:** Well they've both got stripes, but they're different

**Teacher:** In what way are they different?

**Robert:** Well this one (*the* ×4) isn't in lines

**Tamsin:** It's not got as many numbers coloured as the blue (×2) … just every other one

**Robert:** Well that'll be half then, won't it? Half as many coloured in as on the blue one

**Robert:** Hey that's funny 'cos two's half of four

**Teacher:** It's funny but it's a very mathematical observation you've made Robert. I'd like you to share that with the rest of the class in the plenary, if you'd like to

**Robert:** No thanks!

# How was the resource used effectively?

## For inclusion

The resource enabled Robert to be included in the lesson. It was effective because he was able to work independently. By providing him with the table squares he has been given access to the answers that his learning difficulty had prevented him from gaining. A bonus was that another child was able to use the same resource, even though it had not been designed specifically for her. This is often the case with children who have additional needs. It is rare that a resource or an approach will only be useful for one child; there are usually others who will also need or benefit from it. The apparent effort and consequent justification of planning specifically for one child will usually have benefits for at least one other member of the class. The fact that Tamsin needed Robert's resource also helped to put him in the unusual situation in a mathematics lesson where he was seen as 'expert'. This becomes very empowering in terms of inclusion, because it allows Robert to enter into a mathematical discussion using mathematical terminology based on the resource. The resource did not merely allow Robert to access the lesson but it allowed him to include someone else.

## For mathematical thinking

What is seen by the use of the table squares is the way in which it provides more than just the 'right answer' for the child. The visual form of the number squares becomes a focal point for the children. They can see the number patterns at work and their eyes are drawn to them, initially because of the colours and the 'stripes' that appear. In looking at this they begin to examine why the shades are as they are and begin to make some connections. Robert has spent much of his mathematical life being overwhelmed by numbers and although he had found this resource useful in allowing him to participate in lessons, the mathematics behind it had not really clicked into place. As he and Tamsin examined the patterns together, he began to see that there was a relationship between the shaded numbers. He then proceeded to make a link between those tables that he knew and their patterns, recognising that the ones he knew had the most obvious patterns. The resource allowed Robert to spot patterns and the recognition of patterns is a key aspect of mathematical thinking (DfES, 2003a: 22).

It is not clear whether this information would allow Robert to become any more confident in recalling the number tables but what it clearly allows him to do is to begin to understand the relationships between numbers and number patterns. He has demonstrated his understanding of the relationship between the 2× and the 4× tables. He may be good at doubling. His teacher and parents could work with him in seeing the relationship between the 2× and 4× in terms of halving/doubling, perhaps by making a table or comparing answers. This might help him also in seeing the relationship with 5× and 10×. Eventually he might be able to work out other tables using this relationship. For example, if he doubles 4×, he can get 8×. If he learns 3×, he can double to get 6×. By seeing the effect on the patterns on the 100 squares (or the relationships) he might be able to use this newly found information to support his learning of tables that he has struggled with up until now. He has used his logical thinking to build up his mathematics knowledge.

This second case study considers the effective use of a resource for another child with barriers to learning, but this time it is in the Foundation Stage.

## Case Study 2: Jo develops understanding of circles and squares (Y1)

### Context
Jo is in the summer term of the Reception class at school. She has a statement for SEN. Her difficulties are classified as 'global learning difficulties' although it has been noted that there are indicators that she could be on the autistic spectrum. She has a spoken vocabulary of ten words. There is a broad target on her statement relating to mathematics. The target is: 'To develop basic skills in early numeracy'.

This has been broken down into SMART targets on her Individual Education Plan (IEP):

- to count objects accurately to 5;
- to be able to recognise a square and a circle;
- to be able to do simple classification.

### Curriculum links

| | |
|---|---|
| CGFFS | **Stepping Stones (Green)** Use appropriate shapes to make representational models or more elaborate patterns Use language such as 'circle' or 'bigger' to describe the shape and size of solids and flat shapes |
| 2006 PNS Framework | **FS** Use language such as 'circle' or 'bigger' to describe the shape and size of solids and flat shapes |
| 1999 NNS Framework | **Reception:** Use language such as 'circle' or 'bigger' to describe the shape and size of solids and flat shapes |
| OTHER | **IEP target:** Jo should be able to recognise a square and a circle **P levels Shape, Space and Measures** **P6** Pupils search for objects not found in their usual place demonstrating their understanding of object permanence. They compare the overall size of one object with that of another where the difference is not great. They manipulate three-dimensional shapes. They show understanding of words signs and symbols that describe positions. **P7** Pupils begin to respond to forwards and backwards. They start to pick out name shapes and sizes from a collection. They use familiar words when they compare sizes and quantities and describe position. (DfES, 2001b) |

The class is working on shape and space and specifically on the properties and language of the 2D shapes, circle and square. Jo's teacher has seen this as an excellent opportunity to work on Jo's IEP target of 'To be able to recognise a square and a circle'.

The teacher has formalised the mathematics lessons for the Reception class in the summer term, in order to prepare the children for Year 1. Because of this, there is an opening oral/mental starter to the lesson. The teacher uses the oral/mental starter to reinforce the properties of squares and circles. After this, there are a number of activities in the class-room that the children can participate in. The activities are all designed to reinforce the objectives of the lesson and make use of a number of resources. The activities all involve mainly squares and circles but some other shapes have been presented too.

- The sand tray has circle and square cutters.
- The paint corner has an assortment of cardboard boxes and cylinders for printing circles and squares.
- The attribute blocks have been placed on the carpet for construction and investigation.
- Stickers of squares and circles have been placed on a table for picture design.

Jo will be able to access all of these activities. The teacher's priority, however, is to ensure that Jo makes some progress towards her target. The teacher is concerned that Jo begins to understand the mathematical properties of circles and squares and is able to 'recognise a square and a circle'. Jo has limited spoken language and therefore this presents a chal-lenge to the teaching staff.

## Key resource

Although the teacher has carefully selected a variety of resources to help children to engage with the concepts of shape, there is one key resource that will be particularly bene-ficial to Jo. The resource that the teacher carefully selects to help Jo to achieve and to be included in this lesson is the resource of song. Music can be a useful tool to aid learning for children with additional needs. It gives them a medium in which they can develop skills and presents the opportunity for rehearsing and over-learning (Jaquiss and Paterson, 2005: 1). Jo has responded well to music in previous lessons and the teacher has selected this to engage and develop her mathematical thinking.

## The lesson

The teacher has bright appealing large shapes of circles and squares which vary in size. They can be removed from a board on which they are held by Velcro. The teacher begins by selecting a square. She starts the song straight away.

## The Square Song

(sung to the tune of 'Twinkle, twinkle little star')

*Here's a shape that you know well*
*It's a square, how can you tell?*
*Four sides I can see,*
*Four corners there must be,*
*Here's a shape that you know well*
*It's a square, your turn to tell*

The rhythm of the song lends itself to the properties of a square being emphasised. On the third line of the song, the teacher touches a side of the square as she sings the song, point-ing to a side on each of the four beats of the bar:

*Four / Sides / I can / See*

She does the same on the fourth line, touching the four corners according to the four beats of the bar:

*Four / Corners / There must / Be*

After the line 'your turn to tell', a number of children are keen to 'tell' and so they come out and choose a square and sing the song (with support from the teacher), touching the appropriate parts of the square as they proceed. This continues for as long as the teacher deems appropriate, before moving on to explore the circle in a similar fashion. The teacher selects Jo to demonstrate the circle song and although Jo is unsuccessful at choosing the circle, she is given one and then 'sings' it along with the others.

The Circle Song
(sung to the tune of 'The wheels on the bus')

*The circle that I hold goes round and round*
*Round and round, round and round*
*The circle that I hold goes round and round*
*All day long*

*No sides no corners 'cos its round, round, round*
*Round, round round, round, round round*
*No sides no corners 'cos its round, round, round*
*All day long*
[Repeat verse 1]

When the teacher decides that the children have gained as much as possible from this section of the lesson, they then are allowed to choose their activity. As the children go off to their different activities, Jo heads for the attribute blocks. She enjoys sorting these into colours (an earlier target on her IEP). When the teacher joins the group she discovers that Jo has grouped the shapes according to colour. She recognises what Jo has done and praises her for grouping in this way. Next, the teacher steers Jo to focus on the shapes of the attribute blocks. The teacher selects a circle and as she does so she begins to sing the 'Circle Song'. Jo, who had been previously absorbed in her colour-sorting activity, responds immediately to the sound of the music and makes eye contact with the teacher. The teacher rolls the circle between her hands in such a way that Jo is able to make eye contact with the circle. She sings the song to Jo as she rolls the circle.

**Teacher:**  Now you find me a circle Jo, and sing the song too
          [*Jo picks up a red square (the teacher's circle is red)*]
**Teacher:**  Will that one go [*singing*] 'round and round' Jo?
          [*No apparent response from Jo*]
**Teacher:**  I can't make it go round and round, Jo
          [*The teacher then rolls the circle along the mat. It's quite an impressive roll and Jo giggles and the other children nearby exclaim with excitement. The teacher sings the circle song as she rolls the block back towards Jo. Jo now picks up a circle and rolls it. As she does this, the teacher sings the circle song. At this point Jo begins to hum along with the song as she rolls the circle*]
**Teacher:**  Well done Jo, you have chosen the circle, the one that goes 'round and round'

# How was the resource used effectively?

## For inclusion

The song was used at the beginning of the lesson. By using the song in the oral/mental starter, it was seen as a key element and became an integral part of the lesson for all the children. Although the song was designed specifically for Jo, the teacher based the start of her lesson using the song. This was particularly effective as an inclusive device, because what had been designed for one child was used to benefit all the children in the class. It was only later in the lesson that it was used more specifically for Jo.

## For mathematical thinking

Jo has previously been able to demonstrate that she is able to 'sort sets of objects according to a single attribute' (DfES, 2001b). This shows that she has reached P level 5 of Ma1: Using and applying mathematics. The selection of a shape is not just about achieving progress in the area of Ma3: Shape and space but also in the area of Ma1: Using and applying mathematics. If Jo is able to 'sort objects ... according to criteria' then she is moving a stage further in her understanding of mathematics. To do this, Jo needs help to make connections. It may be difficult for Jo to grasp that a square has vertices (referred to as 'corners' in the Foundation Stage) and a circle has none. Sensory stimulation is needed to help children with the most severe barriers to learning (Westwood, 2003: 27). Jo needs to be presented with as many sensory routes as possible to help her to make the connections which give a circle and a square their properties. The use of the tactile and visually bright squares and circles is a very helpful resource, but Jo needs something in addition to this.

The song is powerful, and the actions that go along with it are too. The teacher has carefully chosen to do a different tune for the circle and the square. This is deliberate: Jo needs to make a connection between the song and the shape. If the tune were the same for each shape and only the words changed, that would not help Jo to distinguish between the circle and square. As the song is sung, Jo is beginning to make the links between the shape that is held when one tune occurs and the different shape that is held when the another tune is sung.

Progress with children working at this level can often seem to be slow and can be hard to identify, particularly when considering mathematical understanding. According to Panter (2001: 44), 'it must be appreciated that good teaching of mathematics under such conditions is an immense challenge'. In this situation, the teacher has responded to the challenge by the careful choice of resources. As Jo responds to the music, she is demonstrating an early stage of thinking and categorisation. As she hears the song, feels the shape in her hand and looks at the shape, then connections are being made about the properties of that shape. She sees, hears and touches the round, continuous edge of the circle. The song provides another way for her to 'hear' the properties that make this shape a 'circle'. The fact that the song changes or no song is sung when the 'non-circle' shape is held is a prompt for Jo to recognise that this is 'different', thus helping her to develop the early ability to categorise and recognise the shape. The use of multi-sensory resources is key to utilising children's auditory, visual, tactile and sensory skills (Pickles, 2001: 298). In this situation the use of song combined with tactile, brightly coloured shapes has allowed Jo to develop her mathematical thinking about the properties of shape.

# Resources for children who are more able at mathematics

For many teachers their own confidence in mathematics is an area of anxiety and therefore the thought of teaching a child who is more able in this area can be daunting. It need not be. As for most teaching, what is required is a clearly planned lesson which will meet the child's needs. Able mathematicians often need to have the time and resources to pursue an area in depth and to be allowed to do this can be of great satisfaction (Eyre and McClure, 2001). The teacher can facilitate this by providing appropriate resources and allowing the child the time to investigate their interest. The following case study shows how an able mathematician in the Foundation Stage is provided with the resources to develop his mathematical thinking.

## Case Study 3: William uses attribute blocks to develop his logical thinking (Y1)

### Context

William is in the same class as Jo. He has been assessed as being gifted and talented in the field of mathematics. He has already achieved many of the level 2 targets for mathematics, which has been recognised through teacher assessment. William is in the same lesson on squares and circles as Jo. The lesson objectives are the same as those for Jo. The task for the teacher, having ensured that the lesson can help Jo in her mathematical development, is to plan so that William can also be included and learn in this lesson.

### Key resource

The key resource that the teacher has chosen to aid William's mathematical thinking is attribute blocks.

**Figure 5.3: Attribute blocks**

These are a structured set of three-dimensional shapes designed to develop children's logical thinking. In this lesson the teacher has decided to use them as a representation of two-dimensional shapes. The shapes consist of square, circle, triangle, rectangle and hexagon. Each shape can be thick or thin; large or small; red, yellow or blue. The shapes can be used by all the children, many of whom will focus on the circle and square, but the teacher has included this resource for William because of how she intends to develop his mathematical thinking.

## The lesson

The lesson proceeds as described for Jo. During the oral/mental starter William sings along with the other children.

**Teacher:** There are many other shapes than circles and squares but I haven't got songs for them all yet. They do all have names though and we will look at some now

[*As the teacher holds up the shapes (to show the 2D faces) a few children are able to say the names of the triangle. William is able to name all the shapes and add information about the properties of each of these shapes*]

[*At activity time, the teacher directs William to the attribute blocks and works one-to-one with him to explain how he is going to do some work on classification of shapes. The teacher has designed a 'sorting machine'. The machine is drawn on a large piece of paper (see Figure 5.4). She explains to William that he has to pass all the shapes through the machine and sort them*]

**William:** That's easy

[*William quickly sorts out all the red shapes and passes them through the appropriate side of the machine and the same with the blue, which he puts on the 'non-red' side of the machine. The yellow blocks are left in the box*]

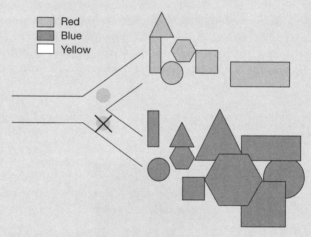

**Figure 5.4: First-stage tree diagram**

**Teacher:** What about the yellow blocks, William?

**William:** Well, I've done some red and those blue

**Teacher:** But all the blocks have to go through the machine, William, they all have to be sorted, so where will the yellow ones go?

**William:** Well they're not red, I know that, but they're not the same as those [*pointing to the blue*]

**Teacher:** But does our machine sort them into the 'same'?

**William:** [*Verbalising to himself as he moves the blocks*] Red or not red. *So these* [*pointing to the yellow ones*] go here with these [*pointing to blue*]

**Teacher:** Yes, that's right. You've now got two groups, 'red' and 'not red'

[*William can't do this task fast enough*]

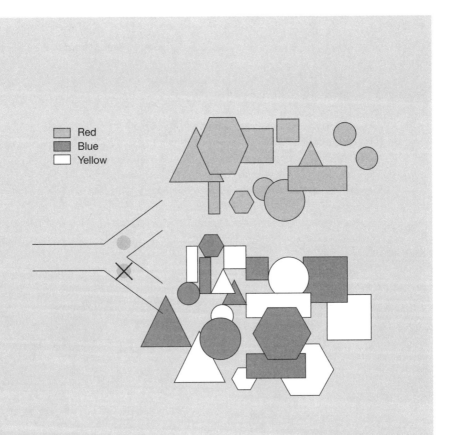

**Figure 5.5: Sorting into 'red' and 'not red'**

**William:** But I don't like these all being mixed up, big, little, thick, thin
**Teacher:** Well, we can add another bit to the sorting machine and take this idea a bit further
        [*The teacher draws two more branches to each of the original branches*]
**Teacher:** How would you like to sort them this time, William?
**William:** Big and small!

The teacher then shows William how he can add other branches, and reminds him that he can use pen and paper if he wants to record anything. William works individually with the blocks for the rest of the lesson. By the time the lesson ends, William has moved the shapes through various sorting machines. He has recorded machines which sort for thick or thin, large or small. The teacher also observed him extending the original machine to sort for size and then thick and thin, although he did not record this.

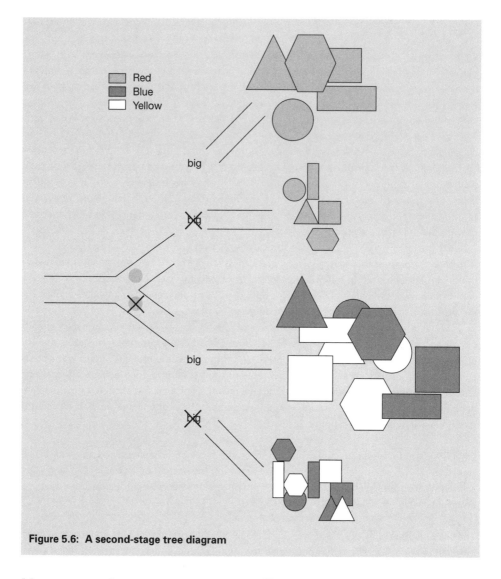

Red
Blue
Yellow

big

big

**Figure 5.6: A second-stage tree diagram**

# How was the resource used effectively?

## For inclusion

William was able to participate in the lesson. He was allowed the same opportunity as the other children to join in the various activities. Many other children were using the attribute blocks but in a different way to William. The use of the 'sorting machine' enabled him to use his existing knowledge of shape but to develop his knowledge of classification (Ma4).

## For mathematical thinking

Within this lesson the teacher provided William with a number of problems to be solved. Problem-solving is one of the ways in which gifted and talented children can be challenged (Clark and Callow, 2002: 121). William was challenged to classify shapes. The use of this resource allowed William to develop his mathematical thinking by giving him concrete materials which enhanced both his understanding of the properties of shape and his classification skills. The sorting machine gave him the opportunity to be able to develop a new aspect of classification; the principle of binary classification.

In working with this resource William began by sorting out the red shapes from all the others. The new concept that William was introduced to was 'not red'. If something is 'not red', that does not mean it is blue or yellow – it is just not red. This was a development in William's mathematical thinking, but once he had grasped it he was then able to develop and refine it further. Like many children, William had grasped the concept of grouping according to colour, a skill with which he was competent. The resource of the sorting machine presented William with only two options, 'red' or 'not red'. Because William had the sorting machine to 'play' with, this allowed him to develop his mathematical thinking by actively performing a binary classification process. This was demonstrated by his verbalisation as he passed each of the attribute blocks through the machine, verbalising 'red' or 'not red'. Each time he selected a yellow or a blue block he verbalised, 'not red', and then he began to internalise this. Handling each of the yellow and blue attribute blocks and moving them through the appropriate side of the machine reinforced the notion that blue and yellow could be considered together as a new group, the 'not red' group.

A further strength of this particular resource, for a child who is very able mathematically, is that it can then be used in a number of ways. Once William had been introduced to the concept of binary classification, he was then able to develop this skill. The attribute blocks and the proforma of the sorting machine provided William with resources that he was then able to use to extend his thinking. He was able to engage in first- and second-stage binary classification as he devised new machines to sort and classify. The provision of paper and the attribute blocks allowed him to experiment with other classifications. William was able to choose a new classification and was then able to draw this onto his machine. The physical task of being able to pass the blocks through whatever criteria he had chosen for his machine gave him the opportunity to develop his thinking about the properties of shapes and the different ways in which they can be classified.

Later, William devised a machine that sorted on the basis of 'four sides' and 'not four sides'. He had a pile of rectangles and squares pass through the sorting machine, in the 'four sides' section. William then refined this set by classifying them according to 'equal sides' and 'not equal sides'.

The resource has allowed William to work alone. It is important that able children can 'work independently, searching with confidence for meaning and pattern in abstract tasks' (Clark and Callow, 2002: 95), however this was only effective because of the teacher's intervention. The resource has also provided him with a model which has enhanced his mathematical thinking by allowing him to take part practically, in a process which has developed his classification skills.

# Resources for children who are learning mathematics with English as an additional language

Raiker (2002) suggests that problems in the teaching and learning of mathematical concepts may be compounded by the inaccurate use of mathematical vocabulary. For children who have English as an additional language it is imperative that they are explicitly taught the precise and correct use of words in order to underpin the development of their mathematical thinking. In order to develop their mathematical ability, children need the opportunity to see the teacher (or TA) demonstrate and model appropriate mathematical language. They then need the opportunity to rehearse and explore this vocabulary in order to consolidate their learning (DfES, 2003a). In the following case study we see how a resource can help to promote learning after the correct modelling has been demonstrated.

## Case Study 4: Xuan (Y3)

### Context

Xuan has moved to England and joined a Year 3 class. She arrived with very little English, which has made life at school quite difficult. An area where she has excelled is in the number aspect of mathematics. This is encouraging because it is often easy to underestimate the mathematical ability of those who are new learners of English (DfES, 2001c). Xuan, however, is able to tackle computation work very easily. This is restricted to the most straightforward aspects of computation, namely worksheets full of calculations. She is working at level 3 for Ma2: Number and algebra. Any problem-solving or mathematics involving word-based questions is difficult for Xuan to attempt. She is unable to deal with this type of question because of her developing English language and specifically the specialist language required for mathematics. The class is working on solving story problems in real life and although Xuan could easily manage the computation aspect of this, she is unable to move from the 'story' and decipher the language. This prevents her being able to translate this into the mathematical calculation. The teacher uses the lesson as an opportunity to develop the language and mathematical understanding of 'more', 'less' and specifically 'more than' and 'less than'.

### Curriculum links

| | |
|---|---|
| NC | **KS2 Ma2: Pupils should be taught to:**<br>4a choose use and combine any of the four number operations to solve word problems |
| 2006 PNS Framework | **Y3 Using and applying mathematics**<br>Solve one-step and two-step problems involving numbers, money or measures, including time, choosing and carrying out appropriate calculations |
| 1999 NNS Framework | **Y3** Solve simple word problems set in 'real life' contexts and explain how the problem was solved |
| Other | Xuan does not have an IEP as she does not have SEN but the teacher is targeting her development of her mathematical language, specifically, 'more', 'less', 'fewer', 'more than', 'less than', 'most', 'least', 'fewest' |

### Key resource

The key resource that the teacher has selected in order to include Xuan in the lesson and to help her develop her mathematical thinking is 'digit pop-ups' (Figure 5.7). As can be seen, the resource only extends to ten characters, but it is the mathematical language and concepts that are being developed, not competence with large numbers.

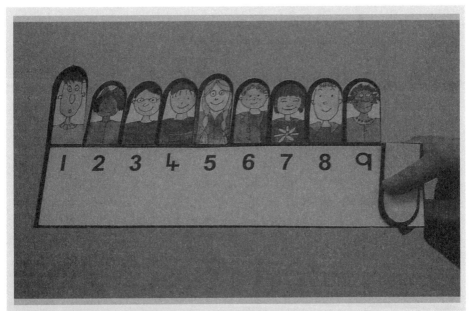

**Figure 5.7: Digit pop-up people**

## The lesson

After the oral/mental starter the children move into groups to continue their problem-solving work. Xuan is in a group of five children who are all assigned to work with the TA. The teacher has carefully prepared with the TA (see paragraph below) the work that she wants the children to do. There are no written questions but the TA works through series of problems with the children. Each child and the TA have a set of the digit pop-ups, which the TA refers to as 'pop-up people'.

| | |
|---|---|
| **TA:** | Let's look at our pop-up people. What do you notice? |
| **Child 1** | They're all the same |
| **TA:** | That's right |
| | [*The TA then spends some time exploring the specifics of 'sameness'. The children, including Xuan, identify the fact that the resource has the same numbers on it and that the children are the same. They look closely at the same hairstyles, same clothes and the same features, eyes, ears*] |
| **TA:** | How many children have I got? |
| **Children:** | Ten |
| **TA:** | [*Begins a story*] There were ten children sitting on the mat when the teacher told five of them to go and read their books |
| | [*The TA counts and puts five children down*] |
| **TA:** | Xuan, have I got more or less children than you now? |
| **Xuan:** | Five |
| **TA:** | Yes, that's right, I have got five children and you have ten, so I have less children than you |
| **TA:** | Xuan, have I got less or more children than Tom? |
| **Xuan:** | Less |
| **TA:** | That's right, I have got less than Tom. Who has got more than me, Xuan? |
| **Xuan:** | Chantelle |

| | |
|---|---|
| **TA:** | Can you tell me in a sentence? |
| **Xuan:** | Chantelle more you |
| **TA:** | Well done, that's right, Chantelle has more than me |

[*After further exploration from the teacher, the children are asked to work in pairs to make up their own story about the ten children using the words 'more', 'less', 'more than' and 'less than'. Xuan is reluctant to work in a pair, conscious that she is not able to communicate as effectively as the other children. The TA observes her on her own, popping the people down and quietly verbalising the words 'less' as she pops some people down and 'more' as she releases them to spring back up again. After Xuan has spent some time playing alone with the pop-up people, the TA works with Xuan*]

| | |
|---|---|
| **TA:** | I'm holding up three children, Xuan. Can you hold up more than I have? [*Xuan holds up six*] |
| **TA:** | You're holding up three more than me [*Xuan looks confused*] |
| **TA:** | You have three more than me, Xuan … one, two, three [*The TA touches the three more. Xuan lets all the children pop up*] |
| **Xuan:** | Seven more! |
| **TA:** | That's right Xuan, seven more than me |

# How was the resource used effectively?

## For inclusion

The resource is appealing to all the children, who enjoy the different faces and characteristics. It includes children from a variety of different ethnic backgrounds and this, along with the detail of clothes and colours, provides a rich stimulus for developing Xuan's language. This is also helpful for Xuan because it allows her to count people in her first language and the resource provides the numeral in English.

## For mathematical thinking

In a situation such as Xuan's, where a child has a high level of attainment in paper-based calculations, it is tempting to overlook the development of their mathematical thinking. While it is important to celebrate the success a child's achievements, the teacher also has a responsibility to develop mathematical thinking and this was a particular issue for Xuan because of her being a new user of English.

The resource gave a very clear 'picture' of the concept that was being taught. The fact that all the children had the same resource and could compare how many children they had, gave the clear picture of 'more' and of 'less'. The same could be achieved with counters or Unifix but this activity engaged Xuan because of the appeal of the people. The fact that the TA was able to place her examples in a story context ('There were ten children sitting on the mat when the teacher told five of them to go and read their books') helped to develop Xuan's thinking about 'more' and 'less' by placing it in a familiar context and understanding that this was connected to the process of addition and subtraction, with which she was very competent.

Xuan was not as confident as the other children to work in a pair to create her own story with the pop-up people, so the TA did not insist that she worked in a pair. Children who are at the early stages of learning English should not be asked to present their work orally but should be allowed to listen to others (DfES, 2001c). The resource allowed her to work on her own. Because the resource has the feature of being physically flexible and the ability to 'pop' the people up and down, Xuan's mathematical thinking continued as she 'played' with the children. This was demonstrated by her verbalising 'more' and 'less' as she moved the pop-up people around.

The resource also allowed Xuan to take control of her own learning. She was able to use the resource independently and refine her understanding of the concepts 'more' and 'less' as she chose how many children to have and whether to add or subtract from her starting position. As can be seen from the lesson extract, Xuan still has to consolidate her understanding of 'more than' and 'less than' and this resource can provide her with the opportunity to do that.

# The significance of the TA as an important resource

Throughout all the case studies it can be seen that the TA is a vital part of the process. Although this section is concerned primarily with the TA as a resource, it is important to recognise the positive role model that the TA can be for children and in particular for learning mathematics (Headington, 2001: 4).

Ideally, the teacher would hope to engage with as many children as possible during the mathematics lesson in order to support the learning going on. The TA is a key resource that the teacher can use in order to double this amount of interaction in the classroom. The significance and importance of their role in developing children's mathematical thinking is enormous. However, as with all resources, the management of them is the teacher's responsibility and the success depends on how well the teacher uses and deploys them. The TA is no different from any other resource in this sense and their use should be planned carefully.

Planning and preparation are crucial for all resources but it is slightly different with the use of a TA. The resources that have been mentioned so far are concrete apparatus which is the same in whatever classroom it is placed; but the use of a person means there are more variables. If the TA is uncertain of their own mathematical knowledge or if they are uncertain about how they are meant to be working with the children, then it is far less likely that they are going to be able to develop the children's mathematical thinking most effectively.

In order to minimise the variables involved in this case careful planning is needed and wherever possible this should be collaborative (Soan, 2005: 76). If a teacher meets to plan and share with the TA then it is much more likely that any misconceptions that are held might be eradicated before they are possibly introduced to any children. Collaborative planning also enables best practice and ideas to be shared, which will be a two-way process. If this is not available then an information sheet guiding the TA through the lesson and directing him/her to the key learning points is the next best thing.

## SUMMARY OF **KEY POINTS**

This chapter has been concerned with the inclusion of all children in mathematics lessons. It is not just the ability to participate in the lessons that has been emphasised, but the ability to undertake mathematical thinking. The mathematical thinking may be very different for each child, depending upon their individual strengths, barriers to learning and backgrounds. The use of resources is a key aspect of making this work successful. Using one of the NC's three principles of inclusion, 'overcoming barriers to learning', it can be seen that appropriate resources can be an important strategy to assist in providing 'access'.

Planning for one specific child can often be used for the benefit of the whole class. A resource that has been carefully selected to develop one child's mathematical thinking will usually have benefits for others. The same resource can be used to develop mathematical thinking for a wide variety of children. The key to a resource being used effectively with such children is in the skill of the teacher. As the teacher cannot be everywhere, it is of great importance that the crucial position of the TA as a resource is recognised. With careful planning of both physical and human resources, the children will not only be included but will also have the opportunity to develop their mathematical thinking.

### REFLECTIONS ON PRACTICE

1. When you are planning a mathematics lesson, do you consider including resources which can actually enable the children to access mathematics and support their mathematical thinking?
2. Which group of children do you feel that you best include by the resources that you use?
3. Is there a group of children where you need to consider inclusion and resources more specifically?
4. How are you going to ensure that the TA you are working with is clear about the mathematical thinking that you are hoping to develop?

**REFERENCES** REFERENCES **REFERENCES** REFERENCES **REFERENCES** REFERENCES

Clark, C. and Callow, R. (2002) *Educating the gifted and talented*. London: David Fulton.

Daniels, H. (2006) The dangers of corruption in special needs education. *British Journal of Special Education*, 33 (1): 4–9.

Department for Education and Employment (1999) *Mathematics. The National Curriculum for England: Key Stages 1–4*. London: DfEE Publications.

Department for Education and Skills (2001a) *Special Educational Needs: Code of Practice*. London: DfES Ref. 581/2001.

Department for Education and Skills (2001c) *Framework for Teaching Maths Y 7,8,9*. London: DfES Ref. 0020/2001.

Department for Education and Skills (2002) *Including all children in the literacy hour and daily mathematics lesson*. London: DfES Ref. 0465/2002.

Department for Education and Skills (2003a) *Primary National Strategy: mathematics and inclusion materials for providers of initial teacher training*. London: DfES Ref. 0605-2003.

Department for Education and Skills (2003b) *Teaching the daily mathematics lesson to children with severe or profound and multiple learning difficulties* London: DfES Ref. 0032/2003.

Eyre, D. (2001) Mathematics, in Eyre, D. and McClure, L. (eds) *Curriculum provision for the gifted and talented in the primary school, English, mathematics, science and ICT*. London: NASEN/Fulton, pp64–89.

Headington, R. (2001) *Supporting numeracy* (2nd ed.). London: David Fulton.

Jaquiss, V. and Paterson, D. (2005) *Meeting SEN in the curriculum: Music*. London David Fulton.

Norwich, B. (1999) The connotation of special education labels for professionals in the field. *British Journal of Special Education*, 26: 179.

Panter, S. (2001) Mathematics, in Carpenter, B. Ashdown, R. and Bovair, K. (eds) *Enabling access: effective teaching and learning for pupils with learning difficulties* (2nd ed.). London: David Fulton, pp36–51.

Pickles, P. (2001) Therapeutic provision in mainstream curricula, in Wearmouth, J. (ed.) *Special education provision in the context of inclusion policy and practice in schools*. London: David Fulton, pp291–304.

Raiker, A. (2002) Spoken language and mathematics. *Cambridge Journal of Education*, 32: 45–60.

Soan, S. (2005) *Achieving QTS reflective reader: primary special educational needs*. Exeter: Learning Matters.

Westwood, P. (2003) *Commonsense methods for children with SEN*. London: Routledge Falmer.

# 6

# Cross-curricular resources to develop mathematical thinking

## John Dudgeon

*Mathematics is of central importance to modern society. It provides the vital underpin-
ning of the knowledge economy. It is essential in the physical sciences, technology,
business, financial services and many areas of ICT. It is also of growing importance in
biology, medicine and many social sciences.*
(Smith, 2004: 11)

Cross-curricular planning offers such a rich potential for mathematical learning that when-
ever opportunities arise it must be the responsibility of the teacher to enthusiastically
embrace them. It is important that children do not see mathematics as just an individual subject, but also a tool that they can use for gaining deeper understanding of other subjects: 'It is
through using mathematics in the contexts of other subjects that pupils develop their ability
to apply mathematics … and learn to appreciate the role that mathematics plays in the real
world' (Coles and Copeland, 2002: 7).

If we analyse aspects of our daily lives it quickly becomes apparent that we do not encounter
experiences in neat and distinct subject-based packages. Life demands that we understand
our own skills and how to apply them. By making links between mathematics and other subjects in school, we provide opportunities for children to see the relevance of their learning
and gain deeper understanding: 'We want pupils to be numerate, not so they can carry out
feats of mental arithmetic in school, but so they can confidently apply their knowledge of
mathematics to a range of situations in their subsequent working and domestic lives'
(Hughes et al., 2000: 119). The *Excellence and Enjoyment* document (DfES, 2003) highlights a
number of ways in which making strong links between curriculum subjects and areas of
learning deepen children's understanding. Cross-curricular mathematics reflects the real
world, cuts through subject boundaries and builds awareness of practical uses.

## Chapter focus

This chapter will discuss how mathematics can be given meaning through the effective use
of resources from a variety of cross-curricular contexts, and demonstrate the value of
embedding mathematics in other subjects in order to develop children's mathematical
thinking. It will focus on:

- **play as a resource for developing mathematical thinking;**
- **cultural artefacts as resources for stimulating mathematical activity;**
- **literature as a starting point for problem-solving.**

# Play as a resource for developing mathematical thinking

Brooker (2002) points out that many attempts have been made to define what constitutes 'play' and, while an actual definition may not have been achieved, the different ways of looking at play have helped in developing theories. These theories have impacted on how we teach children. The importance that the Curriculum Guidance for the Foundation Stage (CGfFS) (QCA, 2000) places on play demonstrates the valuable contribution that educators now place on play as a resource for learning. When children are playing, it allows them to make connections, it reinforces knowledge, encourages creativity, and allows them to take risks without the fear of failure. Tucker (2005) makes the point that as play is not endorsed in the National Curriculum (NC) (DfEE, 1999) it leaves some practitioners feeling it is inappropriate beyond the Foundation Stage. However, with good planning and quality adult involvement, it is possible to provide purposeful, appropriate play activities in all three key stages from Foundation Stage through to the end of Key Stage 2. This chapter will maintain that such activities, whether adult initiated or child initiated, support and develop children's mathematical thinking. The advantage of linking play and mathematics is argued by Griffiths (1994): she claims that this linkage gives mathematics purpose, provides meaningful situations, encourages responsibility and is practically based – an important aspect to kinaesthetic learners.

The CGfFS states that 'there should be opportunities for children to engage in activities planned by adults and those they plan or initiate themselves' (QCA, 2000: 11). When using any form of play as a stimulus or starting point for mathematical thinking it is clear, therefore, that it is necessary to plan in such a way that consideration is given to both adult-initiated and child-initiated activities. Teachers, other practitioners and trainee teachers need to be aware of the complexities involved in these two different requirements. The focus on adult-initiated activities requires planning that identifies specific learning outcomes (this may be connected to subject-specific or mathematical process outcomes). Planning for child-initiated activities requires a focus on more open-ended activities based on a stimulus, or provision of resources, which allow for the creation of independent activities or further development of activities that had started with adult input.

The value of play as a resource to develop children's mathematical thinking is not restricted to the Foundation Stage. Different types of play offer further opportunities for the development of mathematical thinking within Foundation Stage, Key Stage 1 and Key Stage 2 settings.

## Case Study 1: Mathematical thinking related to the concept of 'five' in a Reception class

### Context
The first case study in this section focuses on a Reception class in the autumn term. Tim (the teacher) is developing the children's understanding and thinking related to the cardinal and ordinal value of the number five. He has planned a range of activities which allow for development of conceptual understanding and development of thinking related to aspects of this number.

Tim begins by using a nursery rhyme as a resource for a whole-class focus on the number five. Using the interactive whiteboard (IWB), Tim provides a visual aid of five flowers to act as an iconic image which will relate to the acoustic image of the actual nursery rhyme. In addition, Tim provides a concrete representation of flowers in pots for the children to handle using 'play flowers' in pots. He explains that they are going to play at acting out the rhyme, and picks five children to stand with him and gives them a penny each. He then asks the children to start singing 'Five little flowers in the garden shop' and to follow his actions.

## Curriculum links

| | |
|---|---|
| NC | **KS1 Ma2:** Pupils should be taught to: <br> **1a** approach problems involving number <br> **2a** count reliably up to 20 objects |
| CGfFS | **MD ELGs** Say and use number names in order in familiar contexts <br> Count reliably up to 10 <br> Use developing mathematical ideas to solve problems <br> Use language such as 'more' or 'less' to compare two numbers <br> **Stepping Stone (Green)** Recognise numerals 1 to 5 <br> Representing numbers using fingers, marks on paper or pictures <br> Uses own methods to solve a problem <br> **CLL ELGs** Listen with enjoyment, respond to stories, songs and other music <br> Use talk to organise, sequence and clarify thinking, ideas, feelings and events |
| 2006 PNS Framework | **FS** Say and use number names in order in familiar contexts <br> Count reliably up to 10 everyday objects <br> Find one more or one less than a number from 1 to 10 <br> **Using and applying mathematics** <br> Use developing mathematical ideas and methods to solve practical problems |
| 1999 NNS Framework | **Reception** Say and use number names in order in familiar contexts <br> Count reliably up to 10 everyday objects <br> Recognise numerals 1 to 9 |

(*To the tune of 'Five currant buns in the baker's shop'*)
Five little flowers in the garden shop [*Tim shows the five flowers on the screen, indicates the physical five flowers in pots, and holds up his thumb and fingers*]
Leaves below and petals on top
Along comes Gemma with a penny to pay [*Tim gets Gemma (Reception child) to go towards him and exchanges her penny for a 'flower' pot that has a 1p label attached to it*]
She buys a flower and takes it away [*Gemma goes with her flower and sits down*]

At this point Tim turns to the children and asks, 'How many flowers are left in the shop?' He asks the children to count the flowers with him, using the pictures on the IWB, which now show four flowers, and the 'play pots', which also show four. When they get to four he turns to the children and asks them to say how many flowers are left. Tim explains that they are going to sing the rhyme again but challenges the children by asking how many flowers the rhyme will have to start with. Some of the children quickly recognise the need to start with four and wave their hands holding up four fingers; the other children watch and copy their peers. They sing the rhyme until no flowers are left, with Tim asking questions after each verse.

After the rhyme, Tim sends the children, in groups, to activity areas. Some of the activities have a large picture card attached with a statement (as below) or question to encourage the children to keep a focus on numbers 1–5. The children are free, however, in most of the activities, to initiate their own ideas. Two of these groups will have adult support.

## Activities

1. Make 'bunches' of flowers for the 'garden shop' (teacher-led)
2. In the collection of 'bears' (Compare Bears) find five that are the same in some way
3. Make five snakes using the soft dough
4. Help Percy the puppet to put the numbers on the washing line in the right order (number cards which match pictures of flowers with the correct numeral)
5. In the water tray find something that can be a 'boat' to hold five cubes
6. Play 'Monster munch' using five small toys and a puppet (TA supported)

Tim works with a group of children making 'bunches' of flowers. On the table are many artificial flowers of different types/sizes, numeral cards 1–5, sticky notes, pencils, and ribbons to tie the bunches. The children discuss the items on the table and Tim asks if they can make a bunch of flowers with five or less than five flowers. The children start to sing 'Five little flowers in the garden shop' as they are choosing and counting their flowers. As Tim helps each child to tie the created bunch, he invites the child to put something on a label (sticky note) to show how many flowers are in the bunch. He notes the following:

• some of the children draw pictures to represent flowers;
• some children put simple marks on the note similar to a tally count;
• some children attempt to record a numeral without looking at the numeral cards on the table;
• some children search for, find, and use the numeral card to record their own numeral on the sticky notes.

Tim asks each child to swap their bunch of flowers with that made by another child, to look at the label, and to match the label to one of the number cards on the table. He notes that some of the children struggle to interpret the labels made by others. During a discussion which follows, Tim encourages the children to explain how they knew which number card to match, to talk about the number of flowers they counted, and to think about what they recorded on their own labels. Some of the children explain how they knew that their bunch of flowers held less than five.

Susan, the teaching assistant, uses a monster puppet to play the 'Monster munch' game. Each child has a large 1 × 5 grid on which they count, and place, five small toys, one in each space. They have to close their eyes while the monster decides which toys (if any) it will munch. When they open their eyes they have to tell each other if the monster munched any of their toys, and, if so, how many. Eddie pointed to the empty two spaces on his grid and said the monster had munched two of his toys. Rahina counted the four toys left on her grid and said she was missing one toy: when asked how she knew, she held up five fingers, touch-counted using her other hand and said 'four and one more to make five'. The children begin to take turns at being the 'monster muncher'.

## How was the resource used effectively?

The CGfFS (QCA, 2000: 25) states that 'well planned play is a key way in which children learn with enjoyment and challenge during the Foundation Stage'. By choosing to start with a song that allows the children to act out parts and incorporate the use of fingers, the teacher leads the children through a multi-sensory approach to learning. Acoustic images are particularly helpful for children in the Foundation Stage and those with SEN (see Chapter 5 for a further case study example). The language of the song allows the mathematical concept to be communicated to the children. The language used in such rhymes, and the necessity to recite the language in correct order, gives young children a store of verbal ideas, which assists with creative and logical thinking (Pound, 1999). Providing a range of additional images and 'props' allows all children to participate and make connections between audio, visual and tactile representations. Challenging the children as to how many flowers the rhyme will have to start with after one has been bought encourages them to make a prediction. They then have the ability to check their prediction by singing the song.

The small-group play activities offer the children opportunities to consolidate understanding of the cardinal and ordinal value of numbers 1 to 5, to initiate their own ideas using the resources provided, and to experiment, plan, think through ideas and apply them. Turner and McCullouch (2004: 27) highlight the importance of using 'a wide range of examples to reinforce development of aspects of number'.

The mathematical thinking of young children is often best manifested in well-planned 'play' situations which are enjoyable, purposeful to the children, and underpinned by children's developing communication skills. Using the puppet in the number line activity allows the children to rehearse the rhyme, internalise the related concepts and apply knowledge to a different, but related, context. Finding five bears that are 'the same' extends thinking as well as consolidating practice of counting to five. The selection of the bears involves the children in decision-making based on colour, or size, or involves both attributes. The justification for 'my five bears are the same' involves logical thought – even if that logical thinking may not be verbally expressed by some children.

Adult involvement allows for further development of thinking through use of opportunities to engage children in talking 'mathematically', by showing an interest in how they solve a problem/reach a solution, and by making appropriate interventions in their play. Tim and Susan both participated in the play activities, intervening to challenge and extend the children's thinking in different ways. Tim's activity allowed for consolidation and rehearsal of number concepts linked to the rhyme. In addition, it provided a context for purposeful mathematical recording and opportunities for children to consider the need to connect iconic images, mark making and symbols. As Worthington and Carruthers (2003: 103) point out, 'it is through exploring mathematical graphics on their own terms that young children come to understand the abstract symbolism of mathematics'. Susan's activity placed abstract concepts of 'less' and 'more' in a game context and placed the children in situations where their mathematical thinking could be observed and communicated to others in a variety of ways.

## Role-play as a resource for developing mathematical thinking

There is general agreement among researchers on the importance and value of sociodramatics or role-play (Brooker, 2002). Careful planning and preparation of role-play can allow teachers to create meaningful and creative situations for a range of areas of learning. These situations help children to assimilate information, use resources creatively and develop strategies based on experience and knowledge. Such experiences are helpful in leading children to make links while developing their understanding of the world.

As children take on roles naturally when playing, role-play can be an effective way of practising skills in real-world situations that develop mathematical thinking. Van Ments (1999: 19) states that 'role-play is the experiencing of a problem under an unfamiliar set of constraints in order that one's own ideas may emerge and one's understanding increase'. Practitioners can support and develop children's mathematical thinking through participating in role-play environments. Sensitivity is needed, however, particularly with young children, to ensure that the adult doesn't 'take over' and that the ideas for dialogue and play stem from the children's choices.

It is important to recognise that role-play does not have to be confined to Early Years but can contribute to all levels of learning. The *Excellence and enjoyment* document supports this and discusses how 'effective teaching recognises the critical role in learning played by experiences or interactions with the surrounding environment' (DfES, 2003: 10).

These next two case studies look at role-play situations in Key Stages 1 and 2.

## Case Study 2: Y1 children in the garden centre shop

### Context
A role-play area is shared between Reception (previous case study) and Year 1. Following a visit, and with the help of the children and parents, the teachers have created a garden centre in an area just outside the two classrooms. The teaching assistant has observed and then joined a group of four Year 1 children who have been playing freely in the garden centre 'shop'. She enters the shop and takes on the role of a customer.

### Curriculum links

| | |
|---|---|
| NC | **KS1 Ma2:** Pupils should be taught to:<br>**1c** make decisions about which operations and problem solving strategies to use<br>**2a** count reliably up to 20 objects |
| 2006 PNS Framework | **Y1** Count reliably up to 20 objects<br>**Using and applying mathematics**<br>Describe a problem using numbers, practical materials and diagrams; use these to solve the problem and set the solution back in the original context |
| 1999 NNS Framework | **Y1** Use mental strategies to solve simple problems set in real life, money or measurement context<br>Recognise coins of different values. Work out how to pay an exact sum using smaller coins |

| | |
|---|---|
| **TA:** | I would like to buy some sunflower seeds, please |
| **Paul:** | OK, how many do you want Miss? |
| **Tara:** | Which ones are the sunflower seeds? |
| **Paul:** | Those big ones … we have got lots |
| **TA:** | I would like 15 please. How much are they? |
| | [*Two other children (Aisha and Sarah) are watching and the TA turns to them and asks if they are shopping for anything. Aisha is unsure but Sarah quickly says she wants to buy some seeds as well*] |

| Tara: | [*Looking at the box with the seeds in and noticing the price written on the box*] The seeds are one penny |
|---|---|
| TA: | Is that the price for all of them? |
| Paul: | No! That's the price for one seed. It is one penny for one seed |
| Tara: | So you need 15 pennies because you need 15 seeds |
| | [*The teaching assistant opens her purse and places a 20 pence coin on the counter and asks if that is enough. Paul has started to count the seeds into a bag but stops when the TA asks if he has got a big enough bag. He looks in to see how many he has put in and quickly continues, laughing, saying he could fit loads in the bag*] |
| Tara: | [*Looking at the 20 pence and then the TA for confirmation*] That's 20 pennies isn't it? |
| TA: | Yes it is 20 pence. Have I given you enough money? |
| Tara: | Yeah, too much. You need some money back |
| | [*Tara takes 20 pennies from the till and starts to count. When she gets to 15 she puts these back in the till. She then gives the five pennies to the TA. The TA takes the five pennies and reaches for the 20 pence piece. Quickly Tara tells the TA that that is hers because it is to pay for the seeds*] |
| TA: | Thank you for my seeds and my change. I'm going to have a look to see what else I might buy |
| | [*Sarah starts a conversation with Tara about buying seeds*] |
| | [*The TA is standing with Aisha admiring the bunches of flowers in the buckets*] |
| TA: | They are all so lovely. I don't know which one to choose |
| Aisha: | I'm having this one. It's got five flowers in and I like the yellow ones |
| TA: | Oh, haven't they all got five flowers in the bunch? |
| Aisha: | See, some have only two or three ... smaller |
| TA: | Ah yes, some have less than five. Are they the same price? |
| Aisha: | [*Looking at the labels attached*] Mmm no ... three flowers in that one, three pence |
| TA: | I'll buy this bunch then for three pence. [*Looks in her purse*] Oh dear, I can't find a three pence coin |
| | [*Paul and Aisha both laugh, saying that there is no such thing as a three pence coin*] |
| Aisha: | I'm having these two bunches ... 5p each |
| | [*Aisha looks in her 'purse', thinks for a moment and gives Paul a ten pence piece, saying 'it's for both'. Paul looks unsure*] |
| TA: | You've only given him one coin ... but you've got two bunches of flowers |
| Aisha: | Five and five make ten ... that's a ten pence piece |

## How was the resource used effectively?

Using role-play as a resource encouraged and allowed the children to experiment and demonstrate elements of creative thinking. The resource was enjoyable, visual, practical, and held meaning for the children as it originated from a visit to an actual garden centre within their community. In both the Reception and Year 1 classrooms, activities across a range of subjects had connections to the items being prepared for, or brought into, the role-play area. Each week, the teachers added new items into the 'garden centre and shop' to encourage new initiatives and stimulate the children's thinking.

At the beginning in the free play the children were able to use knowledge in a creative way, initiating their own activity and giving the TA the opportunity to observe. This enabled the TA to use the children's ideas as starting points and consider ways in which the children's understanding and thinking could be assessed and developed further. By taking on the role of the customer, the TA was participating in the children's play, encouraging mathematical dialogue, modelling for some of the children, and supporting their understanding and use of money in problem-solving situations.

In this context the role-play was being used to look at mathematical problems, making them real and allowing the children to test ideas, call upon previous learning and communicate thinking verbally and by actions undertaken. The CGfFS promotes the idea that 'children enjoy mathematical learning because it is purposeful' (QCA, 2000: 70).

By asking specific questions, e.g. 'Have I given you enough money?', the TA was allowing the children an opportunity to reflect on their own learning and to work out a strategy for justifying their responses. Within a role-play situation questions can often be viewed as less threatening to children than if asked in the course of a specific discussion about mathematics. The responses, dialogues and interactions demonstrated a range of ways in which the children were thinking mathematically.

- Tara made a connection between one penny for one seed and the cost of 15 seeds.
- The same child showed understanding that 20 pence was more than 15, that one coin (20 pence) could be worth the same as 20 coins (pennies), and used this knowledge to find a strategy to calculate the change needed.
- Aisha made connections to the number of flowers in a bunch and its cost.
- The same child reasoned that two bunches of five flowers must be ten pence, and communicated her understanding of the connection to this amount and a ten pence piece.

Bruce (2001: 127) points out how play 'helps children to think through ideas and apply them in all sorts of ways safely in the world of play'.

It can be seen from the conversations that the children were listening to each other's ideas and responding accordingly, motivated by the fact that they quickly had feedback on their thoughts and actions. In addition, the TA challenged their thinking further by particular responses (e.g. 'Oh dear, I can't find a three pence coin'). By valuing all the children's responses she encouraged them to further reason and evaluate. Discussion and collaboration could be seen to be assisting the children's mathematical understanding. Van Ments states that role-play 'is an excellent way of developing interpersonal and communication skills' (1999: 36).

## Case Study 3: Y5 become party caterers

### Context
This role-play concentrates on a Year 5 class who were asked to take on the role of party caterers and plan a menu for the staff party at the end of the term. The adults involved took on the role of customers, with the class teacher becoming a 'business adviser'. The teacher is using this scenario to focus on the children's problem-solving strategies, having created a situation that will require them to use mathematical skills and previous learning.

The children worked in six groups and had to work to a budget in order to produce the menu. Half of the groups worked at producing a three-course sit-down menu, and the other half looked at a buffet-style menu.

## Curriculum links

| | |
|---|---|
| NC | **KS2 Ma2:** Pupils should be taught to:<br>**1a** make connections in mathematics and appreciate the need to use numerical skills<br>**1b** identify information needed to carry out the task<br>**1h** present and interpret solutions in the context of the problem<br>**4a** choose use and combine any of the four operations to solve problems involving numbers in real life |
| 2006 PNS Framework | **Y5** Solve multi-step problems, and problems involving fractions, decimals and percentages; choose and use appropriate calculation strategies at each stage, including calculator use<br>**Using and applying mathematics**<br>Solve problems by breaking down complex calculations into simpler steps, choose and use operations and calculation strategies appropriate to the numbers and context; try alternative approaches to overcome difficulties; present, interpret and compare solutions<br>Represent information or unknown numbers in a problem, e.g. in a table, formula or equation; explain solutions in the context of the problem<br>Tabulate systematically the information in a problem or puzzle; identify and record the steps or calculations needed to solve it, using symbols where appropriate; interpret solutions in the original context and check their accuracy |
| 1999 NNS Framework | **Y5** Use all four operations to solve simple word problems involving numbers and quantities based on real life. Explain methods and reasoning |

## Task card

You are to plan a meal for the end-of-term staff party. You must follow the advice on the task card and be prepared to present your results.

You must take into account that five of the staff are vegetarians, the cost of the food, and the cost of the cooking not forgetting the cost of soft drinks and tea and coffee. You have been given a budget of £500 to cater for 20 members of staff. Your task is to make a profit and impress in order to get more business.

### Some important points

- Make sure you are clear on numbers and any other dietary requirements
- Make use of recipe books to get ideas
- Use the internet to look at supermarket websites to obtain prices
- Make sure you cost in the price of cooking (Hourly rates are to be given that include staffing and fuel)
- You are reminded that you are trying to make a profit but also trying to impress in order to gain future business.

The children were given two hours every day to take on their roles as party organisers but could also work on it in their own time if they wished. If the groups required any extra assistance they had to book an appointment with the teacher who took on the role of the client. A letter was sent home to the parents explaining the relevance of the work and the opportunities that it offered in terms of the links to the NC. At the end of the week each group had to present their menu and price; they had also to discuss how they arrived at the decisions that led to the finished product.

The results surpassed the expectations of the class teacher in the quality of the work under-taken, enthusiasm demonstrated, use and application of mathematical and ICT knowledge, communication within the groups and commitment to learning. It was noticeable that each group took the task seriously and had allocated roles to each other within their groups. The class teacher and teaching assistant observed the different ways in which the children:

- gathered the necessary data;
- made choices regarding which sources to access and how to make effective use of such sources – one group sent representatives to some of the teachers to show alternative menus and ask for opinions;
- used a range of number operations and tools to make calculations;
- employed systems and strategies to check their calculations and changes to budgets;
- discussed and made decisions as to how to present their results.

The class teacher was particularly interested in the ways the groups asked his advice as a 'business adviser'. It was apparent that some of the children needed assistance with spe-cific calculations, how to gather and record the relevant data effectively to suit the task, and how to access the internet effectively. By taking on specific roles, the children were able to identify for themselves the areas of learning and expertise which they needed advice on to succeed in the task. One group sought advice on how to construct a database to keep a running total of costs. A different group asked for advice on the use of ICT to present their menus and results.

Each group arrived at results that stayed on budget although there were differences in the quality of the menus. Two groups produced work that showed good profits and menus that looked very professional. It became apparent that many more hours had been spent on the tasks than had been allocated in school, pointing to groups arranging meetings out-side of school. On the basis of the task the class proposed that they be allowed to plan the catering for their end-of-school party when they went into Year 6.

## How was the resource used effectively?

The role-play acted as a resource in which the children could use knowledge acquired from previous learning, pose questions, deal with and overcome new problems: skills that could be used in later life. The scenario set for the children inspired and motivated them. *Excellence and enjoyment* (DfES, 2003) discusses the importance of creating a learning culture and developing motivation. It advocates that children must be given appropriate time, space and materials to collaborate with one another in order for effective learning cultures to develop.

Throughout the role-play the children were demonstrating understanding of the connections between the four rules of number; they used calculation strategies mentally and on paper and made choices as to which tools (i.e. multiplication squares, calculators, computers) to support those calculations. Notably, the children recognised gaps in their own understanding or ability to apply knowledge, seeking advice within a scenario which allowed them to do so without feeling pressured. In a discussion after the role-play, the children were able to:

- recognise the knowledge applied and skills they had used;
- select aspects of learning which they realised needed further work;
- identify the strategies they had used which had been/had not been effective;
- discuss how ICT tools and facilities had been helpful to their 'research' and presentations.

The *Excellence and enjoyment* document also recognises the importance of social skills in children's learning. The evidence from the week's work was that the children were sharing ideas and information, enjoyed being part of a working group and took part in reflective discussion to make sense of the task, even working outside the set times. Pound (1999: 6) argues that mathematical thinking 'depends heavily on the experiences, social interaction and accompanying language that children meet'. The task required the children to work in groups, ask questions and select and record relevant information. In doing this, they were collaborating, discussing roles within the group and having to make decisions regarding strategy. Asking the children to seek advice when necessary from the 'business adviser' maintained the role-play experience and allowed them to organise ideas in order to explain their approach so far, explaining how this had affected future planning. In addition, this aspect to the role-play allowed the teacher to be able to monitor progress, offer advice and, in particular, assess the children's ability to use and apply mathematical and ICT knowledge and skills. The finished results and the attitude of the children while engaged in the task was testament to the motivating effect that the role-play scenario had offered.

# The use of cultural artefacts as a starting point for mathematical activity

This section focuses on the opportunities that cultural artefacts allow in adopting a cross-curricular approach to mathematics. When used effectively, such resources can help children connect mathematical learning with aspects of their lives. It helps us recognise the cultural heritage of all children by drawing upon their own cultural experiences. It can aid understanding that mathematical ideas derive from many historical and cultural contexts, and is embedded in many varied real-life contexts. Nelson et al. (1993: 8) make the point that, 'a multicultural approach helps to promote a holistic view of learning'. As an example, the authors discuss how 'Islamic designs not only introduce spatial notions of pattern, symmetry, transformation and equivalence, but also have spin-offs in other school subjects, notably art, religious studies, history, and social studies' (ibid.: 8). For teachers and their pupils these designs, and other cultural areas, offer a fascinating and purposeful opportunity for cross-curricular investigations. Such investigations allow for the development of specific aspects of mathematical understanding and application of mathematical thinking skills.

### How was the resource used effectively?

## Case Study 4: Year 2 discuss a floor pattern

### Context
This case study follows a class of Year 2 children as they discuss the shapes that they can see in a pattern projected onto the whiteboard. The class had been following a theme on religions and this was work related to a visit to a mosque earlier in the term. The children had been investigating a variety of pictures and books to search for patterns similar to those seen on the walls and floor of the mosque. One of the groups selected the particular picture of a Victorian floor (Figure 6.1) and used the Visualiser to project the picture onto the whiteboard.

The teacher gives time for the children to discuss the projected image with talk partners before inviting specific responses or asking questions.

## Curriculum links

| | |
|---|---|
| NC | **KS1 Ma3:** Pupils should be taught to:<br>**1d** use the correct language and vocabulary for shape, space and measures<br>**2a** describe properties of shapes they can see or visualise using the related vocabulary |
| 2006<br>PNS Framework | **Y2** Visualise common 2D shapes and 3D solids; identify shapes from pictures of them in different positions and orientations<br>**Using and applying mathematics**<br>Describe patterns and relationships involving numbers or shapes, make predictions and test these with examples |
| 1999<br>NNS Framework | **Y2** Use the mathematical names for common 3D and 2D shapes<br>Sort shapes and describe some of their features |

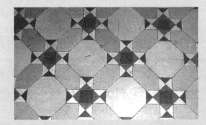

**Figure 6.1: Floor tiles**

**Teacher:** That's a great picture you chose. What have you been talking about?

**Claire:** All the shapes we can see. I can see a triangle there, look [*Claire points at the correct shape in the pattern*]

**Teacher:** Who agrees with Claire that this shape is a triangle?

**Children:** Yes [*indicating by putting their thumbs up*]

**Teacher:** Who can tell me why it is a triangle?

**Neil:** Because it has three sides

**Teacher:** Excellent. Is there anything else you can tell me about a triangle?

**Claire:** It's red and it has three corners

**Teacher:** This triangle is red, but would it matter if it was blue … would it still be a triangle?

**Aaron:** I don't think it matters what colour it is … look, there's a blue triangle on that picture [*pointing to a shape poster on the classroom wall*]

**Teacher:** Well done. It is a triangle because it has three sides and three corners: it doesn't matter what the colour is. What other shapes were you talking about that you could see?

**Sofia:** Well, me and Darren can see a square full of triangles

**Teacher:** Can you show the other children?

[*Sofia points to a large square which encompasses four equilateral triangles. She counts them at the same time*]

**Teacher:** Isn't that amazing – four triangles inside that square … anyone notice anything else?

**Joe:** [*Tilting his head*] Is that another square? A diamond in the middle and more triangles

[*Joe shows the shape he is looking at and all the children tilt their heads to spot the 'diamond' and triangles within the square*]

**Teacher:** Is it really a diamond or another square? [*She shows a picture of a square and then rotates it. This captivates the children and she shows other shapes which can look 'different' when rotated*]

**Teacher:** Now can anyone tell me what that shape is? [The teacher points to the hexagon] [*The children take time to really look at the shape. Many of the children are puzzled and so the teacher asks them to count the sides*]

**Teacher:** Have we talked about any shape with six straight sides?

**Sajid:** We did look at a shape that has six sides but it didn't look like that [*The teacher shows another picture of a different hexagon (a regular hexagon) and begins to talk to the children about 'special' hexagons, 'special' triangles and why a square might be a 'special' type of shape*]

By developing the interest generated by the visit to the mosque and allowing for further investigations through pictures/books, the teacher has placed the significance of learning about shapes in a context that is meaningful for the children. The children viewed the picture holistically to begin with, searching the whole pattern to recognise and discuss recognisable shapes and patterns. This not only reinforced some of the learning that had taken place at the mosque but began to show the children the creativity that can be achieved by the use of geometric shapes. Woodman and Albany (1988: 4) considered that, 'Inherent in many artistic forms, there exists a mathematical precision too often taken for granted.'

Using the image of the pattern gave a visual stimulus for the children and, by being linked to other areas of learning, helped develop their interest. By encouraging the children to talk about what they could see and to listen to all responses, the teacher helped to develop their mathematical language, ideas and thoughts. The question 'Who can tell me why it is a triangle?' demands more than a yes/no answer: it requires explanation and justification based on the properties of a triangle. The teacher was able to extend the children's thinking by challenging the group to consider if colour, or orientation of a shape, matters to its properties.

Encouraging the children to continue to look for further shapes encourages the use of correct language and vocabulary related to those shapes and the vocabulary related to position. The discovery made by one of the children, that the square was made up of triangles, provided the teacher with further opportunity to discuss the pattern and ask the children to collaborate in finding the answer. The teacher then used the irregular hexagon in the pattern to challenge the children's prior knowledge and open up discussion on how we can have different types of hexagons. This was then extended to different types of other shapes.

## Case Study 5: Y6 children explore Vedic squares

### Context

The Year 6 children have been looking at the religion of Islam. The class teacher planned a lesson that made links between mathematics and Islam through studying number patterns and geometry. The class teacher has planned a lesson using Vedic squares. This lesson plan attempts to make links between the work they have been undertaking on Islam, design, numerical patterns and the creation of tiling effects similar to Islamic patterns.

# Curriculum links

| NC | KS2 Ma2: Pupils should be taught to:<br>1a make connections in mathematics and appreciate the need to use numerical skills<br>2b recognise and describe number patterns<br>2h use mathematical reasoning to explain features of shape and space |
|---|---|
| 2006<br>PNS Framework | Y6 Make and draw shapes with increasing accuracy and apply knowledge of their properties<br>**Using and applying mathematics**<br>Identify and use patterns, relationships and properties of numbers or shapes; investigate a statement involving numbers and test it with examples<br>Explain and justify reasoning and conclusions, using notation, symbols and diagrams |
| 1999<br>NNS Framework | Y6 Recognise and explain patterns and relationships<br>Make shapes with increasing accuracy<br>Explain methods and reasoning |

| LESSON PLAN   Objective: To recognise and explain patterns and relationships, generalise and predict. | |
|---|---|

| MENTAL/ORAL | RESOURCES |
|---|---|

**RESOURCES** Interactive whiteboard

| 1 | 2 | 3 | 4 | 5 | 6 | 7 | 8 | 9 |
|---|---|---|---|---|---|---|---|---|
| 2 | 4 | 6 | 8 | 10 | 12 | 14 | 16 | 18 |
| 3 | 6 | 9 | 12 | 15 | 18 | 21 | 24 | 27 |
| 4 | 8 | 12 | 16 | 20 | 24 | 28 | 32 | 36 |
| 5 | 10 | 15 | 20 | 25 | 30 | 35 | 40 | 45 |
| 6 | 12 | 18 | 24 | 30 | 36 | 42 | 48 | 54 |
| 7 | 14 | 21 | 28 | 35 | 42 | 49 | 56 | 63 |
| 8 | 16 | 24 | 32 | 40 | 48 | 56 | 64 | 72 |
| 9 | 18 | 27 | 36 | 45 | 54 | 63 | 72 | 81 |

| 1 | 2 | 3 | 4 | 5 | 6 | 7 | 8 | 9 |
|---|---|---|---|---|---|---|---|---|
| 2 | 4 | 6 | 8 | 1 | 3 | 5 | 7 | 9 |
| 3 | 6 | 9 | 3 | 6 | 9 | 3 | 6 | 9 |
| 4 | 8 | 3 | 7 | 2 | 6 | 1 | 5 | 9 |
| 5 | 1 | 6 | 2 | 7 | 1 | 8 | 4 | 9 |
| 6 | 3 | 9 | 6 | 3 | 8 | 6 | 3 | 9 |
| 7 | 5 | 3 | 1 | 8 | 6 | 4 | 2 | 9 |
| 8 | 7 | 6 | 5 | 4 | 3 | 2 | 1 | 9 |
| 9 | 9 | 9 | 9 | 9 | 9 | 9 | 9 | 9 |

Introduce the lesson by telling the children that numbers can have shapes and that indeed non-European cultures such as the Chinese and the Indians have celebrated the links that mathematics has with subjects like music, art and dance. Within this lesson we are going to use numbers to explore patterns that lead to Islamic design.

- Show the two multiplication squares explaining that the square on the right is called a 'Vedic Square' because of its origins in old Indian texts called the 'Vedas'
- Ask the children to discuss with each other if they can see any patterns in either square
- Can the children see what connects the two squares? How is the second square created?
- Go back to patterns but concentrate on the Vedic square looking at individual numbers.

| MAIN | |
|---|---|

**Resources:** Vedic Squares, Compasses, Squared paper, Tracing paper, Rulers

| 1 | 2 | 3 | 4 | 5 | 6 | 7 | 8 | 9 |
|---|---|---|---|---|---|---|---|---|
| 2 | 4 | 6 | 8 | 1 | 3 | 5 | 7 | 9 |
| 3 | 6 | 9 | 3 | 6 | 9 | 3 | 6 | 9 |
| 4 | 8 | 3 | 7 | 2 | 6 | 1 | 5 | 9 |
| 5 | 1 | 6 | 2 | 7 | 3 | 8 | 4 | 9 |
| 6 | 3 | 9 | 6 | 3 | 9 | 6 | 3 | 9 |
| 7 | 5 | 3 | 1 | 8 | 6 | 4 | 2 | 9 |
| 8 | 7 | 6 | 5 | 4 | 3 | 2 | 1 | 9 |
| 9 | 9 | 9 | 9 | 9 | 9 | 9 | 9 | 9 |

| 1 | 2 | 3 | 4 | 5 | 6 | 7 | 8 | 9 |
|---|---|---|---|---|---|---|---|---|
| 2 | 4 | 6 | 8 | 1 | 3 | 5 | 7 | 9 |
| 3 | 6 | 9 | 3 | 6 | 9 | 3 | 6 | 9 |
| 4 | 8 | 3 | 7 | 2 | 6 | 1 | 5 | 9 |
| 5 | 1 | 6 | 2 | 7 | 3 | 8 | 4 | 9 |
| 6 | 3 | 9 | 6 | 3 | 9 | 6 | 3 | 9 |
| 7 | 5 | 3 | 1 | 8 | 6 | 4 | 2 | 9 |
| 8 | 7 | 6 | 5 | 4 | 3 | 2 | 1 | 9 |
| 9 | 9 | 9 | 9 | 9 | 9 | 9 | 9 | 9 |

**Activities**

In this part of the lesson we are going to look at developing our awareness of these number patterns. When we have done that investigation and explored some of the patterns we are going to use the numbers from the Vedic square around a circle to create some more basic shapes.

- Using a Vedic square ask the children to investigate more shapes created by looking at the numbers.
- Children to then look at creating designs through the use of more than one number
- Children to create a circle and then to equally space the nine numbers from the square around the circle (some children may need to be reminded how to do this)
- Using one line from the square join together the numbers following the line sequence
- Children to experiment with different lines and then combinations of lines
- As an extension some children can use tracing paper over their designs and repeat their shapes creating tiling effects.

**Review** Children to share their work discussing in particular how they created their designs

## How was the resource used effectively?

The Primary National Strategy discussion paper 'Big ideas' (PNS, 2006: 1) states that mathematics is a 'rich medium for identifying and creating patterns, posing questions, predicting and exploring possibilities which help to explain the world we live in'. Through using the Vedic squares as a starting point for investigation, the teacher is able to begin to suggest to the children that mathematics has its origins in many different cultures and has not developed solely from Western cultures. For the children to recognise any patterns in the squares they must use their existing knowledge of number in order to make sense of the challenge, and asking the children to work together encourages discussion and the sharing of theories.

The children's thinking was demonstrated in the logic and reasoning that was required to be successful in recognising the relationship between the two squares, with many strategies being evidenced. Asking the children to explain their reasoning made them communicate their thoughts, deepening understanding and promoting discussion. Further investigation into the patterns created by the numbers led to connections being made with other mathematical disciplines, such as symmetry. The squares themselves allowed investigation to take place and acted as visual clues, helping the children to make sense of the task. The patterns created were surprising and visually motivating: this was particularly helpful to the children who were not perhaps artistic enough to achieve a satisfying result, providing them with ideas that they could apply in other mathematical and cross-curricular tasks.

The development of the lesson continued to challenge the children to use and apply skills, such as the formation of an equally spaced circle to continue to create the patterns. The discussion surrounding these created designs served to extend vocabulary, and gave a natural lead into tessellation, rotating, reflecting and translating shapes.

# Literature as a starting point for problem-solving

The linking of mathematics and literacy is an effective way of introducing children to a problem-solving situation. By using a story that the children enjoy, the mathematics can have meaning for them and gives a context for any work that follows. Whitin and Whitin (2004: 4) state that 'using maths related children's literature can help children realise the variety of situations in which people use mathematics for real purposes'.

It is important to realise that the experiences offered by many texts do not appear at first glance to be mathematics related. Many children's books with no specific mathematical link contain opportunities to introduce mathematical concepts. This makes sense when we consider how interwoven into our lives mathematics is. Stories allow teachers to take problems and give them interest through a character or a situation. This can provide excitement, stimulate learning, and allow children to connect with experiences that, to them, are 'real' and meaningful. This gives the related activities real purpose, motivating children to work through problems.

## Case Study 6: Oliver's vegetables (Reception)

### Context

The Reception teacher has planned a week of work based around a story called *Oliver's vegetables* (French, 1995). The story itself follows a small boy through the days of a week, allowing the teacher to introduce the aspect of time to the children. The teacher has also recognised the many other opportunities for mathematical development and cross-curricular learning that the story provided (and highlighted these by shading the appropriate sections on his weekly plan). He used the plan to frame a holistic approach to the children's development.

### Curriculum links

| | |
|---|---|
| NC | **KS1 Ma3:** Pupils should be taught to:<br>**4a** put familiar events in chronological order, compare the durations of events using a standard unit of time |
| CGfFS | **MD ELGs** Say and use number names in order in familiar context<br>Use developing mathematical ideas to solve problems<br>**CLL ELGs** Listen with enjoyment, respond to stories, songs and other music<br>Use talk to organise, sequence and clarify thinking, ideas, feelings and events |
| 2006 PNS Framework | **FS** Use everyday language related to time; order and sequence familiar events and measure short periods of time |
| 1999 NNS Framework | **Reception** Understand and use the vocabulary related to time. Order familiar events in time<br>Know the days of the week and the seasons of the year |

### Weekly plan

| Week commencing: | MONDAY | TUESDAY | WEDNESDAY | THURSDAY | FRIDAY |
|---|---|---|---|---|---|
| **Activities/Resources** | | | | | |
| Themed activity | *Read the story talking about the days of the week* | *Read the story again asking the children to discuss what will happen* | *Children to investigate days of the week using a calender* | *Children to plant some lettuce seeds* | *Children to make salads* |
| PSED activity | *Sharing news from the weekend* | *Circle time* | *Fruit tasting and discussing* | *Making an interest table* | *Talking about healthy eating* |
| Reading/Writing | *Making labels for days of the week* | *Making price tickets for the garden centre* | *Making labels for vegetables* | *Looking at different books about seeds* | *Looking at books about gardens* |

| Mathematics | Looking at some calendars showing days of the week | Exploring different coins and their value | Sorting seeds for the garden centre | Creating patterns using seeds | Using balances to measure the mass of seeds |
|---|---|---|---|---|---|
| Science | Looking at how things grow | Planting some sunflower seeds | Cutting up and investigating vegetables | Looking at different types of leaves | Cooking vegetables and exploring changes |
| ICT and computers | Making labels | Playing with some control games | Looking at some of the pictures of vegetables | Playing with some control games | Using paint to draw some pictures of sunflowers |
| Sand tray | Investigating the texture of wet and dry sand | Building sand castles and using pots | Playing with diggers in the sand | Investigating the texture of wet and dry sand | Investigating the texture of wet and dry sand |
| Water tray | Investigating different containers | Measuring using jugs | Investigating different containers | Washing salad leaves using water | Investigating different containers |
| Physical activity | Going to the outside garden looking at plants | Going on a minibeast hunt | Planting seeds in the garden boxes | Pretending to grow into a tree | Using small spades to dig weeds |
| Creative area | Constructing junk models | Constructing junk models | | | |
| Sensory area | Using playdough to make fruit | Handling different seeds | Mixing and blending paint | Handling different vegetables | Tasting different vegetables |
| Imaginative play | Using puppets to act out Oliver's vegetables | Making containers for the garden centre | Dolls from the dolls house going out for tea | | |
| Role play | Putting seeds into bags to sell in the shop | Planting seeds in the garden centre | Buying vegetables at the garden shop | Counting the money in the shop till | Shopping at the garden centre |

## How was the resource used effectively?

The story acted as a starting point for a range of problem-solving and investigational activities. This is an important aspect. 'The key skill of problem-solving involves pupils in developing the skills and strategies that will help them to solve problems they face in learning and in life' (DfEE, 1999: 21). In particular, the teacher used the story to introduce the theme for the week, which was based around the concept of time, specifically the days of the week. This stimulated the children's interest, was linked to their own experiences, and benefited learning by linking together many aspects important to the children's development. In terms of the story it allowed the teacher to effectively question the children, challenging them but also giving them the opportunity to refer to the story and the labels for clues.

Pictures and key vocabulary were re-created and used as 'story-board' items to assist with class, group and individual sequencing of the story events. The children made labels for the days of the week: these were used within the story context and also in the role-play area to show opening times on specific days of the week.

The book offered opportunities for the teacher to get the children to practise other areas of their mathematical development such as counting the number of vegetables. The content of the story served as a vehicle for the themed planning for the week: in turn, this provided opportunities for activities that would develop mathematical thinking, such as investigating heavy/light boxes of vegetables, the capacity of different boxes to hold amounts of vegetables, and 'buying' vegetables in the garden shop. With adult support, further investigations involved cutting up some vegetables, observing what they looked like on the inside, cooking vegetables, comparing vegetables to find 'similar' and 'different' ones, and looking at the vegetables on display in a local greengrocer. This allowed for discussions on healthy eating and why it might be important to eat vegetables. These latter activities made strong links between mathematical thinking and scientific enquiry. One of the strengths of using literature is the opportunity it affords to develop key thinking skills.

## SUMMARY OF **KEY POINTS**

A central tenet of the Primary National Strategy is that children need 'to develop as confident, enthusiastic and effective learners' (DfES, 2003: 4). This chapter has illustrated how, with careful planning, a range of cross-curricular resources can be utilised to support children's mathematical understanding, help them make links between mathematics and other subjects, and assist the development of mathematical thinking. It is important to realise that children's learning and progress in all subjects can be dependent on their mathematical knowledge. By using a cross-curricular approach teachers are able to develop and support children's mathematical thinking in a way that can excite, motivate and encourage high-order thinking. Through play, children have the chance to practise and consolidate; they have time and space to think; they have the opportunity to use and apply all of this without the fear of failure.

The challenge for teachers is to plan cross-curricular opportunities that help children see the value of mathematics, its relevance within our world and its creativity. By doing this, children will be encouraged to engage with mathematics leading to opportunities for development of their mathematical thinking.

REFLECTIONS ON PRACTICE

1. When looking at medium term and long-term planning do you look for opportunities in other curriculum areas that would enhance the mathematical objectives you need to teach?
2. How can you develop your teaching so that play becomes an integral part of your lesson planning in all three key stages?
3. Does your teaching demonstrate mathematics as a creative resource allowing children the opportunity to experiment and make discoveries?

**REFERENCES** REFERENCES **REFERENCES** REFERENCES REFERENCES REFERENCES

Bottle, G. (2005) *Teaching mathematics in the primary school.* London: Continuum.

Brooker, E. (2002) The importance of play, in *Teaching mathematics in Reception and Year 1.* London: Department for Education and Skills. Ref. 0501/2002.

Bruce, T. (2001) *Learning through play.* London: Hodder and Stoughton.

Coles, D. and Copeland, T. (2002) *Numeracy and mathematics across the primary curriculum.* London: David Fulton.

Department for Education and Employment (1999) *Mathematics. The National Curriculum for England: Key Stages 1–4.* London: DfEE Publications.

Department for Education and Skills (2003) *Excellence and enjoyment: A strategy for primary schools.* London: Primary National Strategy. DfES Ref. 0377/2003. Available at **www.dfes.gov.uk/primarydocument** (accessed 25/09/06).

Department for Education and Skills (2006) Developing the social and emotional aspects of learning to support children's progress and the achievement of curricular targets. DfES Ref. 0348-2006DWO-EN. Available at **www.standards.dfes.gov.uk/primary/publications/isp/more_supp_pdms/pns_isp034806_seal.pdf** (accessed 15/11/06).

French, V. (1995) *Oliver's vegetables*. London: Hodder Headline.

Griffiths, R. (2005) Mathematics and play in Moyles, J. (Ed) *The Excellence of Play* (2nd ed.) Berkshire: Open University Press.

Harling, P. (1990) *100's of ideas for primary maths a cross-curricular approach*. London: Hodder and Stoughton.

Hughes, M., Desforges, C. and Mitchell, C. (2000) *Numeracy and beyond. Applying mathematics in the primary school*. Buckingham: Open University Press.

Nelson, D., Gherverghese Joseph, G. and Williams, J. (1993) *Multicultural mathematics. Teaching mathematics from a global perspective*. Oxford: Oxford University Press.

Pound, L. (1999) *Supporting mathematical development in the early years*. Buckingham: Open University Press.

Qualifications and Curriculum Authority (QCA) (2000) *Curriculum Guidance for the Foundation Stage*. Available at **www.qca.org.uk/223.html#currguid**.

Smith, A. (2004) *Making maths count*. London: HMSO.

Tucker, K. (2005) *Mathematics through play in the early years*. London: Paul Chapman.

Turner, S. and McCullouch, J. (2004) *Making connections in primary mathematics*. London: David Fulton.

Van Ments, M. (1999) *Effective use of role-play: a handbook for teachers and trainers* (2nd ed.). London: Kogan Page.

Whitin, D. and Whitin, P. (2004) *New visions for linking literature and mathematics*. Urbana, IL: NCTE Consulting Network.

Woodman, A. and Albany, E. (1988) *Mathematics through art and design*. London: Unwin Hyman.

Worthington, M. and Carruthers, E. (2003) *Children's mathematics. Making marks, making meaning*. London: Paul Chapman.

# 7

# The environment and the outdoor classroom as a mathematical resource

Kellie Cunningham

Taking children into a learning environment outside is frequently associated with Early Years practitioners. An underpinning philosophy within Early Years settings is valuing both experiential and sensory learning. *The Curriculum Guidance for the Foundation Stage* (CGfFS) (DfEE, 2000) recommends that an effective Early Years curriculum should be structured around provision within both indoor and outdoor learning environments. However, it can be argued that the value of such learning experiences is not replicated within Key Stages 1 and 2. There are many factors that often discourage trainee teachers, newly qualified teachers and experienced teachers from taking the indoor classroom outside. These factors range from the content coverage constraints of the National Curriculum (NC) (DfEE, 1999a), environmental factors (such as weather and school location), and the introduction of the standards for educational visits (DfES, 2002). This latter requirement, while necessary, has increased the administration of supporting educational visits and outdoor excursions in an already demanding profession.

This chapter will argue that the outdoor classroom (and the many various resources it provides) can provide a rich and real-life context for learners to develop and apply their mathematical thinking. With creative and effective planning, such resources can be used to develop children's communication skills, reasoning skills and problem-solving skills; namely, the key strands identified in Attainment Target 1: Using and Applying, within *Mathematics: The National Curriculum for England* (DfEE, 1999a).

## Chapter focus

This chapter will explore and evaluate the notion of using school grounds and local environments as a mathematical resource to support the development of children's mathematical thinking. It will focus on:

- **a rationale for selecting the outdoor environment as a resource to promote creativity in mathematics learning and teaching;**
- **outdoor learning in the Foundation Stage;**
- **exploiting school grounds to use and apply children's mathematical thinking;**
- **devising mathematical trails to develop mathematical thinking.**

# The outdoor environment as a resource to promote creativity

The *Excellence and enjoyment* document (DfES, 2003) advocates the notion of creativity within the delivery and implementation of the core subjects. Schools are being encouraged to become more innovative and creative with the NC and provide enrichment through a wide range of learning experiences.

Humble (2002) suggests that in order to teach children to use and apply mathematics, we need to provide them with well-structured learning contexts in which their existing mathematical knowledge and thinking can be applied, developed and enriched. Such contexts need to be varied, motivating, challenging and capable of making mathematical discovery. The research by Askew et al. (1997) into the features of effective mathematics teachers suggests that the most effective teachers establish creative ways to make connections and links both within the mathematics curriculum and across the wider curriculum.

The 'outdoor classroom' provides a stimulating environment with great potential for creative mathematical learning. With skilful planning, the outdoor classroom could be used to introduce or consolidate aspects of the *Primary Framework for literacy and mathematics* (DfES, 2006) and programmes of study within the NC for mathematics.

The outdoor classroom provides many resources to promote mathematical thinking: the challenge is identifying them and being creative. The idea that all that is required is to take the indoor activities outside is incorrect, and every effort must be made to avoid simply replicating indoor mathematics sessions outdoors. While some indoor resources can be incorporated into planned outdoor activities (Tucker, 2005), practitioners need to look at what the outdoor classroom naturally provides in the way of resources and utilise them to create connections across the curriculum. This does create some challenges for class teachers who are working within an objective-driven climate: the selected resource must facilitate the learning process in order for the child to achieve the selected objective.

The outdoor classroom cannot be seen as a singular resource: there are many dimensions to outdoor learning:

- environmental learning can develop lifelong learning skills such as decision-making skills and thinking skills (North American Association for Environmental Education, 2001);
- the outdoor classroom lends itself to the many concepts taught in the indoor classroom (Wagner, 2000);
- there has been a push to develop the emotional development of children through *Social and Emotional Aspects of Learning materials* (SEAL) (DfES, 2005), which focus on the generic skills of problem-solving.

There have been significant initiatives in the last decade to support outdoor learning across the curriculum. Working with the DfEE, the Learning through Landscapes Trust (Adams, 1990) has enabled schools to utilise their school grounds as places for learning and extending the learning within the classroom. Providing the potential for learning within the school grounds and local community is harnessed, children's learning experiences can be enriched and their knowledge applied in a real-life context. More recently, education authorities have made funding available for schools to upgrade and refurbish their school grounds, making connections with the curriculum and providing enrichment during children's playtimes.

Such a move will be welcomed by OFSTED, who reported in 2005 that their observations demonstrated limited evidence of such creative modifications of the curriculum. They claimed that there is an increasing need for the integration of mathematics teaching across subjects. They proposed that there should be fresh ways of introducing creativity into mathematics teaching and learning. Such an observation supports the notion that creative development and implementation are integral to a broad, balanced and relevant curriculum.

The proposal in this chapter is that the outdoor classroom provides many mathematical resources, opportunities and real-life experiences, which will facilitate and maintain the high standards of attainment achieved through the effective delivery of the National Numeracy Strategy Framework (NNS) (DfEE, 1999b), and will promote the flexibility in approach advocated by the Primary Framework for mathematics (DfEE, 2006).

# Outdoor learning in the Foundation Stage

Outdoor learning is a key principle underpinning effective practice in Early Years settings (DfEE, 2000). Extending the learning environment to the outdoors provides Early Years practitioners with a stimulating, real environment in which to plan purposeful learning opportunities and provides children with a rich and stimulating experience. Bilton (1998) argues that the provision of high-quality outdoor activities offers children greater creative and intellectual freedom than indoor experiences. For some children, this freer environment may offer a more appropriate mode of learning which enables better access to, and understanding of, mathematical concepts. Many Early Years settings provide a purpose-built outdoor area in which children can make connections with their learning through cross-curricular links and through self-exploration. Using the outdoor classroom as a medium to promote and develop children's mathematical understanding provides practitioners with an opportunity to be creative with their planning, and opportunities for children to make connection with their learning through cross-curricular links (Pound, 2006). Making connections with different aspects of learning is fundamental to children's mathematical development.

## Planning for mathematical development through outdoor learning

Planning for mathematical development in the Early Years is a complex process. While the CGfFS provides practitioners with a clear set of early learning goals (ELGs), planning for progression in learning needs to consider how best to develop children's mathematical understanding and thinking skills within a holistic approach to learning. Play, enjoyment and responding to children's interests need to be central to such an approach. As Pound (2006: 124) advocates, planning should 'allow for time and space for play, flexibility and interaction'. The notion of flexibility produces an interesting conflict within an objective-driven curriculum: the individual learning needs of the children must remain central to planning, with a clear mathematical objective, while unplanned and spontaneous learning must also be harnessed. Gifford (1995) argues that mathematics without a clear objective can result in missed opportunities to exploit children's mathematical development. The learning setting for creating and striking the balance between flexibility and rigidity can be identified through the outdoor classroom. An Early Years outdoor environment is not only stimulating and natural, it also provides a suitable, playful environment that is relevant and real to children and allows them to connect mathematically with the world around them at their own level.

The first case study illustrates how planning can achieve a balance between objective-driven teaching and child-initiated access.

## Case Study 1: Outdoor learning in the Foundation Stage

### Context

A class of 29 Reception children who have easy and open access to an outdoor area. The children are working in mixed attainment groups and can choose to access the outdoor space at their own accord. The class teacher frequently uses the large outdoor area as a learning resource and the children are very comfortable working outside. The teacher, or TA, always joins children in this outdoor area. The children are used to working within a child-initiated ethos, and respond very well to working collaboratively.

As part of her short-term planning, the teacher has prepared activities for outdoor learning (see Table 7.1). She plans to observe the children while they complete the tasks, so as to allow her to build up a profile of the children's mathematical development.

### Curriculum links

| | |
|---|---|
| NC | **KS1 Ma3:** Pupils should be taught to:<br>**1d** use the correct language and vocabulary for shape, space and measures<br>**1f** use mathematical communication and explanation skills |
| CGfFS | **ELGs** Count reliably up to 10<br>Use developing mathematical ideas and methods to solve practical problems<br>Talk about, recognise and recreate simple patterns<br>Use everyday words to describe position<br>Use language ... to describe the shape and size of solids and flat shapes<br><br>**Stepping Stones (Green)**<br>Count an irregular arrangement of up to 10 objects<br>Describe a simple journey<br>Find items from positional/directional clues<br>Use appropriate shapes to make representational models |
| 2006 PNS Framework | **FS** Talk about, recognise and recreate simple patterns<br>Say and use number names in order in familiar contexts<br>Use familiar objects and common shapes to create and recreate patterns and build models<br>Use language such as 'circle' or 'bigger' to describe the shape and size of solids and flat shapes<br>Use everyday words to describe position<br><br>**Using and applying mathematics**<br>Use developing mathematical ideas and methods to solve practical problems |
| 1999 NNS Framework | **Reception** Order a given set of numbers<br>Count reliably up to 10<br>Count reliably in other contexts<br>Use language such as more, less, longer, shorter, heavier and lighter<br>Talk about, recognise and recreate simple patterns<br>Use everyday words to describe position |

**Table 7.1 Foundation Stage planning**

**Short-term plan: Foundation Stage weekly plan for outdoor learning**

| | Key learning intentions and assessment opportunities *ELGs and stepping stones Children will be able to:* | Activities *Adult supported. How will we enable the learning to take place?* | Target groups *Which children?* | Activities *Adult planned, children choose independently What challenges might we set up for children?* | Links *with other areas of learning* | Evaluation to inform next steps *What have the children learnt?* |
|---|---|---|---|---|---|---|
| MD | **Early learning goals for shape, space and measures** *Use language such as 'circle', 'bigger' to describe shapes and the size of shapes* *Use language such as 'greater', 'smaller', 'heavier' or 'lighter' to compare qualities* *Use developing mathematical ideas and methods to solve practical problems* *Talk about, recognise and recreate simple patterns* *To develop one-to-one and stable-order counting principles* | **Log jump, one to one Counting.** Problem-solving activity set up outside, children to organise number logs (1–10 or 1–20 depending on children's individual needs) to cross grass area, avoiding obstacles. (Either one-to-one or counting or ordering numbers.) T and TA to model and discuss possible strategies. **Active patterns with natural objects spider's webs, logs, stones, leaves.** Building on from previous repeating pattern work, children to devise their own patterns using natural materials, number of attributes to vary according to the children's individual needs. T / TA to discuss pattern with children and discuss possible pictorial symbols to represent pattern. | All children to access throughout the week. Profile children to be observed in adult-initiated and child-initiated play. | Children to identify the shape and size of natural materials within the wooded area and then move to the construction site, where they will sort according to size, shape, or any other key variables. Moving natural materials with play digger. Observe and encourage children to use key language. | Creative development Language and literacy | |

T: Teacher  TA: Teaching Assistant

### How was the resource used effectively?

As part of her planning, the teacher has selected to use the outdoors as a context in which to set a variety of mathematical activities. The selected resource could result in learning which the class teacher may not have planned or intended. Relying heavily upon the natural resources and open space, the class teacher has created a spectrum of learning opportunities, linked directly to achievable learning outcomes and intended objectives, which would be difficult to duplicate in the indoor classroom.

Children's mathematical thinking has to be meaningful for it to be effective; mathematical activities have to be relevant and linked directly to the children's lives. Current models of teaching within Early Years emphasise the importance of meaningful learning (Pound, 2006) and harnessing and capturing real-life experiences that children bring to the classroom. This short-term plan exemplifies how such real-life experiences can be harnessed through outdoor learning and how teachers can provide children with the opportunity to apply their knowledge and draw on previous learning within a real context.

The role of the imagination is a vital component in learning through the outdoors. For each of the activities listed in the case study, the children are required to hypothesise, guess, categorise or identify relationships between patterns. Such processes are suggested by Devlin (2000) as being essential in developing children's ability to think mathematically. Within Early Years teaching, the rich experiences that play and imagination offer contribute vastly to the mathematical development of a child through supporting a child to think abstractly (Pound, 2006: 33). In the case study, the notion of play and encouraging children to think abstractly underpins each activity, which consequently encourages the development of mental imagery.

The teacher includes adult involvement within her plans for this outdoor learning not only for health and safety reasons. She believes that quality adult involvement is an important factor in supporting the development of children's creativity, communication skills, problem-solving skills and social interaction. Tucker (2005) maintains that all play needs adult involvement at some level in order to support children's mathematical development.

# Log jump

In this activity the teacher has chosen to develop children's problem-solving strategies through encouraging them to use and apply their counting skills. The outdoor environment allows the children sufficient room and space to physically develop the one-to-one principle (Gelman and Gallistel, 1986) where children can co-ordinate, touch and count the logs. This can also reinforce the stable-order principle (ibid.), as the children repeat the counting words in order. Drawing upon their problem-solving skills, the children can engage in collaborative learning, and they are encouraged to think strategically and abstractly. Although this activity could easily be replicated in the classroom across a large carpet area, a sense of role-play and imagination can be created outside. Children require adequate space to try out a variety of possibilities and make mistakes, and the obstacles can vary in shape and size.

# Active patterns

The class teacher has devised an activity which is clearly differentiated by outcome: this allows access and engagement at a child's individual level. Underpinning this activity is the opportunity for the development of key aspects of the children's mathematical thinking.

- Children are developing their reasoning skills through choosing and selecting their material.
- They are developing their systematic thinking skills through planning and reviewing.
- They are developing their communication and reasoning skills through describing their pattern.

The natural environment provides an abundance of resources which children can select to make patterns and sequences. The attributes will vary from texture, colour, size, shape, smell and touch, which allow children to make mathematical connections to the world around them using their senses. Such an activity is differentiated by outcome as the selected attribute or pattern will vary according to children's knowledge and understanding of pattern and sequences. Within this activity, children could select an attribute and either:

- describe an order or pattern;
- describe and make line patterns;
- copy a sequence;
- create a sequence;
- recognise a cyclic pattern or,
- develop a mathematical idea and method to solve a problem.

Although artificial materials could be used as an alternative, the natural environment does provide a rich and unusual resource which allows children to personalise learning and make connections between indoor and outdoor learning experiences.

## Construction

Similarly to the pattern activity, the children are being asked to make a connection with their environment using their senses. The children are free to classify the objects according to a variety of attributes. A key feature of this activity is the crucial development of mathematical language that the children use as they complete the activity. Although the children are working within a 'construction site', they are working with objects that are real to them and can make connections with other areas of the learning, such as knowledge and understanding of the world. It would be difficult to replicate this activity indoors; there are few manufactured resources that can provide such richness and endeavour to engage the children's senses in such a meaningful way.

As illustrated, the outdoor environment provides a medium through which to develop and expand key thinking processes and abstract thinking. Equally as important, the planned activities use the outdoor area as a comfortable and safe learning environment in which children can use their imagination and find creative uses for the specific resource items.

# Exploiting school grounds to use and apply children's mathematical learning

Although the outdoor learning area is viewed as an important extension of the classroom within Foundation Stage settings, this is not necessarily the case within Key Stages 1 and 2. Most primary schools have playgrounds, walls, and sometimes grassed areas, ponds, purpose-built play areas, or even small woodlands. These outdoor resources can often be overlooked or underused, yet they offer opportunities to provide a different, and meaningful, context in which children could apply their mathematical learning. Markings such as number grids, patterns or specific shapes can be created on hard-surfaced areas. Colour can be applied to identify straight lines, curved lines or even specific tessellation patterns in different walls. Scale drawings and scaled models could be created of the school and its grounds (either by teaching staff or Year 5/6 children), which could be used as starting points for surveys, data collection, monitoring of growth of plants/trees or construction of a specific mathematics trail.

## Case Study 2: Exploring shape within the school grounds (Y3)

### Context

A Year 3 class are classifying shapes by their properties by exploring the notion of 'shape families'. The school grounds consist of a playground which has markings and basketball nets, walls of different heights and different sized brick patterns, a field with goal posts and a few trees at the end of the field. The children, their teacher and a TA are searching for, and recording, a range of shapes within this environment. The children have brought pictures of shapes (three-dimensional and two-dimensional) from the classroom to assist their thinking and their search. The children are in mixed groups: each group has boards, paper to sketch and access to a digital camera as a means of recording. The teacher plans to use the digital pictures to model the key vocabulary in the review of work undertaken and to introduce/reinforce the properties of 3D shapes. The use of photographs back in the classroom also links to aspects of the children's ICT work.

During this lesson the teacher has asked his TA to focus on Liam, a child working towards level 2 accessing Wave 2 support. Tracking back within the Primary Framework for mathematics end-of-year expectations (key objectives) to Year 2 for shape and space, the teacher wants Liam to use this outdoor resource to develop the mathematical language of the shapes he can see, and to describe some of their properties. Liam often struggles to concentrate in the classroom and is usually reluctant to express his thinking in front of other children.

### Curriculum links

| | |
|---|---|
| NC | **KS2 Ma3:**<br>**1h** use mathematical reasoning to explain features of shape and space<br>**2b** visualise and describe 2D and 3D shapes |
| 2006 PNS Framework | **Y2** Visualise common 2D shapes and 3D solids; identify shapes from pictures of them in different positions and orientations; sort, make and describe shapes, referring to their properties |
| 1999 NNS Framework | **Y2** Use mathematical names for common 2D and 3D shapes ... describe some of their features ... number of sides, corners and faces<br>Find the 2D shapes and faces of 3D shapes, according to a specific criteria |
| Other | QCA ICT Scheme of Work Unit 3A Manipulating graphics and texts |

*Liam and the TA are standing at the edge of the playground looking onto the school and a small wooded area.*

**TA:**    Liam, can you tell me what shapes you can see in front of you? Have a good look around; there is a lot to see

| Liam: | I can see loads of trees and things and the playground, I suppose that's [*pointing at the school*] a shape, loads of shapes |
| TA: | Great spotting! Can you see any shapes that you can recognise? ... The pictures might help |
| Liam: | What – do you mean the flat ones and ... ones you can pick up? |
| TA: | That might be a useful way of naming them. The flat ones only have the one face ... do you remember? We call them two-dimensional or 2D. The others have more than one face: we call them three-dimensional or 3D<br>[*she writes the two terms on Liam's board as a memory prompt*] What do you think the school building is? |
| Liam: | Well it's mmm ... 3D?, with some 2D shapes [*he looks at the windows*] and some 3D shapes joined on [*he looks at the pipes*] |
| TA: | Can you show me which shapes you think are 2D? [*Liam leads the TA to the window of his classroom*] |
| Liam: | See Miss [*he draws with his fingers*] this is a square, just like the number square! [*He can see this through the classroom window*] |
| TA: | Oh yes, I can see that, but can you tell me why it is a square and not say, a triangle? |
| Liam: | 'Cos it has four sides and corners and it looks the same as the ones in the classroom |
| TA: | I like your thinking! Let's see if we can find any other four-sided 2D shapes on our school building |
| Liam: | Yep! Easy! I know that the main entrance is a rectangle. It has two long sides and two short sides, and the entrance to Mrs Murray's room is also 2D, but there is no door there |
| TA: | Well spotted! Remember that we can also call that shape an oblong. OK Liam [*she hands him a digital camera*], can you take some digital pictures of different 2D shapes and different 3D shapes that you can find in our school grounds. I will be with you and I want you to tell me why it is a 2D or 3D shape |
| Liam: | Yeah, but there are loads and I can't remember their names |
| TA: | What do you see when you look at this shape? [*pointing to the pipe*] |
| Liam: | Well ... it's not flat ... it's not really got straight sides and it has one round face |
| TA: | You're right – it hasn't got straight edges ... it is also hollow inside. If I cut this in two, what shape do you think I will see? |
| Liam: | Er ... I think it will be a circle |
| TA: | Excellent, you see we've described them. This is a cylinder, Liam, and now we know what it looks like [*She writes the name on his board and makes a quick sketch of the pipe*]<br>[*Liam collects photographs of windows, a tree trunk, playground markings and a goal post*] |
| TA: | OK Liam [*pointing to tree trunk*], why have you chosen this one? |
| Liam: | It's a 3D one 'cos it has no sides and I can walk around it, do you know Miss, there are loads of shapes I can walk around out here! They are everywhere |
| TA: | What do you think about its shape? |
| Liam: | Mmm, no straight-side edges and round. Oh, it's like the pipe only fatter [*looking at his board*]. What's that again...? |
| TA and Liam: | [*together*] Cylinder |
| TA: | Well done. What about the green zone [*playground marking a circle*], what shape is this? |
| Liam: | It's a circle, I know that is 2D because it is flat and round. Miss, there are lots of shapes on the playground, they are all 2D you know |

> **TA:** OK Liam, look at one of the shapes you have taken a picture of. Can you think about where you might have seen similar shapes ... maybe at home, in the classroom or even out here?
>
> **Liam:** [*Taking time to look at his pictures and think*] Well, my window, it has four straight sides, four corners ... mmm, I think the corners are all the same, just upside down. It looks like the school gate and the Reception gate. It's the same shape as my door at home!
>
> **TA:** How is it the same shape, Liam?
>
> **Liam:** It has the four corners and four sides ... but they are not the same size.
>
> **TA:** What's not the same size?
>
> **Liam:** These sides ... two are long and two are short. Is it a square Miss, or a rectangle?
>
> **TA:** It's a type of rectangle Liam, because they all have the opposite sides the same length

## How was the resource used effectively?

In most primary schools, progression is often illustrated through a variety of differentiated resources. When developing understanding of the properties of shape, the many manufactured resources (plastic or wooden 3D or 2D shapes) can often leave children without a sense of purpose. Looking at and using shapes within their environment will provide children with a sense of connecting mathematical ideas to objects/materials they see in the world around them. Some of these outdoor learning experiences can be brought into the classroom by drawing upon, in the case of shape, packaging materials to enable children to identify shapes belonging to the same 'families' but which look different in texture, materials, colour or size.

However, the outdoor classroom provides practitioners with an abundance of resources that can be differentiated through support and selection. In the case study the class teacher and TA use the notion of 'home learning' (Anghileri, 1995), in which learning is placed in a real-life context; the learning is achieved through physical experiences and connections, not taught.

The class teacher selected an outdoor environment which the children could readily relate to – their own school grounds. Within this environment, and with the sympathetic support of the TA, the transcript shows that Liam did not experience any difficulty in identifying shapes, although there were some discrepancies with his definitions and descriptions of properties. Clemson and Clemson (1994: 45) believe that 'when environments are mathematical, mathematics happens'. This is only likely to take place with appropriate adult intervention. Liam made a significant and 'real' connection with his world, which enabled him to apply his previous knowledge in a meaningful and personal way. His ability to respond in this situation enabled the TA to facilitate his mathematical development and support his thinking skills.

Further analysis of Liam's transcript indicates that he made connections in other areas of mathematics; he made the connection with the number square and was able to relate the shape to a resource he uses every day, and he is familiar with the term 'square'. Making such connections is vital when developing mathematical thinking. Although the TA did not prompt or encourage Liam to make such connections, she did promote mathematical thinking when she encouraged Liam to visualise an additional 2D or 3D shape – an important aspect involved in the formation of mental images. (Chapters 2 and 3 discuss mental imagery in more depth.)

The outdoor environment provided a rich learning environment in which Liam could communicate and reason more easily through the shapes around him. He quickly noted that we live in a 3D world, or 'shapes are everywhere', and that there are many to choose from. Although there were some errors with his terminology, and a misconception surrounding properties of 3D shapes and squares, Liam was able to communicate and describe the shapes around him. The TA used this as an opportunity to expand his use of terminology and correct any misconceptions he had.

The role of the TA was critical in the case study: she encouraged Liam to discuss and expand upon his definitions and was able to model key vocabulary. Similarly in the Reception case study, the role of the TA did not alter according to indoor learning and outdoor learning. In the outdoor lesson the TA was able to observe and make assessments against the success criteria of the lesson, ask probing questions and identify key misconceptions. However, it must be noted that the effective conditions for learning were deeply embedded within the ethos and teaching approaches developed by the class teacher. Part of this approach involved providing access to learning for all the children. In this case study the digital camera, and the clipboard notes/sketches made by the TA, acted as a recorder for Liam and therefore any recording barriers were removed. He was able to use these recording devices to connect the shapes around him with the images on camera or paper. This helped him to visualise certain shapes, memorise their names/properties, and make connections with 2D recorded images and the shapes around him. With the help of the TA, Liam made use of the recorded prompts to allow him to participate fully in the lesson plenary.

Even though this activity could have been replicated within the classroom using a variety of shapes and resources, the level of engagement and motivation that Liam channelled into the activity was encouraging. The activity set within the outdoor environment appeared to help Liam overcome potential classroom-based barriers to learning. Using the school grounds as part of the unit of work resulted in enrichment and allowed greater scope for decision-making, communication, teamwork and application of knowledge. Liam was successful in applying his previous knowledge and was able to reason and explain his selection of shapes.

# Devising mathematical trails to develop mathematical thinking

Skinner (2005) suggests that mathematical trails provide clear opportunities for children to make connections between mathematics and other areas of learning, such as physical development, space awareness, literacy and language, and creative development.

## What is a mathematical trail?

A mathematical trail based around a particular location has fixed features of mathematical interest and involves aspects of orienteering such as 'map' interpretation/reading, position and direction. The features on a mathematical trail could include signs, 'street furniture', walls, railings, buildings, and living items which change through the seasons, such as trees. In primary schools, such trails are usually presented to children in a diagrammatic and/or photographic form, with specific instructions to follow, information to find, and questions to answer. To develop mathematical thinking, the most effective trails will combine closed questions with open questions: this will allow children more opportunities to develop estimation skills, decision-making skills, and choice in data-gathering/recording methods. The latter is important in moving children towards a recognition of efficient and effective problem-solving strategies and the need for appropriate forms of recording in given situations. Many schools have developed their own trails and often these trails will have expanded into the community, such as parks, town centres, villages and beaches.

# What is the value of mathematical trails?

El-Naggar (1994: 8) suggests that there are some key benefits to specific mathematical trails:

- they cater for different learning styles and levels of attainment;
- they allow all children to 'do mathematics' through engaging in discussion, exploration, interpretation of the task and sharing ideas;
- they provide a motivating and exciting context for learning and the application of knowledge;
- they can allow for a wider perspective of assessment for learning.

In addition, mathematical trails encourage children to be more aware of how mathematics is all around them, that mathematical concepts and ideas are needed in the creation of manufactured items, and that the natural world illustrates many mathematical ideas in practice. Mathematical trails can be specific to a strand within the Primary Framework for mathematics (DfES, 2006), or cover a broader range of mathematical themes. There are some advantages to mathematical trails having a specific focus, as this will enable more effective relationships between the 'trail' and the specific mathematics unit of study. A broader trail may enable greater links to other subject areas. Whatever the choice, the trail should be used alongside classroom learning so that connections are made between the two learning environments. It is the effective use of the questioning that will provide class teachers with sufficient information to inform their assessment and for the activity to be meaningful to the child.

The final case study in this chapter follows a team of teachers, TAs and school governors as they develop their ideas related to mathematical trails using the school grounds (playgrounds), local shops and an adjacent park.

## Case Study 3: Planning mathematics trails (Key Stage 2)

### Context

A junior school in an urban environment adjacent to a small park. Within the park is a nineteenth-century building now housing a museum. The teachers, TAs and some of the governors are at the planning stage but have already decided that their environment provides enough scope for two mathematical trails. One trail will focus on aspects of shape and space and the second will focus on aspects of number and measurement. They split into two 'development teams': within each team are representatives from the lower junior (Years 3/4) teachers and upper junior (Years 5/6) teachers. Part of the planning involves walking, photographing and analysing the local environment for opportunities for mathematical development and application of knowledge.

## Curriculum links: shape and space trail

| | |
|---|---|
| NC | **KS2 Ma2**: Pupils should be taught to:<br>**1c** approach spatial problems flexibly, including trying alternative approaches to overcome difficulties<br>**1h** use mathematical reasoning to explain features of shape and space<br><br>**KS2 Ma3**: Pupils should be taught to:<br>**2a** recognise right angles, perpendicular and parallel lines<br>**2b** visualise and describe 2D and 3D shapes and the way they behave, making more precise use of geometrical language<br>**2c** recognise reflective symmetry in regular polygons<br>**3b** transform objects in practical situations; transform images using ICT; visualise and predict the position of a shape following a rotation, reflection or translation |
| 2006 PNS Framework | **Y3/4** Read and record the vocabulary of position, direction and movement, using the four compass directions to describe movement about a grid<br>**Y5** Visualise 3D objects from 2D drawings<br>**Y5/6** Estimate, draw and measure acute and obtuse angles using an angle measurer<br>**Y5/6** Describe, identify and visualise parallel and perpendicular edges or faces; use these properties to classify 2D shapes and 3D solids<br>**Using and applying mathematics**<br>**Y3/4** Identify patterns and relationships involving numbers or shapes, and use these to solve problems<br>**Y6** Suggest, plan and develop lines of enquiry; collect, organise and represent information, interpret results and review methods; identify and answer related questions |
| 1999 NNS Framework | **Y3/4** Identify lines of symmetry in simple shapes<br>Identify right angles in 2D shapes and the environment<br>Recognise positions and directions using compass directions<br>**Y5/6** Recognise reflective symmetry in regular polygons<br>Recognise perpendicular and parallel lines<br>Describe and visualise properties of 3D and 2D shapes<br>Recognise properties of reflective and rotational symmetry |

## The shape and space trail

It was agreed that position and direction should feature strongly in this trail. The language involved would be inclusive for the children of all attainments, e.g. left, right, forwards, turn, towards, in between, 90° degree turn, less than 90° turn, more than 90° turn. For more able/upper juniors this would develop into using compass directions and estimation of angle as appropriate. The use of this language would be evident on the 'shape trail in and around our school' booklet which would be used for the children to follow/read/interpret and record.

Recognition of 3D and 2D shapes would be built into the trail, and it was agreed that this recognition would include shapes that the children should be familiar with and shapes they may not be familiar with. Questioning would be a mixture of closed questions, e.g. 'What shape are all the windows on the part of the school facing East Street?', and more open questions, e.g. 'What do you notice about the shapes in the park railings?'. The upper juniors would have more focus on relating shapes they could identify within 'shape families' to aid classification skills.

Patterns (tessellating and non-tessellating) in brickwork, specific buildings and the children's 'adventure playground' area would feature within the trail. Year 5 and Year 6 children would be expected to develop this further using knowledge related to aspects of transformational geometry.

## Curriculum links: number and measurement trail

| | |
|---|---|
| NC | **KS2 Ma2:** Pupils should be taught to:<br>**1a** make connections in mathematics and appreciate the need to use numerical skills and knowledge when solving problems in other parts of the mathematics curriculum<br>**Ma2, Ma3 and Ma4:** Pupils should be taught to:<br>**4c** estimate answers by approximating and checking that their results are reasonable by thinking about the context of the problem, and where necessary checking accuracy<br>**Ma3 and Ma4**<br>**4a** recognise the need for standard units of measurement, choose ones which are suitable for a task and use then to make sensible estimates in everyday situations<br>**Ma4**<br>**2b** construct and interpret frequency tables, including tables for grouped discrete data |
| 2006 PNS Framework | **Y3/4** Choose and use standard metric units and their abbreviations when estimating, measuring and recording length<br>**Y4/5** Answer a set of related questions by collecting, selecting and organising relevant data; draw conclusions, using ICT to present features, and identify further questions to ask<br>**Y5/6** Read and interpret scales on a range of measuring instruments, recognising that the measurement made is approximate and recording results to a required degree of accuracy |
| 1999 NNS Framework | **Y3/4** Make and measure clockwise and anti-clockwise turns<br>Suggest suitable units and measuring equipment to estimate or measure<br>Solve a problem by collecting, organising and representing data<br>**Y5/6** Solve mathematical problems or puzzles, recognise and explain patterns and relationships<br>Understand and use angle measure in degrees<br>Identify, estimate and order acute and obtuse angles |

## The number and measurement trail

It was agreed that 'counting' would only feature within the trails where it was a reasonable number for counting or could be easily estimated. Information boards/headings could be utilised for finding out data such as the opening/closing times of the local shops, the park, the local museum, or the date of construction of specific buildings. Year 5/6 children could develop this by creating questionnaires to determine shopping patterns at particular times.

The existing furniture within the school grounds could be utilised to make predictions on new additions. For example, 'If we wanted to add more benches along the East Street facing the playground, how many could sensibly fit in the space?' The Year 5/6 children would be encouraged to incorporate these ideas with notions of planning within a budget.

Estimation of the length of the park path and the height of buildings/trees would feature: children would be encouraged to suggest their own methods for undertaking the estimations. Measurement tools appropriate to the children's learning would be made available for checking the estimations. It was anticipated that the children could find ways in which to gather data on the types of trees in the park, and represent the data in appropriate forms.

When both planning groups came together, it was agreed that two 'trail' booklets would be produced for the children to use. The booklets would provide photographic clues, sketches, text and information clues.

## How was the resource used effectively?

All parties involved in the planning process recognised that the school grounds and local area held great potential for linking classroom mathematical learning with application to real-world contexts. The planning that each team put into their own mathematical trail ensured that the trail would be developed, used, and become a permanent part of the school's mathematical scheme of work. Because it was expected that the mathematical trail would become part of the school's identity longer-term, over the years a wide range of resources (such as photographs, rubbings, maps, task cards, markings, virtual school tours on the school website, etc.) would continue to be developed. These could be used in and out of the classroom in order to develop the children's mathematical thinking in a wide variety of ways.

Both trails utilised open and closed questions in order to engage and challenge children of all attainment levels. For example, in the number and measurement trail, the planning group discussed how asking children to count the number of bricks in the school gym wall was unrealistic, but that encouraging them to estimate the answer would provide an opportunity for the children to solve the problem in a variety of ways, prompting valuable discussion that could happen while on the trail or later in the classroom.

When both trails were discussed it became apparent to all involved that mathematical understanding was not the only aspect of learning to benefit: many of the skills involved gave opportunities for the development of interaction and team collaboration, communication skills and the explanation of mathematical thinking. It was agreed that the process of planning had enabled everyone involved to see, and better understand, relevant links between mathematics, thinking skills, geographical aspects and, crucially, the type of questioning needed to challenge children's thinking.

## SUMMARY OF KEY POINTS

The case studies in this chapter have provided a brief overview of the advantages of using the 'outdoor classroom' to facilitate and develop children's mathematical thinking. However, although a rich resource, there are some limitations that often prevent and restrict many teachers from planning to use the outdoor classroom. The second case study in this chapter illustrates the use of the outdoors during a unit of work related to a specific mathematics focus. Within units of work, time is often considered to be a constraint. This chapter has advocated that, providing this is planned for, the school grounds can, and should, be utilised within units of work. Teaching assistants can be involved in the planning of and use of outdoor areas for individual or small groups of children. It is essential that trainee teachers are accompanied by a qualified teacher when taking children out of the classroom. This is a legal health and safety requirement.

Unpredictable weather can often be a constraint and, as with all aspects to teaching, flexibility really does count. Having a contingency plan should, therefore, always be included in the preparation. Alternatively, planning an activity that can be used as a carousel activity that children can access throughout a week, may prevent cancelling a session due to weather.

A key factor involved in creating the effective conditions for learning in the outdoor classroom has been shown to be an ethos regarding team working, listening to and learning from others, and a recognition that learning in the 'outdoor' classroom holds as much merit as learning in the 'indoor' classroom.

Finding opportunities to use the outdoors to facilitate mathematical thinking can be created in different ways. Specific ELGs or units of work for mathematics can be identified from within the CGfFS or the Primary Framework for mathematics. A themed-based approach could be used which draws upon specific aspects of mathematical learning as well as units of work associated with other subject areas. Whichever approach is adopted, it should be remembered that the Primary Framework for mathematics suggests that, in order for mathematics to be successful, using and applying mathematics must be embedded within all strands of the framework, and that teachers should strive to find creative approaches to delivery, planning and provision of resources. Outdoor learning environments offer a medium in which such expectations can be achieved.

REFLECTIONS ON PRACTICE

1. What would you consider to be the key issues from the early year's case study? Why?
2. What are the advantages of using the outdoor environment as a resource, within Key Stage 2, to deliver a unit of work?
3. Reflect upon a unit plan you have taught. Consider opportunities that you may have overlooked for making effective use of the environment.
4. Are there any key issues surrounding assessment for learning when working within an outdoor setting?

**REFERENCES** REFERENCES **REFERENCES** REFERENCES **REFERENCES** REFERENCES

Adams, E. (1990) *Learning through landscapes: The final report.* Winchester: Learning through Landscapes Trust.

Anghileri, J. (ed.) (1995) *Children's mathematical thinking in the primary years: perspectives on children's learning.* London: Cassell.

Askew, M. (1999) It ain't (just) what you do: effective teachers of numeracy, in Thompson, I. (ed.) *Issues in teaching numeracy in the primary schools.* Buckingham: Open University Press.

Askew, M., Brown, M., Johnson, D., Rhodes, V. and Wiliam, D. (1997) *Effective teachers of numeracy: Summary of findings.* London: King's College, pp2–3.

Bilton, H. (1998) *Outdoor play in the early years: management and innovation.* London: David Fulton.

Clemson, D. and Clemson, W. (1994) *Mathematics in the early years.* London: Routledge.

Department for Education and Employment (1999a) *Mathematics. The National Curriculum for England: Key Stages 1–4*. London: DfEE Publications.

Department for Education and Employment (1999b) *The National Numeracy Strategy. Framework for Teaching Mathematics from Reception to Year 6*. London: DfEE Publications.

Department for Education and Employment (2000) *Curriculum Guidance for the Foundation Stage*. London: QCA.

Department for Education and Skills (2002) *Standards for educational visits*. London: DfES.

Department for Education and Skills (2003) *Excellence and enjoyment: A strategy for primary schools*. London: DfES. Primary National Strategy. Ref. 0377/2003. Available at **www.dfes.gov.uk/primarydocument** (accessed 25/09/06).

Department for Education and Skills (2005) *Excellence and enjoyment: Social and emotional aspects of learning*. DfES 1378-2005 G. Available at **www.standards.DfES.gov.uk/primary/publications/banda/seal/pns_seal137805_guidance.pdf** (accessed 15/11/06).

Department for Education and Skills (2006) *Primary Framework for literacy and mathematics*. **www.standards.dfes.gov.uk/primaryframeworks/**.

Devlin, K. (2000) *The maths gene*. London: Weidenfeld and Nicolson.

El-Naggar, O. (1994) *Differentiation through maths trails*. Stafford: NASEN Enterprises.

Gelman, R. and Gallistel, C.R. (1986) *The child's understanding of number*. Cambridge, MA: Harvard University Press.

Gifford, S. (1995) *Number in early childhood. Early Childhood Development and Care*, 109: 95–119.

Humble, M. (2002) Investigating numeracy in Key Stage 2, in Koshy, V. and Murray, J. (eds) *Unlocking numeracy*. London: David Fulton.

North American Association for Environmental Education (2001) *Annual report*. Washington, DC: NAAEE.

OFSTED (2005) *The Annual Report of Her Majesty's Chief Inspector of School 2004/5. Mathematics in primary schools*. London: OFSTED Publications.

Pound, L. (2006) *Supporting mathematical development in the early years* (2nd ed.). London: Open University Press.

Skinner, C. (2005) *Maths outdoors*. London: BEAM Education.

Tucker, K. (2005) *Mathematics through play in the early years*. London: Paul Chapman.

Wagner, C. (2000) *Planning school grounds for outdoor learning*. Washington, DC: National Clearinghouse for Educational Facilities.

# 8

# Exploiting interactive whiteboard technologies to support the development of mathematical thinking

## Mike Toyn

Both the National Curriculum (DfEE, 1999a) and the National Numeracy Strategy (DfEE, 1999b) refer to the use of information and communication technology (ICT) in teaching and learning activities.

Where teaching is concerned, better standards in mathematics occur when teachers:

- devote a high proportion of lesson time to direct teaching of whole classes and groups, making judicious use of textbooks, worksheets and ICT resources to support teaching, not to replace it;
- use and give pupils access to number lines and other resources, including ICT (DfEE, 1999b: 5).

This chapter focuses on the use of interactive whiteboards (IWBs) to support the development of mathematical thinking. Wheeler (2005: 58) comments that 'ICT can offer many opportunities for developing children's mathematical understanding and improving their reasoning skills'. He goes on to say, 'The key strengths of ICT can allow children to focus on the higher order reasoning aspects of problem solving rather than simply on the calculations required' (Wheeler, 2005: 58).

In order to go beyond the use of ICT because 'many pupils enjoy using computers' (Thompson, 2003: 172), it is necessary to be aware of the reasons why ICT might be incorporated into mathematics teaching and learning.

IWBs are one of the technologies that fall under the banner ICT and they are becoming increasingly widespread in primary classrooms. Several writers are prepared to make bold statements about the potential of IWBs; for example, Williams and Easingwood (2004: 45) opine, 'this piece of equipment alone has the power to completely revolutionise the way that teachers teach, and learners learn'.

## Chapter focus

This chapter will explore the contribution that IWBs can make to the development of mathematical thinking and how their power may be utilised for maximum benefit. It will focus on:

- **the IWB as a tool to promote discussion;**
- **using an IWB to develop problem-solving skills in conjunction with automatic functions;**
- **using an IWB to embed using and applying skills;**
- **children using the IWB**

# What is an interactive whiteboard?

Firstly, to clarify, an IWB 'is essentially a large computer screen, which is sensitive to touch' (Gage, 2005: 1). In this chapter, it is being thought of as part of a package that includes a touch-sensitive board and a data projector connected to a computer or laptop. Indeed, Gage (2005: 3) goes on to say, 'an IWB can be thought of as a mix of a computer, an overhead projector and a whiteboard', although regular users will probably want to add 'flipchart' to that list.

The essential element of these descriptions is the aspect that goes beyond simply using the technology as a large display: the interactive element. Indeed, the DfEE (2000) states what might seem obvious when it says, 'An interactive whiteboard facilitates interactivity.' It is this facilitation of interactivity that this chapter is concerned with: what does an IWB offer that simply using a large computer image does not? Merrett and Edwards (2005: 12) suggest this point in their statement: 'There is recognition that the IWB, in some lessons, is a more useful resource than a projector for a PowerPoint presentation or simply as a non-interactive whiteboard.'

# What does an IWB offer to support the development of mathematical thinking?

One reason often cited for using IWBs in primary teaching is that they increase children's motivation (Richardson, 2002; Knight *et al.*, 2005). While it is agreed that any resource that increases children's motivation is to be welcomed, increased motivation alone will not support children's development of mathematical thinking. In addition to this it is an expensive way to increase pupil motivation. Indeed, there is also evidence to suggest that the motivational increase is short lived: as Knight et al. (2005: 13) go on to explain, 'as the task became more complex, the technology itself was not able to hold the high levels of motivation'. In short, any justification for using IWBs to enhance mathematical thinking must be clear. The emphasis in the following extract from the DfEE summarises the approach this chapter will take.

*Three key principles, which should underpin any decision to use Information and Communication Technology (ICT) in daily mathematics lessons:*

- *ICT should enhance good mathematics teaching. It should be used in lessons only if it supports good practice in teaching mathematics.*
- *Any decision about using ICT in a particular lesson or sequence of lessons must be directly related to the teaching and learning objectives for those lessons.*
- *ICT should be used if the teacher and/or the children can achieve something more effectively with it than without it.*
  (DfEE, 2000) (emphasis in original)

In particular, it is the final emphasis that forms the focus for this section: looking at how an IWB can be exploited to develop mathematical thinking. What is it that an IWB can do that cannot be done in any other way or cannot be done as effectively by other means? An IWB is nothing more than a resource, or as Gage (2005: ix) points out, 'An IWB is a tool which, when used well, will help a teacher to teach well.' It must be remembered that an IWB alone will not transform poor teaching into good teaching. The board alone will not develop children's mathematical thinking – it is the teacher who creates the opportunities for learning and uses the IWB to maximise the potential of those opportunities: 'It is not the board which determines how much interaction occurs, but the teacher using it' (Gage, 2005: x).

IWBs are one of the digital technologies that allow users to do things more effectively, or to do things that could not otherwise be done, by exploiting one or more of the following features: 'provisionality, interactivity, capacity, range, speed and automatic functions' (DfEE, 1998: Annex A1: 5).

'Provisionality' is the non-permanent nature of information stored electronically. It covers the idea that ideas can be changed and data edited and refined all at the touch of a button. As the user of an IWB can control the computer from the board with a finger, the potential for making the most of provisionality is high. It is important to distinguish between the interactive nature of ICT and the 'interactive' in the name 'interactive whiteboard': the interactive nature of ICT concerns the user being able to interact with software to make changes, to see effects, to receive feedback, etc. The 'interactive' in IWBs refers to the facility where the user can interact with the hardware and control the computer from the screen. Some examples might help to clarify this point. Firstly, a child working individually on a single computer using LOGO to test out and modify a sequence of instructions is interacting with the software and might well be developing their mathematical thinking. It is the interactive nature of the ICT that the pupil is interacting with. Secondly, a teacher using an IWB to advance a PowerPoint presentation about fractions is interacting with the hardware. The presentation might simply be delivering information to the class with no interaction on their part; the only interaction is between the board and the teacher's finger as they advance each slide. 'Capacity' refers to the ability of ICT to deal with things like very large (or small) numbers or huge volumes of calculations. 'Range' refers to the wide range of information ICT allows us to access, for example data on heights of mountains for ordering or weather data for graphing. 'Automatic functions' is reasonably self-explanatory: it refers to such things as using a spreadsheet to automatically calculate the cost of a teddy bears' tea party or getting instant feedback on a drill-and-practice number bonds test.

All these examples ensure 'that the computer is used in such a way that it provides a "value added" component to teaching and learning, that it provides something that otherwise would not be available' (Williams and Easingwood, 2004: 6).

# The IWB as a tool to promote discussion

It appears that the use of IWBs in classrooms has a positive effect on the quantity and quality of discussion that takes place. For example, Gage (2005: 8) notes that 'some research has suggested that high IWB use leads to more questioning, both of children and by them, more stimulating discussion, and better explanations'. The reasons for this increase have yet to be researched but it is interesting to note that it would seem to be something about the IWB and the way it is used by the teacher that is the cause. As (Merrett and Edwards, 2005: 12) explain: 'The IWB is a good medium to generate class discussions: student interaction was limited when students worked independently on laptops using the same interactive software.'

Gage (2005: x) suggests that the reason might be that 'an IWB can provide a focus for children to contribute their ideas, and to listen to those of others'. Whatever the cause, effective questioning and use of discussion are integral to the development of children's mathematical thinking skills.

## Case Study 1: Using an IWB for a shape-reveal activity to promote discussion (Y4)

### Context

As part of a unit of work on 2D shapes in a Year 4 class the teacher, James, uses a shape-reveal activity on an IWB as part of the oral/mental starter. He has prepared a shape on screen using Smart Notebook (Figure 8.1) and has covered it with rectangles of the same colour as the background. He reveals part of the shape and questions the class about the part of the shape that can be seen.

### Curriculum links

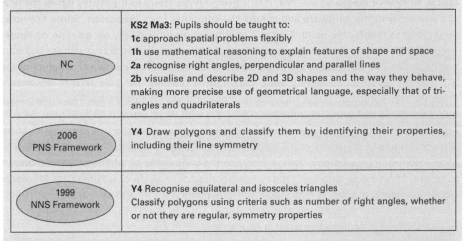

| | |
|---|---|
| NC | **KS2 Ma3:** Pupils should be taught to:<br>**1c** approach spatial problems flexibly<br>**1h** use mathematical reasoning to explain features of shape and space<br>**2a** recognise right angles, perpendicular and parallel lines<br>**2b** visualise and describe 2D and 3D shapes and the way they behave, making more precise use of geometrical language, especially that of triangles and quadrilaterals |
| 2006 PNS Framework | **Y4** Draw polygons and classify them by identifying their properties, including their line symmetry |
| 1999 NNS Framework | **Y4** Recognise equilateral and isosceles triangles<br>Classify polygons using criteria such as number of right angles, whether or not they are regular, symmetry properties |

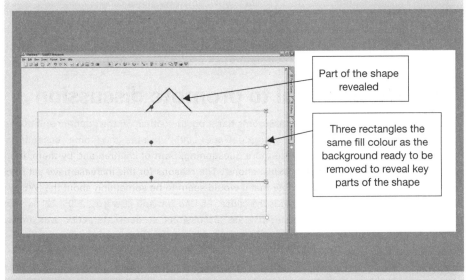

Part of the shape revealed

Three rectangles the same fill colour as the background ready to be removed to reveal key parts of the shape

**Figure 8.1: Screenshot from Smart Notebook**

**James:** You can see part of a shape shown here; the rest is hidden. Discuss with your talk partner what shape could be hidden

*[After a short discussion time]*

| James: | Emma, what shape did you and Sanjay think could be hidden? |
|---|---|
| Emma: | We thought it could be square |
| James: | Sanjay, why did you think that? |
| Sanjay: | Because it looks like a right angle at the top |
| James: | That is right. How could we check? |
| | *[children raise hands]* |
| Harry: | We could put a book against the screen to see if it matched |
| James: | Do you mean that we could compare the angle to something we know is a right angle? |
| Harry: | Yeah |
| | *[James does this with a sheet of A4 paper and confirms the angle to be 90°]* |
| James: | Now that we know it is a right angle, what other shapes could it possibly be? Take one minute to talk with your partner about this |
| James: | Dominique, what shapes did you think it could be? |
| Dominique: | We thought it might be a rectangle |
| James: | Are there any other options? |
| | *[several children raise their hands]* |
| James: | Mohammed, what else could it be? |
| Mohammed: | It could be a right angle triangle or a quadrilateral … like a kite? |
| James: | Well done. I would like you all to discuss shapes that it could not be. Remember, we know it has one right angle |
| Kai: | It can't be an equilateral triangle, because their angles are all 60° |
| James: | Yes, that is right. Anyone else? |
| Ellen: | It can't be a pentagon |
| | *[Kai's hand shoots into the air]* |
| Kai: | But it could be an irregular pentagon |
| James: | Well done. I am going to show you some more of the shape now |
| | *[He removes another section to reveal another vertex (Figure 8.2)].* |

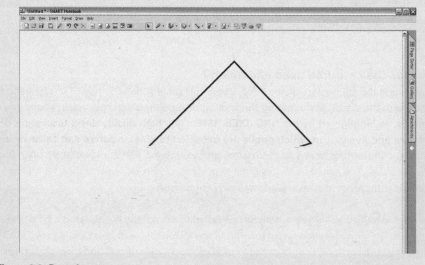

**Figure 8.2: Part shape**

James:    When we could see the first part of the shape, we thought it could be a square, a right-angle triangle, a quadrilateral, a rectangle or an irregular polygon. Now you can see some more, I would like you to discuss this list and see if there are any shapes we can cross off it. I am going to give you two minutes to discuss this with your talk partner

James:    Sunil, has the list of possible shapes changed?

Sunil:    It can't be a square or a rectangle because the new vertex isn't a right angle

James:    That is right. Would you like to guess the shape?

Sunil:    I think it is a right-angle triangle

James:    Let's have a look

          [reveals all of shape (Figure 8.3)]

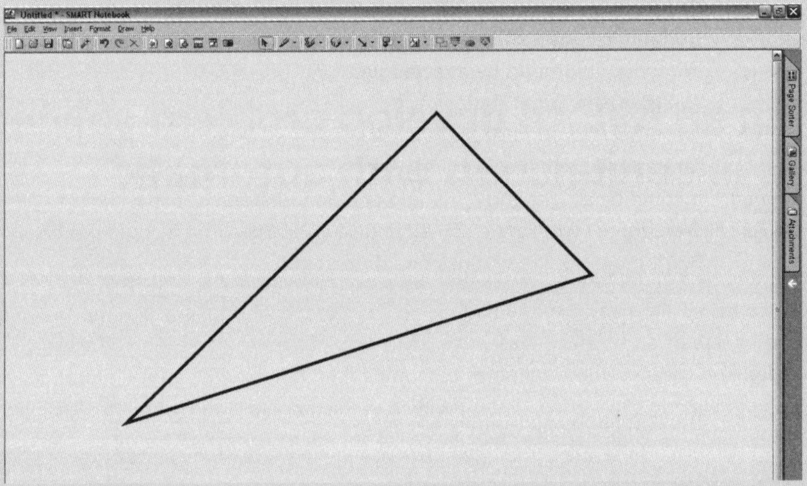

**Figure 8.3: Whole shape**

James:    You were right!

## How was the resource used effectively?

By presenting the shape partially covered, James presented the activity as a challenge to the children with the aim of encouraging the level of discussion about the hidden shape and its properties, as highlighted by the NNS (DfEE, 1999b:11): 'high-quality direct teaching is oral, interactive and lively ... in which pupils are expected to play an active part by answering questions, contributing points to discussion, and explaining and demonstrating their methods to the class'. The activity was designed to present numerous opportunities for children to discuss ideas, apply strategies, reason and solve problems.

James had identified some key questions he wished to ask as part of the activity. he began the activity with an open question about the part of the shape that was revealed, in order to allow the children to draw upon their knowledge of 2D shapes, their names and their properties. He then clarified the known property of the shape (it had a right angle) and redirected the discussion in two ways: what shapes could it be if it must have a right angle and what shapes could it not be? This twofold discussion allowed Kai to demonstrate how he applied his knowledge of regular and irregular shapes to the problem in a logical and reasoned argument.

The IWB was used effectively as a tool to reveal parts of the shape quickly and easily. The provisional nature of ICT was exploited in this example as James changed the display several times during the exercise in a quick, easy and accurate way. This allowed James to select exactly how much more of the shape he wished to reveal. Shape-reveal activities can be carried out using an OHP with a shape on a transparency partially covered by a sheet of paper. The advantage of the IWB is that the user can easily control how much more of the shape will be revealed at each stage and can be sure the there will be no accidental reveals caused by stray draughts, etc. The increased level of control over the revealing allowed James to concentrate on the questioning and discussions of the children. It is worth noting that the success of this activity is reliant on children having a firm understanding of the properties of common 2D shapes and this understanding is rooted in practical experience, a point highlighted by Merrett and Edwards (2005: 9): 'the enjoyment of practical lessons in the shape, space and measurement area of the curriculum could not be replaced by watching an example on the IWB, as we recognised that some lessons needed to be a "hands on" experience'.

# Using an IWB to develop problem-solving skills in conjunction with automatic functions

While it could be argued that software that makes use of automatic functions such as answer checking removes the need for any significant mathematical thinking, appropriate planning and effective use of an IWB can exploit this function of programs. If the software is suitably open ended and can provide a range of outcomes then opportunities for children to develop their problem-solving skills arise. Good practice in this area is summarised by DfEE guidance (2000) when they describe the effective use of ICT for such purposes.

> *Teachers should support the demonstration by clear explanation and well-targeted questioning. This can stimulate children's discussion and invite predictions and interpretations of what is displayed. The children analyse the problem, work out a strategy, arrive at a solution (this could be mentally or with paper and pencil), and compare their solution with others.*
> (DfEE, 2000)

Employing software with automatic functions allows all of these activities to take place as children discuss their strategy in the context of a clearly presented problem; they can discuss their ideas with others; they predict what might happen if a given course of action or strategy is followed. Finally, they can see if the outcome of their thinking has the expected result by comparing their ideas to the answer provided by the software. Indeed, the point raised about predicting is developed further by Richardson (2002), who investigated the effect of different questions in mathematics lessons using IWBs such as 'What would happen if...?' Richardson's research demonstrated that these types of questions were 'extremely productive in extending the children's thinking. I was able to pose a problem to be investigated, prompt discussion through questioning and work with the children towards a solution' Richardson (2002: 12).

The ability of IWB software to quickly recall previous screens allows for 'what if...?' questions to be easily investigated. For example, a question can be posed and a variety of responses explored. Children's responses can be recorded and revisited; this appears to be especially effective when the mathematical process is clearly annotated, as the visual image often prompts a pupil's memory as a stimulus to further learning (Knight et al., 2005: 11).

However, as with all the examples, it must not be forgotten that children's mathematical thinking will only be developed if the IWB is used as part of an effective mathematics lesson; in other words, 'where combined with good communication skills and well planned questions techniques, ICT can act as a powerful influence on the reasoning and problem solving skills of children as they learn' (Wheeler, 2005: 58).

## Case Study 2: Using an automatic function to develop problem-solving skills (Y2)

### Context
As part of a topic of work on money, the Year 2 class teacher (Sally) introduced the children to the program Toy Shop. The children had done work on coin recognition, finding different ways to make given totals and giving change. Sally wished to use this context to develop the pupil's mathematical thinking and chose Toy Shop as it offered many different ways to solve each problem. Figure 8.4 explains the main features of the activity.

### Curriculum links

| | |
|---|---|
| NC | **KS1 Ma2:** Pupils should be taught to:<br>**1a** approach problems involving number, and data presented in a variety of forms, in order to identify what they need to do<br>**1c** make decisions about which operations and problem-solving strategies to use<br>**1e** use the correct language, symbols and vocabulary associated with number and data<br>**1i** explain their methods and reasoning when solving problems involving number and data<br>**4a** choose sensible calculation methods to solve whole-number problems (including problems involving money or measures), drawing on their understanding of the operations<br>**4b** check that their answers are reasonable and explain their methods or reasoning |
| 2006 PNS Framework | **Y2** Add or subtract mentally a one-digit number or a multiple of 10 to or from any two-digit number; use practical and informal written methods to add and subtract two-digit numbers<br>**Using and applying mathematics**<br>Solve problems involving addition, subtraction, multiplication or division in contexts of numbers, measures or pounds and pence<br>Identify and record the information or calculation needed to solve a puzzle or problem; carry out the steps or calculations and check the solution in the context of the problem |
| 1999 NNS Framework | **Y2** Solve mathematical problems or puzzles, recognise simple patterns and relationships, generalise and predict<br>Use mental addition and subtraction, simple multiplication and division, to solve simple word problems involving numbers in 'real life', money or measures, using one or two steps<br>Explain how the problem was solved. Recognise all coins and begin to use £.p notation for money<br>Find totals, give change, and work out which coins to pay |

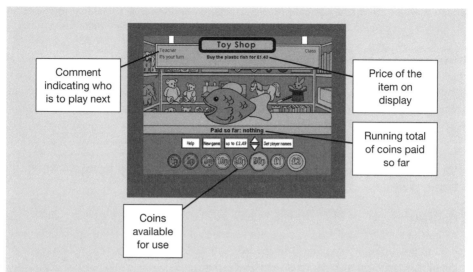

**Figure 8.4: Toy shop**

The program was displayed on the IWB and Sally played against the class. The IWB in Sally's class is mounted close to the floor, enabling the class to sit around it for 'carpet time' at the beginning of lessons. The plastic fish costs £1.43 and Sally is to play first. The follow-ing extract shows some of the discussions and conversations that took place. Sally invited children out to the IWB to select the coins to make the payment choices. The children were using small whiteboards to help them with jottings and to record their decisions.

**Sally:** What shall I start with? I think I will choose £1 as that will leave 43p for you to pay and you won't be able to do that with one coin
*[Sally pays using £1.00. £1.00 has been paid. 43p is left to pay]*

**Children's comments:** We can't use £1 or 50p because there is only 43p left to pay. What if we use a 20p, will Miss be able to win? How much will be left? Well £1 has been paid so far and if we pay 20p that makes £1.20 so that will leave … 23p. You can't pay 23p with one coin. OK, choose 20p
*[The children pay with 20p. £1.20 has been paid. 23p is left to pay]*

**Sally:** I will choose 10p this time
*[Sally pays using 10p. £1.30 has been paid. 13p is left to pay.]*

**Children's comments:** What do you think? I think we should pay with 5p. Will that work? £1.30 and 5p is £1.35, from £1.35 to £1.43 is 8p. She can't pay 8p in one coin so it is OK, isn't it? But if Miss then pays 5p, that will leave 3p, and we will lose then. Why? Well, we can only pay 1p or 2p. Whatever we choose, Miss can then pay the rest with one coin and win. Oh, I see. Shall we choose 2p then?
*[The children pay with 2p. £1.32 has been paid. 11p is left to pay]*

**Sally:** Hmm, I have some stiff competition here. 11p left to pay. I better hadn't use 1p because you could pay with 10p and win. I will go for 5p. That will make the total £1.37 and leave you 6p to pay
*[Sally pays using 5p. £1.32 has been paid. 23p is left to pay]*

**Children's comments:** OK £1.37. That leaves 6p to pay. What coins can we use? 1p, 2p or 5p. Well 1p will leave 5p to pay – we lose – and 5p is just the other way round. We will have to use 2p. That's good, because that will mean Miss has 4p to pay, she will use 2p and we can then win next time
*[The children pay with 2p. £1.39 has been paid. 4p is left to pay]*
*[Sally pays with 1p. £1.40 has been paid. 3p is left to pay]*

**Children's comments:** She didn't pay with 2p. What do we do now? Let's use 1p. But that will mean Miss has 2p to pay next time; we will lose. OK, let's use 2p. No, that is no good either, because Miss can pay with 1p and win. Oh no! We can't win

## How was the resource used effectively?

In choosing to use the IWB in conjunction with this content-specific software, Sally was exploiting the automatic function characteristic of ICT. Each time a coin was selected, the software displayed the price paid so far, giving instant and accurate feedback to the children. However, because there is a strategy element to the game, Sally encouraged the children to predict the effect of each coin choice using their whiteboards and the software was therefore used to confirm and record the coin choices.

Sally supported her use of the program with effective questioning and creating the expectation that children would offer an answer and support it with reasons. Children were asked how they had calculated totals and they were questioned about how that choice might influence the outcome of the game.

Sally made her coin choices explicit to the children by clearly explaining her choices at each stage as well as the calculations she was performing to help her with her decision-making. She encouraged the class to do the same and fostered discussions about coin choices and consequences among the children.

Wegerif et al. (1998) provide a framework to assess if software is likely to support and sustain discussion

- Challenges and problems that have meaning for the children, and which provide a range of alternative choices that are worth discussing.
- A clear purpose or task which is made evident to the group and which is kept in focus throughout.
- Resources for discussion, including information on which decisions can be based and opportunities to review decisions in the light of new information.

(Wegerif et al., 1998; cited in Thompson, 2003: 176)

Using this framework, it can be seen that Sally's choice provided a suitable challenge that presented a range of options to the children. The purpose was clear and as it was displayed at all times during the lesson, the focus on it was maintained. Finally, the children were able to review their choices in light of their discussions.

# Using an IWB to embed using and applying skills

Having the opportunity to use and apply skills in new contexts in conjunction with communicating and reasoning form the three elements of Attainment Target 1 of the NC (DfEE, 1999a). IWBs offer a variety of ways in which children can be challenged to develop and extend their skills in this area. The TTA (1999) suggest some ways in which ICT can contribute to this:

- develop logical thinking and learn from immediate feedback
- make connections within and across areas of mathematics
- develop mental imagery

(TTA, 1999; cited in Briggs and Pritchard, 2002: 7)

The ability to create mental imagery and present problems visually in ways which can be quickly and easily manipulated is a powerful aspect that IWB technologies can contribute to. If the problem that is presented requires children to employ skills and strategies they have developed in other mathematical settings, they then begin to identify links and patterns between these areas, a point which is further developed by Briggs and Pritchard (2002: 5): 'looking for and finding patterns in numbers and other mathematical situations is fundamental to, and essential for, the development of an understanding of many of the fundamentals of mathematics'.

Many of the interactive teaching programs (ITPs) developed by the Department for Education and Skills (**www.standards.dfes.gov.uk**) have been created to support the teaching of specific mathematical topics, for example grid multiplication or the use of a protractor. However, these and the other ITPs can be used for purposes other than demonstrating techniques and can develop using and applying skills. While some users find the simple interface offered by these programs hard to master, the ease with which the user can interact with them makes them a flexible and adaptable tool. ITPs lie somewhere between two distinct groups of software: content-free and content-specific. Content-free software 'does not have any specific content. It is possible to view content-free software as a tool with a specific job that it can undertake, but in no particular subject domain' (Briggs and Pritchard, 2002: 24). An example would be Microsoft Excel: it can do many things, but it is up to the user as to how it is used. Content-specific software, on the other hand, 'is also very common. There are many examples of programs that are specifically written to encourage the learning of a particular mathematical topic' (Briggs and Pritchard, 2002: 25). Interestingly, no mention is made of the development of mathematical skills such as mathematical thinking. An example here would be Maths Circus (4Mation), where the user is presented with a number of challenges that are to be solved though a mix of trial and improvement and logic; there is little room to use the software for any purpose other than that for which it was created.

The Primary National Strategy ITPs fall somewhere in between these two categories as they have a specific function, but the user is free to control the way that they are used. In order to maximise the impact of these kinds of software, it is important to be sure the 'interaction' that takes place when using an ITP is interaction between the teacher and the pupils, between the pupils and other pupils, as well as between the people and the software. This is a point emphasised by Williams and Easingwood (2004: 34): 'the best lessons are those that make extensive use of interactive teaching and learning'.

# Case Study 3: Using the interactive features of an ITP in a shape and space lesson (Y5)

## Context

As part of a unit of work on area and perimeter, the class teacher decided to use an ITP to develop children's problem-solving and reasoning skills. The children were adept at calculating areas and perimeters. The teacher also wanted the children to explore the relationship between area and perimeter.

## Curriculum links

| | |
|---|---|
| NC | **KS2 Ma2:** Pupils should be taught to:<br>**1a** make connections in mathematics and appreciate the need to use numerical skills and knowledge when solving problems in other parts of the mathematics curriculum<br>**Ma3**<br>**1h** Use mathematical reasoning to explain features of shape and space<br>**4e** Find perimeters of simple shapes; find areas of rectangles using the formula, understanding its connection to counting squares and how it extends this approach; calculate the perimeter and area of shapes composed of rectangles |
| 2006 PNS Framework | **Y5** Draw and measure lines to the nearest millimetre; measure and calculate the perimeter of regular and irregular polygons; use the formula for the area of a rectangle to calculate the rectangle's area |
| 1999 NNS Framework | **Y5** Understand, measure and calculate perimeters of rectangles and regular polygons |

The lesson began with the teacher creating a shape on the ITP 'Area' (Figure 8.5) and asking the children about the area of the shape (12 units$^2$) and the perimeter (14 units). The children were then asked to visualise what the shape would look like if a square were removed from one corner.

**Figure 8.5: Area**

The teacher then removed a square from one corner on the ITP to show the shape in Figure 8.6.

**Figure 8.6: Calculating area and perimeter**

The children were again asked to calculate the area (11 units$^2$) and the perimeter (14 units). They were also asked to discuss with a partner how the second shape differed from the first.

This prompted an enthusiastic discussion about how the area had changed but the perimeter had remained the same. The teacher then asked the children to predict what would happen if another square were removed from a different corner. Some of the predictions were recorded and another square was removed, to show the shape in Figure 8.7.

**Figure 8.7: Checking predictions**

The area (10 units$^2$) and the perimeter (14 units) were calculated and children were asked if their predictions were correct.

The teacher then clarified that each time a square had been removed the area of the shape had been reduced by 1 unit$^2$ while the perimeter had remained unchanged. She then asked the children to discuss whether this pattern could continue and how long it could continue for.

The children discussed in pairs and small groups. There was much pointing at the board as children expressed their ideas to their peers. As the intensity of the discussion waned, the teacher stopped the children and asked for the outcome of their conversations.

Some children had thought that only the corners could be removed, while others had realised that a number of squares could be removed leading to a shape such as the one in Figure 8.8, with an area of 6 units$^2$ and a perimeter of 14 units.

**Figure 8.8: Investigating area**

The children then began independent work to investigate how area varies in rectangles of different dimensions but with the same perimeter (e.g. 1cm × 10cm and 2cm × 9cm).

## How was the resource used effectively?

The teacher used a familiar shape where the area and perimeter calculations would allow the children to draw upon their prior learning, but would not take so long as to detract from the pace of the lesson. The use of the ITP 'Area' allowed the teacher to show the different shapes in a clear way that could easily be changed. Indeed, if it had been required, the squares that had been removed could have been added again to compare previous areas and perimeters. This draws on the interactivity and provisional functions of ICT.

The teacher provided the children with opportunities to develop the strategies they would need in order to continue investigating this problem: she asked them to begin visualising what the shape would look like with a square removed. The ITP provided a quick and easy way for the children to see if their visualisation matched the actual result on the board.

By asking children to calculate the area and perimeter after each square had been removed, their ability to use and apply known facts and calculation methods to a new problem was being extended. It also made explicit the process the children should use as the problem was opened out and they were asked 'how many squares can be removed without changing the perimeter?'

The paired discussion was key to developing the children's mathematical thinking in this activity as they were required to draw upon and develop their reasoning and communication skills. The IWB was used effectively to support this as a visual aid to be left on display while the children discussed the above question. They were able to refer to it as they talked about the problem in pairs/small groups: many children were seen to point at the board as they shared their ideas with their peers.

# Children using the IWB

Up to this point, this chapter has focused on the ways in which teachers can use an IWB to develop mathematical thinking. Due to the nature of the boards being installed at the front of the class, often in place of a black or whiteboard, the temptation is to view them solely as a tool for teachers to employ. However, there is wide scope to involve children in their use and for this to have impact on the way they think mathematically.

Williams and Easingwood (2004: 61) suggest this approach when they state that the IWB 'has the potential to completely transform teaching learning through the ability to connect teacher, child and computer'. It is the connection of the child to the computer which opens new opportunities, especially for the development of mathematical communication, as children can be invited to use the board as a means to help explain their thinking, strategies and methods. It can also act as a catalyst to boost children's confidence by empowering them and putting them in a position of control where they have access to a powerful tool to help them articulate their thoughts. This point is illustrated by this example from Gage (2005: 18):

> standing at the IWB, taking the part of the teacher, gave Melanie the confidence to become part of the group. Although she found maths hard, asking questions of the others helped her to think about the reasoning needed to choose a symbol, so that she was then ready to join in with the group.

Further weight to this argument is provided by Smith et al. (2006: 445), who point out that the British Educational Communications and Technology Agency (BECTA, 2003, p. 3) states that students are motivated in lessons incorporating an IWB because "students enjoy interacting physically with the board, manipulating text and images", thereby providing "more opportunities for interaction and discussion".'

## Case Study 4: Children using the IWB to share their ideas (Y6)

### Context
While on his final block placement in a Year 6 class, Mohammed, a trainee teacher, wanted to use the school's recent netball tournament as the basis for some problem-solving work. Mohammed began the lesson by getting the children to concentrate on the semi-final match. In this match, the score at full time had been 2–1.

### Curriculum links

| | |
|---|---|
| NC | **KS2 Ma2:** Pupils should be taught to:<br>**1f** organise work and refine ways of recording<br>**1h** present and interpret solutions in the context of the problem<br>**1i** communicate mathematically, including the use of precise mathematical language<br>**1j** understand and investigate general statements<br>**1k** search for pattern in their results; develop logical thinking and explain their reasoning<br>**4b** choose and use an appropriate way to calculate and explain their methods and reasoning |
| 2006 PNS Framework | **Y6 Using and applying mathematics**<br>Tabulate systematically the information in a problem or puzzle; identify and record the steps or calculations needed to solve it, using symbols where appropriate; interpret solutions in the original context and check their accuracy<br>Explain reasoning and conclusions, using words, symbol or diagrams as appropriate |
| 1999 NNS Framework | **Y6** Identify and use appropriate operations (including combinations of operations) to solve word problems involving numbers and quantities<br>Explain methods and reasoning |

Mohammed began by clarifying that the '2' meant the home team had scored two while the visitors had only scored one.

| | |
|---|---|
| **Mohammed:** | What could the score have been at half time? |
| **Xavier:** | It was 1–1 |
| **Mohammed:** | Yes, the score was 1–1 at half time, but imagine you did not see the first half and all you knew was the full time score; what could the half time score have been? |
| **Sam:** | Do you mean, like, it could have been 1–-0? |
| **Mohammed:** | Yes, would you come and write that on the board? |
| | *[Sam records the score on the board (Figure 8.9)]* |
| **Mohammed:** | I am going to give you three minutes to work in pairs to see if you can think of all the possible half time scores for our netball match. Use your whiteboards to make a note of your ideas |
| | *[After three minutes Mohammed stops the class and asks children to come to the front and record the different scores on the IWB]* |

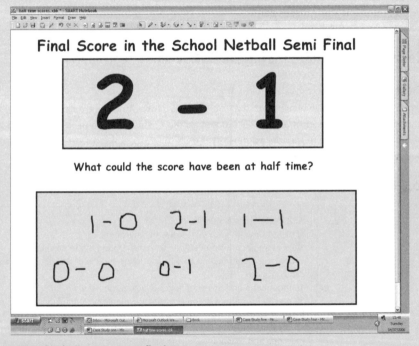

**Figure 8.9: Netball tournament final score**

| | |
|---|---|
| **Mohammed:** | Have we got them all? |
| **Kylie:** | I think so. We made a really long list but then we realised that some scores were already on the list and so we had to go through and cross off the ones we already had. Then at the end we have got the same list that is on the board |
| **Mohammed:** | How could we check if we have got them all? |
| **Brad:** | We could all check our lists. If anyone has got a score that is not on the board, then we can't have them all |

*[The children check their lists and find that all scores are on the board]*

**Mohammed:** I would like you to think about the score at the end of the final match: 2–3. In your groups, I am going to give you ten minutes to think about all the scores that there could have been at half time. But when I ask you for the scores I want you to be sure that you have got them all. That means you will need to have a system for recording them

After ten minutes, Mohammed stops the children and explains that he is going to ask each group to come to the front and to write their scores on the IWB in a way that shows how they know they have got all the scores. He asks each group not to say anything as they write and groups who are not writing are asked to look for two things: what system has the group used; and have they made any mistakes? Figures 8.10, 8.11 and 8.12 show the children's recordings.

Mohammed then showed each page again and asked children from other groups to explain how the scores had been organised. Some sample comments are included below.

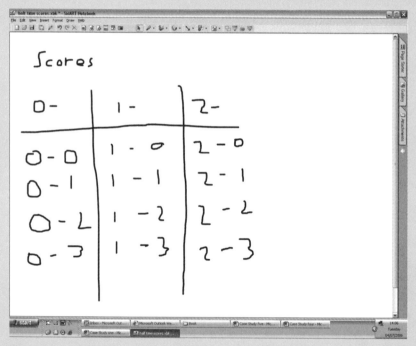

**Figure 8.10: Team scores**

**David:** I think they have looked at the home team's score and then made a list of all the away team scores that there could have been. It looks like they have gone from smallest to largest

**Niamh:** I don't think there is any system here. It just looks like a list of scores. It doesn't work very well because they have got 2–2 on the list twice

**Mohammed:** Group 2, this is your work. What do you say to Niamh's comments?

**Isaac:** Ooops! We didn't mean to have 2–2 on the list twice

*[He then circles it using the highlighter tool]*

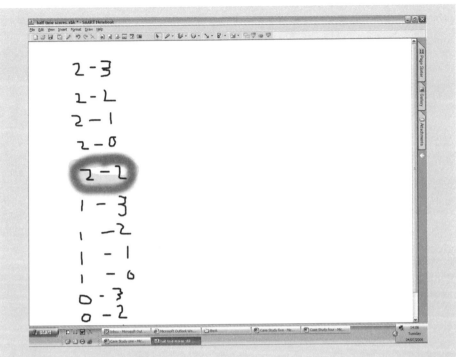

**Figure 8.11: Checking scores**

**Archie:** I can see how they have done it. They started with the final score and then worked down. They took one off the second score until they got to zero and then took one off the first score and did it again

**Niamh:** Oh, it is a bit like the first group's but in the opposite way

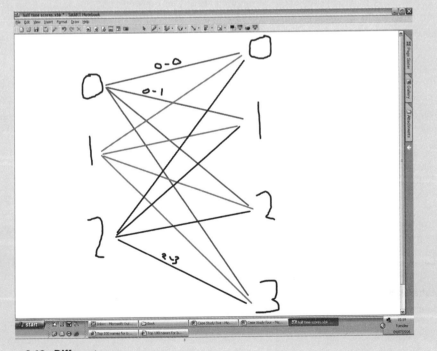

**Figure 8.12: Different scores**

| Mohammed: | Can anyone work this out? No? Well, could someone from group 3 try and explain it? |
| Ewan: | Well, the numbers on the left are all the possible scores that the home team could have got. The numbers on the right are all the scores for the home team. The lines are all the different scores *[He then writes 0–0, 0–1, and 2–3 as examples]* |

Mohammed then explains that they are going to investigate how many different half-time scores there could be for a variety of different full-time scores and they are going to choose a recording system to do this. He shows the class each slide again and asks groups to discuss which they would choose and why. For the remainder of the lesson the class investigate potential half-time scores for different final results and start trying to predict how many there would be for any given full-time score.

## How was the resource used effectively?

Mohammed has taken advantage of the interactive nature of ICT in his use of the IWB. He presented the material in an easy-to-see manner in order to explain the problem to the class. He also got each group to record their results on the board, thereby encouraging the children to interact with the technology. He effectively exploited the interactive feature of the technology by revisiting the pages of children's work. This allowed all the class to clearly see and revisit the work. Each group had a large, clear space to record their work and some groups made use of features such as the line tool and different colours to show their work. The ease with which children were able to revisit the examples allowed Mohammed to focus on his teaching. He used the children's examples effectively as he made no attempt to explain them himself, neither did he allow the group that drew them to explain them. Instead, he asked other groups to work out what system the diagram represented. This allowed the class to consider ways in which they could refine their recording methods and encouraged the use of mathematical language. Finally, he made use of the ability to revisit the work when he showed the work at the end and asked children to choose a recording system to use for the rest of the lesson.

The case study is an example of 'structured interplay between teacher and pupils. Here the teacher is leading the discussion and controlling the use of the IWB but inviting pupils to engage with the interactivity of the IWB to demonstrate understanding or develop a point' (Knight *et al.*, 2004: 14).

## SUMMARY OF KEY POINTS

This chapter has looked at what IWBs are and why a teacher might choose to use one. Its main focus has been on how teachers can maximise their use of an IWB to develop children's mathematical thinking. It is important to ensure that the technology is used to its best effect in order to avoid a powerful piece of technology simply being used as a large display screen. As Williams and Easingwood (2004: 46) point out, 'when used effectively, there is more to an interactive whiteboard than simply electronically mimicking something from a previous generation purely for the sake of it'.

There are likely to be many studies in the near future that will investigate how effective the widespread use of IWBs has been; some have already been conducted, for example Smith et al. (2006: 454), who argue that 'while our findings support some of the claims being made for IWBs, they do not suggest a fundamental change in teachers' underlying pedagogy'. They also make the point that 'while it could be argued that the IWB is a useful presentational tool to have in the classroom, the findings suggest that such technology by itself will not bring about fundamental change in the traditional patterns of whole class teaching' (Smith *et al.*, 2006: 455). Thus, if IWBs are to have an impact on children's mathematical thinking, then careful thought will be needed to ensure that they are used to support good practice in mathematics, with activities that are directly related to the lesson objectives and take opportunities presented by ICT that are not available by other methods (DfEE, 2000).

Research by Wall *et al.* (2005) into the views of children on the impact of IWBs across all subjects found that mathematics had the most number of positive comments made. If this is to be a continuing trend then IWBs must be exploited to their full extent to develop children's mathematical thinking.

## REFLECTIONS ON PRACTICE

1. How does your IWB use exploit the functions of ICT? (Provisionality, interactivity, speed, capacity, range and automatic functions)
2. How does your use of the IWB contribute to good practice in mathematics teaching?
3. Could you plan extended opportunities for your pupils to use the IWB to explain their ideas?
4. Do you plan key questions based on IWB resources that will extend and develop children's communication, reasoning and using and applying skills?

**REFERENCES** REFERENCES **REFERENCES** REFERENCES REFERENCES REFERENCES

Briggs, M. and Pritchard, A. (2002) *Using ICT in primary mathematics teaching*. Exeter: Learning Matters.

Department for Education and Employment (1998) *Teaching: high status, high standards. requirements for the courses of initial teacher training*. Circular 4/98. London: DfEE.

Department for Education and Employment (1999a) *Mathematics. The National Curriculum for England: Key Stages 1–4*. London: DfEE Publications.

Department for Education and Employment (1999b) *The National Numeracy Strategy. Framework for Teaching Mathematics from Reception to Year 6*. London: DfEE Publications.

Department for Education and Employment (2000) *Guide to your professional development: Using ICT to support mathematics in primary schools*. London: DfEE. Available at: **www.standards.dfes.gov.uk/primary/profdev/mathematics/UsingICTtosupportmathematics/** (accessed 30/08/06).

Gage, J. (2005) *How to use an interactive whiteboard really effectively in your primary classroom*. London: David Fulton.

Knight, P., Pennant, J. and Piggott, J. (2004) What does it mean to 'Use the Interactive Whiteboard' in the daily mathematics lesson? *Micromath*, 20(2): 14–16.

Knight, P., Pennant, J. and Piggott, J. (2005) The power of the interactive whiteboard. *Micromath*, 21(2): 11–15.

Merrett, S. and Edwards J-A. (2005) Enhancing mathematical thinking with an interactive whiteboard. *Micromath*, 21 (3): 9–12.

Richardson, A. (2002) Effective questioning in teaching mathematics using an interactive whiteboard. *Micromath*, 18 (2): 8–12.

Smith, F., Hardman, F. and Higgins, S. (2006) The impact of interactive whiteboards on teacher–pupil interaction in the National Literacy and Numeracy Strategies. *British Educational Research Journal*, 32 (3): 443–457.

Thompson, I. (ed.) (2003) *Enhancing primary mathematics teaching*. Maidenhead: OUP.

TTA (1999) *Using information and communication technology to meet teaching objectives in mathematics – initial teacher training: primary*. London: TTA. Cited in Briggs, M. and Pritchard, A. (2002) *Using ICT in primary mathematics teaching*. Exeter: Learning Matters.

Wall, K., Higgins, S. and Smith, H. (2005) The visual helps me understand the complicated things: pupil views of teaching and learning with interactive whiteboards. *British Journal of Educational Technology*, 36 (5): 851–867.

Wegerif, R., Mercer, N. and Dawes, L. (1998) Software design to support discussion in the primary classroom. *Journal of Computer Assisted Learning*, 14(3): 199–211. Cited in Thompson, I. (2003).

Wheeler, S. (ed.) (2005) *Transforming primary ICT*. Exeter: Learning Matters.

Williams, J. and Easingwood, N. (2004) *ICT and primary mathematics. A teacher's guide*. London: RoutledgeFalmer.

# Glossary

**Acoustic image:** Internalised sounds and rhythms which are drawn upon to represent ideas.

**Attribute:** A characteristic of an object or image.

**Autistic spectrum disorder (ASD):** A developmental disorder affecting largely social understanding, communication and flexibility of thought.

**Automatic functions:** The ability of ICT to perform processes without user intervention. Examples include checking the results of calculations or drawing graphs from entered data.

**Calibrated number line:** A line with fixed, spaced numbers recorded in a sequential order.

**Capacity:** A feature of ICT technologies to deal with data beyond the scope of the user's mind. Examples might be; large amounts of data, multiplying very large numbers, subtracting very small numbers.

**Circles of inclusion:** A term derived from the National Curriculum's three principles for inclusion and adapted by the Primary National Strategy. The circles of inclusion are a useful guide when planning lessons in order to check that every aspect of the lesson is inclusive.

**Compare bears:** A commercially produced set of plastic bears in different sizes and colours used for mathematical activities such as grouping and sorting.

**Concrete operational:** A stage of learning defined by Piaget as indicative of children between the ages of 7 and 12 (Harries and Spooner, 2000). Within this stage, children start to think operationally with the help of manipulation of objects and use of images.

**Constructivism:** A theory of learning which believes that knowledge is not passively received: instead, learning is active and allows learners to build up and construct their own meanings through instruction, interaction and experiences.

**Cross-curricular planning:** Planning across subject boundaries.

**Cuisenaire rods:** A set of rods utilising 1cm increments in length from 1cm to 10cm to represent ordinal number.

**Cultural artefact:** An object used, modified or made by humans.

**Decimal fractions:** Numbers recorded and described using base 10. A decimal point is used to separate the whole numbers from the fraction.

**Difference dolls:** A pair of dolls which have some attributes identical and some different.

**Digit pop-ups:** A commercially made resource with pictures of ten children, each of which bends flexibly.

**Dyscalculia:** A condition that affects the ability to acquire arithmetical skills.

**Empty number line:** A blank line with no fixed recording.

**Factor:** A whole number that can be multiplied by another to create a number. For example, the factors of 6 are 1, 2, 3 and 6.

**Fraction bag:** A collection of materials which can be used to practically experience finding a fractional quantity.

**Global learning difficulties:** A generic term which refers to a child who has difficulties across academic areas.

**Iconic representation:** A 'system of representation that depends upon visual or other sensory organization and upon the use of summarizing images' (Bruner, 1966: 10).

**Images:** Images are active constructions that are content-specific representations. Images are more likely to represent concrete ideas (for example, a house) than abstract ideas (such as justice) (English and Halford, 1995).

**Individual Education Plan (IEP):** A plan devised for a child with SEN at School Action, School Action Plus, or with a statement, as explained in the SEN Code of Practice.

**Interactive:** A feature of ICT applications where interaction between the user and the computer or between users occurs.

**Interactive teaching programs (ITPs):** Free applications from the Primary National Strategy to support the teaching of specific areas of mathematics, e.g. multiplication using the grid method.

**Learning trajectory:** 'A hypothetical learning trajectory is made up of three components: the learning goal that defines the direction, the learning activities, and the hypothetical learning process – a prediction of how the students' thinking and understanding will evolve in the context of the learning activities' (Simon, 1995).

**Logicblocs:** A commercially produced structured set of shapes.

**LOGO:** A programming language developed by Seymour Papert for educational purposes, particularly for constructivist teaching and learning.

**Kinaesthetic learners:** People who learn through manipulation of tactile objects, or by moving their bodies and using their muscles.

**Mathematising:** Gravemeijer and Doorman (1999) identify mathematisation as a method of developing tools as a model of mathematical understanding to a model for mathematical understanding.

**Mental model:** 'Mental models are representations that are active while solving a particular problem and that provide the workspace for inference and mental operations' (Halford, 1993: 23); 'Mental models may be retrieved from memory or may be constructed to meet the requirements of a particular task' (English and Halford, 1995).

**Meta-cognition:** Developing an awareness of our own intellectual processes.

**Mixed numbers:** A number which consists of a whole number and a fraction, e.g. $2\frac{1}{2}$.

**Model:** A 'system' that is used to describe, think about, make sense of, explain or to make predictions of another system (Lesh *et al.*, 2000).

**Multibase 10:** A resource also known as Diene's apparatus which is constructed from 1cm cubes representing base 10 place value. A $1 \times 1 \times 1$ cube represents one unit, a $1 \times 1 \times 10$ cuboid represents ten, a $1 \times 10 \times 10$ cuboid represents 100 and a $10 \times 10 \times 10$ cube represents 1000.

**Multilink:** A brand-named resource of cubes which allow each of the six faces to be fitted together.

**Number tracks:** A grid in which numbers are placed in a sequential order.

**One-to-one principle:** Using a different number name for each item counted, counting each item only once and including all items in the count.

**Oblong:** A quadrilateral which has opposite sides of equal length, two sets of parallel sides and four right angles.

**Parallelogram:** A quadrilateral which has opposite sides of equal length, two sets of parallel sides and opposite angles equal in size.

**Place value arrow cards:** Cards which use the digits 1–9 and any number of 0s as place holders as required to represent number. They are placed on top of one another to make a number with the digits showing in particular columns.

**PowerPoint:** Presentation software produced by Microsoft.

**Pre-operational:** A stage of learning defined by Piaget as indicative of children between the ages of 18 months to 4 years (Harries and Spooner, 2000). Within this stage, children start to demonstrate the ability to represent ideas through manipulation of objects and drawing images.

**Prime number:** A positive integer whose only two factors are 1 and itself.

**Provisionality:** Refers to the non-permanent nature of material stored electronically.

**Proper fraction:** The name given to a fraction where the numerator is smaller than the denominator.

**Range:** How ICT allows users to access a broad array of data. Typical examples might be historical data on the internet or sound clips from orchestral instruments on CD-ROM.

**Rational number:** The name given to a number which can be shown as a fraction or as an exact decimal.

**Rectangular number:** Any positive integer that can be represented as a rectangular array: it has more than two factors.

**Rectilinear arrangement:** An arrangement (in this case an array) which is characterised by or bound by straight lines which are always parallel to axes at right angles.

**Rhombus:** A quadrilateral which has four sides of equal length, two sets of parallel sides and opposite angles equal in size.

**Schema:** An organised structure of knowledge in which experience and new knowledge may fit.

**Stable-order principle:** Being able to recite number names consistently in order.

**SEAL:** An acronym representing social and emotional aspects of learning.

**SMART targets:** An acronym applied to targets: specific, measurable, achievable, realistic and time-related.

**Square:** A quadrilateral which has four sides of equal length, two sets of parallel sides and four right angles.

**Square number:** A number that is the product of two equal integers.

**Smart Notebook:** Software provided by Smart Tech (manufacturers of Smart interactive whiteboards). It combines features of standard whiteboards and flipcharts in an electronic format.

**Slavonic abacus:** An abacus where the beads are grouped in blocks of five or ten.

**Statement:** A legal document outlining a child's SEN and the strategies and resources which must be provided to meet those needs.

**Structured set:** A set of objects/images possessing identifiable attributes and characteristics. Each item in the set is unique.

**Triangular number:** A number that can be arranged in the shape of an equilateral triangle. It is created by the sum of consecutive integers.

**Unifix:** A brand-named resource of interlocking cubes which can only fit together in two directions.

**Visualiser:** Sometimes called a digital presenter, ICT equipment that projects materials on to a large screen.

**Wave 2:** Additional targeted support in the form of small group intervention to accelerate progress. The intention is to enable targeted children to work at age-related expectations.

# Objectives index

NC National Curriculum Objectives

| Key Stage 1 Objectives | Chapter: Case Study |
|---|---|
| Ma2: 1a. Approach problems involving number, and data presented in a variety of forms, in order to identify what they need to do | 6:1; 8:2 |
| Ma2: 1b. Develop flexible approaches to problem solving and look for ways to overcome difficulties | 4:2; 4:7 |
| Ma2: 1c. Make decisions about operations and problem solving strategies to use | 4:2; 4:7; 6:2; 8:2 |
| Ma2: 1e. Use the correct language, symbols and vocabulary associated with number | 3:1; 8:2 |
| Ma2: 1f. Communicate in spoken, pictorial and written form, at first using informal language and recording, then mathematical language and symbols | 4:2; 4:7 |
| Ma2: 1i. Explain their methods and reasoning when solving problems involving number and data | 4:2; 8:2 |
| Ma2: 2a. Count reliably up to 20 objects | 6:1; 6:2 |
| Ma2: 2c. Read numbers to 100 or beyond; recognise that the position of a digit gives its value and know what each digit represents, including zero as a place-holder | 3:1 |
| Ma2: 4a. Choose sensible calculation methods to solve whole-number problems (including problems involving money or measures), drawing on their understanding of the operations | 8:2 |
| Ma2: 4b. Check that their answers are reasonable and explain their methods or reasoning | 4:7; 8:2 |
| Ma2: 5a. Solve a relevant problem by using simple lists, tables and charts to sort, classify and organise information | 4:2 |
| Ma2: 5b. Discuss what they have done and explain their results | 4:2 |
| Ma3: 1d. Use the correct language and vocabulary for shape, space and measures | 4:1; 6:4; 7:1 |
| Ma3: 1f. Use mathematical communication and explanation skills | 4:1; 7:1 |
| Ma3: 2a. Describe properties of shapes they can see or visualise using the related vocabulary | 6:4 |
| Ma3: 2b. Observe, handle and describe common 2D shapes; name and describe the mathematical features | 3:4 |
| Ma4: 1h. Explain and justify their methods and reasoning | 4:3 |
| Ma4: 2a. Try different approaches and find ways of overcoming difficulties when solving problems. | 3:4 |
| Ma3: 4a. Put familiar events in chronological order, compare the durations of events using a standard unit of time | 6:6 |
| **Key Stage 2 Objectives** | **Chapter: Case Study** |
| Ma2: 1a. Make connections in mathematics and appreciate the need to use numerical skills and knowledge when solving problems in other parts of the mathematics curriculum | 3:5; 4:4; 6:3; 6:5; 7:3; 8:3 |
| Ma2: 1b. Break down a more complex calculation into smaller steps; identify the information needed to carry out tasks | 3:2; 6:3 |
| Ma2: 1c. Approach spatial problems flexibly, including trying alternative approaches to overcome difficulties | 7:3 |

156

| | |
|---|---|
| Ma2: 1d. Find different ways of approaching a problem in order to overcome any difficulties | 4:3; 4:4; 4:5; 4:6 |
| Ma2: 1f. Organise work and refine ways of recording | 3:5; 8:4 |
| Ma2: 1h. Present and interpret solutions in the context of the problem | 3:5; 4:4; 4:5; 4:6; 6:3; 7:3; 8:4 |
| Ma2: 1i. Communicate mathematically, including the use of precise mathematical language | 4:4; 8:4 |
| Ma2: 1j. Understand and investigate general statements | 8:4 |
| Ma2: 1k. Search for pattern in their results; develop logical thinking and explain their reasoning | 3:3; 4:3; 4:5; 4:6; 8:4 |
| Ma2: 2b. Recognise and describe number patterns | 4:6; 6:5 |
| Ma2: 2D. Understand unit fractions and use them to find fractions of shapes and quantities | 4:4 |
| Ma2: 2h. Use mathematical reasoning to explain features of shape and space | 6:5 |
| Ma2: 3e. Work out what they need to do to add or subtract any pair of two-digit whole numbers | 3:2 |
| Ma2: 3f. Recall multiplication facts to 10 × 10 | 5:1 |
| Ma2: 4a. Choose, use and combine any of the four operations to solve problems involving numbers in real life | 5:4; 6:2 |
| Ma2: 4b. Choose and use an appropriate way to calculate and explain their methods and reasoning | 4:4; 8:4 |
| Ma2: 4c. Estimate answers by approximating and checking that their results are reasonable by thinking about the context of the problem, and where necessary checking accuracy | 7:3 |
| Ma3: 1c. Approach spatial problems flexibly | 8:1 |
| Ma3: 1d. Use checking procedures to confirm that their results of geometric problems are reasonable | 4:7 |
| Ma3: 1g. Present and interpret solutions to problems | 4:7 |
| Ma3: 1h. Use mathematical reasoning to explain features of shape and space | 4:7; 7:2; 8:1; 8:3 |
| Ma3: 2a. Recognise right angles, perpendicular and parallel lines | 7:3; 8:1 |
| Ma3: 2b. Visualise and describe 2D and 3D shapes and the way they behave, making more precise use of geometrical language, especially that of triangles and quadrilaterals | 4:7; 7:2; 7:3; 8:1 |
| Ma3: 2c. Recognise reflective symmetry in regular polygons | 7:3 |
| Ma3: 3b. Transform objects in practical situations; transform images using ICT; visualise and predict the position of a shape following a rotation, reflection or translation | 7:3 |
| Ma3: 4a. Recognise the need for standard units of measurement. Choose ones which are suitable for a task and use then to make sensible estimates in everyday situations | 7:3 |
| Ma3: 4e. Find perimeters of simple shapes; find areas of rectangles using the formula, understanding its connection to counting squares and how it extends this approach; calculate the perimeter and area of shapes composed of rectangles. | 8:3 |
| Ma4: 2b. Construct and interpret frequency tables, including tables for grouped discrete data | 7:3 |

## CGfS — Curriculum Guidance for the Foundation Stage Objectives

| Green Stepping Stones | Chapter: Case Study |
|---|---|
| *Numbers as labels and for counting* | |
| Represent numbers using fingers, marks on paper or pictures | 6:1 |
| Recognise numerals 1 to 5 | 6:1 |
| Count an irregular arrangement of up to 10 objects | 7:1 |
| *Calculating* | |
| Use own methods to solve a problem | 6:1 |
| *Shape, space and measures* | |
| Use appropriate shapes to make representational models | 5:2; 7:1 |
| Use language such as 'circle' or 'bigger' to describe the shape and size of solids and flat shapes | 5:2 |
| Show curiosity and observation by talking about shapes, how they are the same or why some are different | 4:1 |
| Describe a simple journey | 7:1 |
| Find items from positional/directional clues | 7:1 |
| **Early Learning Goals (Mathematical Development)** | **Chapter: Case Study** |
| *Numbers as labels and for counting* | |
| Say and use number names in order in familiar contexts | 6:1; 6:6 |
| Count reliably up to 10 everyday objects | 6:1; 7:1 |
| Use developing mathematical ideas and methods to solve practical problems | 4:1; 6:1; 6:6; 7:1 |
| *Calculating* | |
| Use language such as 'more' or 'less' to compare two numbers | 6:1 |
| *Shape, space and measures* | |
| Talk about, recognise and recreate simple patterns | 7:1 |
| Use everyday words to describe position | 4:1; 7:1 |
| Use language … to describe the shape and size of solids and flat shapes | 7:1 |
| **Early Learning Goals (Communication, Language and Literacy)** | **Chapter: Case Study** |
| *Language for communication* | |
| Listen with enjoyment, respond to stories, songs and other music | 6:1; 6:6 |
| *Language for thinking* | |
| Use talk to organise, sequence and clarify thinking, ideas, feelings and events | 6:1; 6:6 |

**2006 PNS Framework** ▶ **Primary National Strategy Objectives**

**Bold** text signifies end-of-year (EOY) objectives within Mathematics and Early Learning Goals (ELG) within the Foundation Stage

| Foundation Stage Objectives | Chapter: Case Study |
|---|---|
| *Using and applying mathematics* | |
| **Use developing mathematical ideas and methods to solve practical problems** | 4:1; 6:1; 7:1 |
| Sort objects, making choices and justifying decisions | 4:1 |
| Describe solutions to practical problems, drawing on experience, talking about their own ideas, methods and choices | 4:1 |
| **Talk about, recognise and recreate simple patterns** | 7:1 |
| *Counting and understanding number* | |
| **Say and use number names in order in familiar contexts** | 6:1; 7:1 |
| **Count reliably up to 10 everyday objects** | 6:1 |
| *Knowing and using number fact* | |
| Find one more or one less than a number from 1 to 10 | 6:1 |
| *Understanding shape* | |
| Use familiar objects and common shapes to create and recreate patterns and build models | 7:1 |
| **Use language such as 'circle' or 'bigger' to describe the shape and size of solids and flat shapes** | 5:2; 7:1 |
| **Use everyday words to describe position** | 7:1 |
| *Measuring* | |
| Use everyday language related to time; order and sequence familiar events and measure short periods of time | 6:6 |
| **Year 1 Objectives** | **Chapter: Case Study** |
| *Using and applying mathematics* | |
| Solve problems involving addition, subtraction, multiplication or division in contexts of numbers, measures or pounds and pence | 8:2 |
| Describe a problem using numbers, practical materials and diagrams; use these to solve the problem and set the solution back in the original context | 6:2 |
| Describe simple patterns and relationships involving numbers or shapes; decide whether examples satisfy given conditions | 4:7 |
| Describe ways of solving puzzles and problems, explaining choices and decisions orally or using pictures | 4:7 |
| *Counting and understanding number* | |
| Count reliably up to 20 objects | 6:2 |
| *Understanding shape* | |
| **Visualise and name common 2D shapes and 3D solids and describe their features; use them to make patterns, pictures and models** | 3:4 |

| | |
|---|---|
| Identify patterns and relationships involving numbers or shapes, and use these to solve problems | 7:3 |
| Read and record the vocabulary of position, direction and movement, using the four compass directions to describe movement about a grid | 7:3 |
| Report solutions to puzzles and problems, giving explanations and reasoning orally and in writing, using diagrams and symbols | 4:3 |
| Describe patterns and relationships involving numbers or shapes, make predictions and test these with examples | 4:7 |
| *Understanding shape* | |
| Draw polygons and classify them by identifying their properties, including their line symmetry | 8:1 |
| *Measuring* | |
| Choose and use standard metric units and their abbreviations when estimating, measuring and recording length | 7:3 |
| *Handling data* | |
| Answer a set of related questions by collecting, selecting and organising relevant data; draw conclusions, using ICT to present features, and identify further questions to ask | 7:3 |
| **Year 5 Objectives** | **Chapter: Case Study** |
| *Using and applying mathematics* | |
| Represent a puzzle or problem by identifying and recording the information or calculations needed to solve it; find possible solutions and confirm them in the context of the problem | 3:3; 6:3 |
| Plan and pursue an enquiry; present evidence by collecting, organising and interpreting information; suggest extensions to the enquiry | 3:3 |
| Explore patterns, properties and relationships and propose a general statement involving numbers or shapes; identify examples for which the statement is true or false | 3:3; 4:5; 4:7; 5:1 |
| *Knowing and using number facts* | |
| Recall quickly multiplication facts up to 10 and use them to multiply pairs of multiples of 10 and 100; derive quickly corresponding division facts | 5:1 |
| *Understanding shape* | |
| Visualise 3D objects from 2D drawings | 7:3 |
| **Describe, identify and visualise parallel and perpendicular edges or faces; use these properties to classify 2D shapes and 3D solids** | 7:3 |
| Estimate, draw and measure acute and obtuse angles using an angle measurer | 7:3 |
| *Handling data* | |
| Answer a set of related questions by collecting, selecting and organising relevant data; draw conclusions, using ICT to present features, and identify further questions to ask | 7:3 |
| Read and interpret scales on a range of measuring instruments, recognising that the measurement made is approximate and recording results to a required degree of accuracy | 7:3 |

| Year 6 Objectives | Chapter: Case Study |
|---|---|
| *Using and applying mathematics* | |
| Solve multi-step problems, and problems involving fractions, decimals and percentages; choose and use appropriate calculation strategies at each stage, including calculator use | 4:4; 6:3 |
| Tabulate systematically the information in a problem or puzzle; identify and record the steps or calculations needed to solve it, using symbols where appropriate; interpret solutions in the original context and check their accuracy | 3:5; 8:4 |
| Suggest, plan and develop lines of enquiry; collect, organise and represent information, interpret results and review methods; identify and answer related questions | 3:5; 7:3 |
| Represent and interpret sequences, patterns and relationships involving numbers and shapes; suggest and test hypotheses; construct and use simple expressions and formulae in words then symbols | 3:5; 4:6 |
| Explain reasoning and conclusions, using words, symbols or diagrams as appropriate | 3:5; 4:4; 8:4 |
| Explain and justify reasoning and conclusions, using notation, symbols and diagrams | 6:5 |
| *Understanding shape* | |
| Explore patterns, properties and relationships and propose a general statement involving numbers or shapes; identify examples for which the statement is true or false | 4:7 |
| Make and draw shapes with increasing accuracy and apply knowledge of their properties | 6:5 |
| Estimate, draw and measure acute and obtuse angles using an angle measurer | 7:3 |
| Describe, identify and visualise parallel and perpendicular edges or faces; use these properties to classify 2D shapes and 3D solids | 7:3 |
| *Measuring* | |
| Read and interpret scales on a range of measuring instruments, recognising that the measurement made is approximate and recording results to a required degree of accuracy | |

## NNS National Numeracy Strategy Objectives

Objectives **emboldened** are key objectives. Bracketed references following the objectives refer to the NNS Framework section and page where each objective can be found.

| Reception Objectives | Chapter: Case Study |
|---|---|
| **Say and use number names in order in familiar contexts** (4:2) | 6:1 |
| **Count reliably up to 10 everyday objects** (4:4,5) | 6:1; 7:1 |
| Count reliably in other contexts (4:6) | 7:1 |
| **Recognise numerals 1 to 9** (4:9) | 6:1 |
| Order a given set of numbers (4:12) | 7:1 |
| **Use developing mathematical ideas and methods to solve practical problems involving counting and comparing in a real or role play context** (4:20) | 4:1 |
| **Use language such as more, less, longer, shorter, heavier and lighter** (4:22) | 7:1 |
| Understand and use the vocabulary related to time. Order familiar events in time. Know the days of the week and the seasons of the year (4:23) | 6:6 |
| Talk about, recognise and recreate simple patterns (4:26) | 7:1 |
| Use language such as 'circle' or 'bigger' to describe the shape and size of solids and flat shapes (4:24, 25) | 5:2 |
| **Use everyday words to describe position** (4:27) | 7:1 |
| Year 1 Objectives | Chapter: Case Study |
| Solve mathematical problems or puzzles, recognise simple patterns and relationships, generalise and predict (5:62) | 4:7 |
| **Use mental strategies to solve simple problems set in real life, money or measurement context** (5:66, 68, 70) | 6:2 |
| Recognise coins of different values. Work out how to pay an exact sum using smaller coins (5:68) | 6:2 |
| Investigate general statements about familiar shapes by finding examples that falsify it (5:80) | 3:4 |
| Year 2 Objectives | Chapter: Case Study |
| **Read and write numbers to at least 100 in figures and words** (5:9) | 3:1 |
| Solve mathematical problems or puzzles, recognise simple patterns and relationships, generalise and predict (5:63) | 4:7; 8:2 |
| **Explain how a problem was solved orally and, where appropriate, in writing** (5:65) | 4:2 |
| **Explain how the problem was solved.** Recognise all coins and begin to use £.p notation for money (for example, know that £4.65 indicates £4 and 65p) (5:65) | 8:2 |
| Use mental addition and subtraction, simple multiplication and division, to solve simple word problems involving numbers in 'real life', money or measures, using one or two steps (5:67, 69, 71) | 8:2 |
| Find totals, give change, and work out which coins to pay (5:69) | |

| | |
|---|---|
| **Use mathematical names for common 2D and 3D shapes ... describe some of their features ... number of sides, corners and faces** (5:81) | 6:4; 7:2 |
| **Sort shapes and describe some of their features** (5:81) | 6:4 |
| Find the 2D shapes and faces of 3D shapes, according to a specific criterion (5:81) | 7:2 |
| Solve a given problem by sorting, classifying and organising information in a simple way (5:91, 93) | 4:2 |
| **Year 3 Objectives** | **Chapter: Case Study** |
| Use informal pencil and paper methods to support, record or explain HTU+/–TU (5:43, 45) | 3:2 |
| Solve mathematical problems or puzzles, recognise and explain patterns and relationships, generalise and predict (5:63) | 4.7 |
| **Explain methods and reasoning** (5:65) | 4.7 |
| Solve simple word problems set in 'real life' contexts and explain how the problem was solved (5:67, 69, 71) | 5:4 |
| Suggest suitable units and measuring equipment to estimate or measure (5:75) | 7:3 |
| Classify/describe/visualise 3D and 2D shapes (5:81) | 4.7 |
| **Identify lines of symmetry in simple shapes** (5:85) | 7:3 |
| Recognise positions and directions using compass directions (5:87) | 7:3 |
| **Identify right angles** in 2D shapes and the environment (5:89) | 7:3 |
| **Solve a problem by collecting, organising and representing data** (5:91, 93) | 7:3 |
| **Year 4 Objectives** | **Chapter: Case Study** |
| Explain methods and reasoning, orally and in writing (6:76) | 4:3; 4:7 |
| Solve mathematical problems or puzzles, recognise and explain patterns and relationships, generalise and predict (6:78) | 4:3; 4:7 |
| Suggest suitable units and measuring equipment to estimate or measure (6:92, 94) | 7:3 |
| Recognise equilateral and isosceles triangles (6:102) | 8:1 |
| **Classify polygons using criteria such as number of right angles, whether or not they are regular, symmetry properties** (6:102) | 8:1 |
| Classify/describe/visualise 3D and 2D shapes (6:104) | 4.7 |
| Identify lines of symmetry in simple shapes (6:106) | 7:3 |
| Recognise positions and directions using compass directions (6:108) | 7:3 |
| Make and measure clockwise and anti-clockwise turns (6:110) | 7:3 |
| Solve a problem by collecting, organising and representing data (6:114, 116) | 7:3 |
| **Year 5 Objectives** | **Chapter: Case Study** |
| Recognise and explain patterns and relationships, generalise and predict (6:17) | 3:3 |
| **Know by heart number facts up to 10 × 10** (6:59) | 5:1 |

| | |
|---|---|
| Choose and use appropriate number operations to solve problems and appropriate ways of calculating mental with jottings written methods, calculator (6:75) | 5:1 |
| Explain methods and reasoning, orally and in writing (6:77) | 4:5; 4:7 |
| Solve mathematical problems or puzzles, recognise and explain patterns and relationships (6:79) | 7:3 |
| Solve mathematical problems or puzzles, recognise and explain patterns and relationships, generalise and predict (6:79) | 4:5; 4:7 |
| **Use all four operations to solve simple word problems** involving numbers and quantities based on real life. Explain methods and reasoning (6:82–89) | 6:3 |
| Classify/describe/visualise 3D and 2D shapes (6:105) | 4.7; 7:3 |
| Recognise reflective symmetry in regular polygons (6:107) | 7:3 |
| Recognise properties of reflective and rotational symmetry (6:107) | 7:3 |
| **Recognise perpendicular and parallel lines** (6:109) | 7:3 |
| Understand and use angle measure in degrees (6:111) | 7:3 |
| Identify, estimate and order acute and obtuse angles (6:111) | 7:3 |
| **Year 6 Objectives** | **Chapter: Case Study** |
| Recognise and extend number sequences (6:17) | 4:6 |
| Identify and use appropriate operations (including combinations of operations) to solve word problems involving numbers and quantities (6:75) | 8:4 |
| Explain methods and reasoning orally and in writing (6:77) | 3:5; 4:4, 4:6; 4.7; 6:5; 8:4 |
| Solve mathematical problems or puzzles, recognise and explain patterns and relationships, generalise and predict (6:79) | 3:5; 4:6; 4:7; 7:3 |
| Recognise and explain patterns and relationships (6:79) | 6:5 |
| **Solve a given problem** by sorting, classifying and organising information in a simple way (6:115, 117) | 4:4 |
| Recognise perpendicular and parallel lines (6:103, 109) | 7:3 |
| Classify/describe/visualise 3D and 2D shapes (6:105) | 4.7; 7:3 |
| Make shapes with increasing accuracy (6:105) | 6:5 |
| Recognise properties of reflective and rotational symmetry (6:107) | 7:3 |

# Index

Added to the page number 't' denotes a table.